INTERNATIONAL ENCYCLOPAEDIA OF ISLAM

Vol.-7

Islam and Social Justice

INTERNATIONAL ENCYCLOPAEDIA OF ISLAM

Vol.-7

Islam and Social Justice

Editor

A.H. Qasmi

ISHA BOOKS

DELHI-110 033

International Encyclopaedia of Islam
(*Religion*)

ISBN: 81-8205-320-X (Set)

ISBN: 81-8205-327-7

Published in 2006 in India by
Isha Books, D-43, Prithviraj Road,
Adarsh Nagar, Delhi-110 033

Printed at : Rajdhani Printers, Delhi.

Contents

Preface

Man is a social creature. It is the society where he learns how to live in this vast cosmos. Apart from society, people are divided into different castes, cultures and creeds. All these factors go in developing a man's personality. Of all the factors, mentioned above, religion is most important.

There exist about more than two thousand religions in the world today. A religion is regarded as a sacred institution, which governs a man's life here and hereafter and teaches him how to lead a happy and prosperous life.

What's unique to Islam is its endowment to humanity from the divine creator or the Almighty. It is not a set of principles and dogmas scribed by a scholar or thinker. It was sent on the earth circa fifteen hundred years ago, but its principles and preachings hold good even today. Besides showing humanity a straight way to the eternal success, it also has a say in various other walks of human life, such as economy, politics, human rights, social relations, judiciary, marriage and so on and so forth.

Another distinguished feature of Islam is that apart from being the latest religion, it is also the last one. That is to say, whatever is there in Islam, it is valid upto to the doomsday. Now, there will not come any other religion till the Day of Judgement. Therefore, it is the most powerful and as well as the most human-nature-friendly.

Given the present global scenario, there was being felt a dire need to bring out such a mini-encyclopaedia of Islam which may cater to the maximum needs of man in the least possible sheet of paper.

The present series is an humble attempt in the same direction. It comprises ten volumes which cover all the major disciplines of human life like, Prayer, marriage, justice, human rights, social justice and so on.

We are sure that the endeavour would prove to be a capsule of treasure of knowledge about Islam, prepared perfectly. Nevertheless, considering the adage 'to err is human', we would be obliged if the readers suggest some improvements for further editions.

Editor

1

Concept of Social Justice

We have already examined the theoretical bases of society as they are outlined in the Quran and the Traditions, and we have looked briefly at Muslim society as it evolved in the course of history. It now remains for us to ask: Is it possible today to renew something similar to that form of Islamic life for the present and for the future? It is not sufficient that Islam should have been a living force in the past; it is not enough that it has produced a sound and well-constructed society in the time of the Prophet and in the age of the Caliphate.

Since that distant time, there have been immense changes in life—mental, economic, political, and social. There have even been material changes on the Earth, and in its powers relative to man. All these things must be carefully considered before an answer can be given to our question. There is also the further consideration which cannot be overlooked in any discussion which is directed to a practical and particular end, rather than to a theoretical and general; we must discover why it was that the spread of the Islamic spirit came to a halt in matters of political and economic theory only a short time after the era of the Prophet. Was this the longest possible span of life which the inner spirit and resources of Islam could command? Before dealing with these two considerations, we must emphasize the following truths:

> "That Islamic society today is not Islamic in any true sense." We have already quoted a verse from the Quran which can not in any way be honestly applied today:

"Whoever does not judge by what Allah has revealed is an unbeliever."

In our modern society, we do not judge by what Allah has revealed; the basis of our economic life is usury; our laws permit rather than punish oppression; the poor-tax is not obligatory, and is not spent in the requisite ways. We permit the extravagance and the luxury which Islam prohibits; we allow the starvation and the destitution of which the Messenger once said:

> "Whatever people anywhere allow a man to go hungry, they are outside the protection of Allah, the Blessed and the Exalted."

The Imam Ibn-Hazm also delivered a fatwa on the same subject, to the effect that if a man dies in starvation in any town, the people of that town are regarded as having killed him, and the blood-money may be demanded of them. We permit this and similar things which have long been the subject of vain protest. Yet, the Quranic text is undeniably applicable to such things.

It refers to the existence in our modern society of such laws as those which permit usury, adultery, and refusal to pay the poor-tax, which thereby prove themselves to be in opposition to the divine laws laid down in the Quran. So long as Muslim society adhered to Islam, it manifested no weakness and no tendency to abdicate its control of life. It was when it fell away from Islam that these things took place. Emphasis on this fact will compensate for the idle aspersions which Western scholars have cast on our faith, and which they have evidenced from history.

These aspersions have been taken up by some in the East who were either gullible or mercenary, and have been the cause of the sullying of hundreds of pages by such men, under the claim of being liberal thinkers and accurate scholars. This is nonsense, and can only serve as a pretext for the false, the gullible, or the mercenary mind. We may now return to treat the two considerations whose discussion we deferred until we had noted the above points. We may start by answering the second question, why did the spread of the Islamic spirit come to a halt a short space after the time of the Prophet? Here again, we must emphasize two historical facts:

> "This halt was only partial, never complete. It took place only in a limited sphere, that of politics."

The tolerant Caliphate became a tyrannical monarchy:

> "The public funds were made accessible to the monarch, his relatives, his courtiers, and his flatterers, while they became inaccessible to those who had a true claim on them by the laws of Allah and His Messenger. But the remainder of the teachings of Islam remained in force; the charity and benevolence, the mutual help and responsibility tolerance and freedom of conscience and human equality, the payment of the poor-tax and the alms, and all the other positive and negative ordinances of Islam—all these continued in force to a greater or a lesser extent in many Muslim communities. " The Shariah even continued in force as the system of civil law until the nineteenth century, when we introduced French law, thus giving the coup de grace to another tie which bound us to the beliefs of Islam.

The change which overtook the system and the development of politics—a partial change, as we have just said—was the product of an unfortunate mischance, as we have already contended. The mischance was that the control should fall into the hands of the Umayyads, first in an indirect way in the reign of Uthman, and later quite openly in the reign of Muawiyya. If we are to be fair to Islam we cannot hold it responsible for the Umayyads; for it was injured far more by this clan of the Quraish than by the fiercest of its enemies.

It is certain that, if the life of Umar had lasted several years longer, or if Ali had been the third Caliph, or even if Uthman had become Caliph when he was twenty years younger, then the course of Islamic history would have been very considerably changed. For the policy which Umar enunciated was:

(a) to take excessive wealth from the rich and give it to the poor;

(b) to equalize the stipends assigned to the people, as had been the practice under Abu-Bakr.

If Umar had done this, there could have been no opposition to a policy so consistent with Islam. Umar's conscience was above all question, as was his zeal for the faith; the reverence in which he was held for his fidelity to the faith was similarly above the attacks of jealousy and doubt.

If this programme had been carried out by Umar, it would have restored economic and social equity to the Islamic world, and the civil war would have been averted at its very beginning, or, at the least, would have been postponed for a long time. Or if Ali had succeeded Umar, he would have guided the people in Umar's policy, whatever might have been the position of the Quraiship, who had more self-confidence in dealing with Ali than they had in dealing with Umar.

In this case, the matter would not then have come to the stage of rebellion or civil war. The Umayyads would not have later aspired to power; for their nobles had no high standing in Islam because of their early conversion or their renown in the early wars; they were only among the "forced" converts who embraced Islam at the conquest of Mecca, when the success of the new faith was already assured. Under such circumstances they could have held office in the army or in provinces, but with no special reason for holding or being kept out of office, such as they gained in thirteen years under the reign of Uthman.

But it will be asked: How were the Umayyads able to effect such a speedy revolution during a period of turmoil in Islam? Does this not indicate that the Islamic system is unsteady by nature, or at least unsuited to permanency? Does it not indicate that by nature Islam provides no adequate safeguards against such revolution? We must here take account of the conditions of the Islamic state in that age, and we must reckon not only with factors of external power, but also with those of internal agitation.

The truth is that, at that stage Islam was in a ferment, and the really strange thing is that the Umayyads did with it only as much as they could. For "the fact is that the astonishing speed of the conquests, to which history can produce no parallel, added to Islamic society a huge territory, teeming with various races and skills, intellects and languages, systems, traditions, and heritages.

However strong the spirit of Islam may have been, and however powerful in suppressing all these heritages, an element of time was essential before all this new material could be homogenized, before a change could be wrought in the old moral ideas, the rooted traditions, the cherished social systems and customs. Thus, the Umayyad attack on the spirit of Islam just at this juncture took place at a unique point of time; if it had been stayed for a space, it could never have accomplished all that it did.

We have seen that the bulk of Muawiyya's support lay in Syria, a conquered country, rather than in Arabia itself. Those of his supporters who did hail from the Peninsula, such as Amar ibn al-As, were of a nature akin to Muawiyya himself, men who trampled down the moral element in their reckonings, who justified the means by the end, and who justified the end simply on the grounds that they desired it.

As for the suggestion that the Islamic system does not provide by nature adequate safeguards against revolution, for one thing we must bear in mind that this system was assailed by revolution before it had properly struck roots; and for another thing we must remember that in practice no system has any such real safeguards. Where, for example, are the safeguards of democracy in Europe? This is a strongly entrenched system, which has achieved a definite form, and which has had time to establish itself and to spread its influence over a long period into every quarter of life.

Yet, where were its safeguards at the time of the Nazi revolution, or the Fascist, or the Spanish? Or again take the institution of free speech in the United States, whose people fled from Europe to form a free society—where are its safeguards? Today a few newspaper and radio companies can hold a monopoly of both information and opinion, and can forbid any contrary opinions to find their way to the eyes, the ears, or the thoughts of the people.

The truth is that any suspicion that the Islamic system does not afford safeguards against revolution is due to ignorance of what is practically feasible in any system. It betrays also an ignorance of the true facts of Islamic history; we have the evidence of the minor rebellion in the Hejaz, and of the great rebellion against Uthman; we have the evidence of the Qarmatian rebellion and of many others, all of which were directed against exploitation, arbitrary power, and class distinctions. The spirit of Islam has continually and successfully resisted all such things, in spite of the grievous injuries which it has suffered at their hands throughout thirteen hundred years.

The spread of the spirit of Islam, then, was not halted because that spirit was unable to establish itself, nor because it was found inadequate to cope with the demands of the life. As we shall shortly see, this spirit has been continuously operative in many of the aspects of life and society. The halt in its spread was the product of an unfortunate mischance at a unique point of time. And it was when that mischance brought to Islam a Caliph who retained something of the true spirit of the caliphate in the person of Umar II, that the spread of Islam became again apparent, and the government again truly Islamic. But then the times were not propitious for such a truly Muslim Caliph to restore what had been destroyed, or to establish the roots of Islamic traditions in the political system.

But, nonetheless the attempt of Umar II does give us a clear indication that the inner power of Islam was really strong and capable of application in very different times. For his attempt followed the oppressive and evil age of the Umayyads, and it indicated clearly that a renaissance of Islamic government was possible, and not out of question.

We must repeat our contention that even when the spread of the Islamic spirit came to a halt in the realm of politics—though even here it was only a partial halt—it still continued to operate in other aspects of both social and individual life. It continued to realize many of its ideals, and to achieve many of its aims; indeed even to the present day it is still effective in such spheres as are not strongly under the influence of politics. As the Frenchman, Gouilly, says in Islam and the Great Powers:

> "The number of Muslims in Madagascar is not less than three quarters of a million. Most European authorities explain the spread of Islam in the native villages by the fact that it is a unifying religion which ensures for the negro an equality and justice for which he longs; it emancipates him finally from the bondage of priesthood and superstition, and even from the nightmare of evil spirits."

H.A.R., Gibb writes in Whither Islam?:

> "Islam still has it in its power to render a conspicuous service to mankind. There is no other society which

> can show such a record of having united various races in one unity based on equality. The great Islamic community in China, and the still smaller community in Japan, all show that Islam has still the power completely to reconcile such divergent elements as those of race and class. If ever the opposition of the great states of the East and West is to be replaced by understanding, this can only be done through the medium of Islam." Muslim*'s Conduct during Crusades:* The conduct of the Muslims during the Crusades showed the full inspiration of the strong spirit of Islam, as it rose superior to worldly considerations, treachery and ruthlessness. It showed a belief in the unity of mankind and the relationship of humanity beyond all differences of faith, and above all temporal and ephemeral enmities. Salahuddin was not the only one whom the history of the Crusades has recorded as being of the true and lofty Islamic spirit; rather would this description apply to all the Muslim armies which took part in these long and bitter wars. And this remained true despite the foul deeds of the Crusaders. These may be exemplified in the fall of Jerusalem on the fifteenth of July, 1099 A.D. (492 A. H.), during the first Crusade.

The Muslims sought refuge and sanctuary in the Aqsa Mosque, but the Crusaders followed them inside and dispatched them with their swords, so that blood flowed through the sacred precincts in a flood. In this act, the Crusaders violated a solemn treaty which their leader had made with some of the Arabs. This was only one example of the barbarity of the Crusaders, involving as it did a violation of their honour, punishment of the living, and retaliation on the infirm and the children.

Even after that, when fate turned against the barbarians, their treatment at the hands of the Muslims was imbued with the Islamic spirit, which was strong enough to check the desire for vengeance in Muslim hearts, and to keep them within the bounds of humanity and religion.

Again, within our own times, the recent war against the Jewish settlers in Palestine had revealed the penetration of the Islamic spirit. Even after the long interval during which Muslims have been divorced from the spirit and traditions of their faith, these have proved effective in keeping the Arab forces from taking vengeance for the most horrible and inhuman crimes committed by the Zionists in the Holy Land. They have been effective in keeping Muslim armies tune to the lofty tradition which their religion has maintained for fourteen centuries, and that in the midst of a constant record of inhumanity.

While we are discussing the inner vitality of Islam, we must not overlook the succession of disasters and calamities, both internal and external, to which Islam has been subjected throughout its long history. Yet, it is still a powerful element in human history, and commands the attention even of some occidentals as a means of saving humanity from it present dilemma, as we have already seen in the quotations from Gouilly and Gibb.

Despite the fact that such men are unable fully, to comprehend the Islamic spirit, but confine themselves rather to a review of its practical profit as it now exists, than to an appreciation of its profound spiritual content. For it is difficult for occidentals who have been brought up in the shadow of a deeply rooted materialistic civilization—and such we shall later see that it is to appreciate this subtle spiritual element.

We have already indicated that the first internal disaster which overtook Islam, namely its subjugation by the Umayyads. This was an interlude which neither permanently affected the practical traditions of Islam nor altered its spiritual exhortations and laws. It did not produce any permanent social principles, any accepted practical traditions, or any rooted practices.

We must now examine quickly the more important developments which befell Islam, and mark their influence through the following centuries. The first of these is to be found in the rise of the Abbasid state, with its reliance on racial elements newly converted to Islam. The attitude of these people to their new religion was never whole-hearted, because of the national loyalties whose roots remained strong within them.

But as time passed on, the Abbasid state deserted these elements on which it had been founded, and which were now beginning to acquire a tincture of Islam, for others whose nucleus was a body of Turks, Circassians, Dailamites and such like. So, this dynasty continued to find its support in elements which were opposed to the spirit of Islam, and to which it gave a favoured position because it relied on them. There was nothing to withstand these racial elements – and hence to withstand the power of the dynasty – except the spirit of Islam, with all the inner force and vitality which it could muster.

Then followed the destructive raids of the Tartars, bursting with savage ferocity on the Islamic world. Without delay Islam turned aside the force of the onslaught, swallowed it up, and assimilated it. Yet, this was not accomplished without causing in the spirit of Islam itself a profound upheaval in which the practices and traditions of this religion were forcibly modified.

Nonetheless in spite of the humiliation of the state by the Tartar onslaught, the Islamic community continued powerful and loyal to its ideals, and constant in the fundamentals of its religion, no matter how far it may have wandered from them in a few purely official aspects.

We must also bear in mind here that the Roman Empire, the building and growth of which had occupied almost a thousand years, was cut off and fell into pieces in a single century, as a result of the incursions of the Huns and Goths; nothing was left of it except a few scattered traces.

However, the Islamic state remained in occupation of a

wide territory, although its building had occupied little more than half a century, and though it had to contend with a number of internal struggles between ruling families, as well as the external attacks of the Tartars, and others. Such factors demonstrate the intense vitality of Islam, in that it was able to meet these circumstances.

As we trace the development further, in the West we find the war in Spain, and in the East the disaster of the Crusades. In the first of these Islam was worsted, in the second it was victorious. But from that time to this it has had to contend with ferocious enemies of the same spirit as the Crusaders, enemies both open and hidden.

But the final overthrow of Islam took place only in the present age, when Europe conquered the world, and when the dark shadow of colonization spread over the whole Islamic world. East and West alike. Europe mustered all its forces to extinguish the spirit of Islam, it revived the inheritance of the Crusaders'-hatred, and it employed all the materialistic and intellectual powers at its disposal. With these it sought to break down the internal resistance of the Islamic community and to divorce it gradually over a long period from the teachings and the heritage of its religious faith.

When we speak of the hatred of Islam, born of the Crusading spirit, which is latent in the European mind, we must not let ourselves be deceived by appearances, nor can we let their hypocrisy blind us to the fact that they deny to us any freedom of religion. They say, indeed, that Europe is not as unshakably Christian today as it was at the time of the Crusades and that there is nothing today to warrant hostility to Islam, as there was in those days. This is entirely false and inaccurate. General Alien by was no more than typical of the mind of all Europe, when, entering Jerusalem during the First World War, he said:

"Only now have the Crusades come to an end."

Similarly, the Governor of Sudan was no more than typical

of the European mind when he placed all governmental power at the disposal of missionaries in the Southern Sudan, while forbidding any Muslim trader even to enter the country. It happened once that a certain official was stationed for a rather long time in South, and so asked for a transfer to the North; it was not granted. He then bethought himself to try lifting up his voice in the Muslim call to prayer; that single act sufficed to ensure his transfer the following day. And England is, of all the European countries, the most tolerant and patient and skilful in reconciling questions of religion.

People sometimes wonder how this obstinate spirit of resistance to Islam can persist so strongly and to such a pitch in a Europe which has discarded Christianity, and where the exhortations of preacher and monk no longer fill European ears as they did in the age of the Crusades. But this fact ceases to be surprising when we take into account two facts:

> "The enmity which the Crusaders stirred up was not confined to the clangour of arms, but was, before all else and above everything, an intellectual enmity. The European mind was poisoned by the slurs which the Crusaders' leaders cast on Islam as they spoke of it to their ignorant Western compatriots. It was in that age that there grew up in Europe the ridiculous idea that Islam was a religion of unbridled passion and violent sensuality, that it consisted merely of formal observances, and that it had no teaching of purity or of regeneration of heart. And this idea had remained as it started.

"This loathing spread space. The ignorant mass of Crusaders had dependents in many places throughout Europe; and the process was hastened by the Spanish Christians in their war to deliver their country from 'the yoke of the idolaters".

But the downfall of Muslim Spain was to require many centuries before it was completed; when this protracted struggle and the constraint which it involved grew too great, a hostility to Islam started to take root in Europe, and ultimately became permanent.

Finally, it took the form of a complete extirpation of Islam throughout Spain after a conflict which reached a pitch of ferocity and bitterness hitherto unknown. The cries of joy which all over Europe greeted this event were unfortunately uttered in ignorance of the consequences which would arise; for the result was that science and learning were blotted out, and in their place came the ignorance and the barbarity of the Middle Ages.

But before the echoes of these happenings in Spain had died away, there took place a third event of immense significance, which was to hasten the breaking of the ties between the Western world and Islam. This was the fall of Constantinople to the Turks. Europe had always looked to Byzantium as a relic of the glory of ancient Greece and Rome, and had regarded it as the fortress of Europe against Asiatic barbarism. In the centuries which followed, and which were filled with wars, the hostility of Europe to Islam was no longer a question of merely academic importance; it was now a question of political import also. And this fact further increased the violence of that hostility.

In addition to all this, Europe derived great profit from this cleavage. The Renaissance or rebirth of European arts and sciences in the widest sense arose particularly from an Islamic and Arab source; in most cases it can be traced back to material contacts between the East and the West. Europe profited more than did the Muslim world, but it did not acknowledge the gift, because it was blinded by its loathing of Islam. Or, more correctly, the reverse is true, that loathing increased with the passage of time, until it was second nature.

At this point, loathing swamped all understanding whenever the word 'Muslim' was mentioned; it entered into all their thoughts until it came to form a permanent part of the thinking of every European, man or woman. And still stranger than this is the fact that this feeling continued to flourish even after all the movements of intellectual exchange. Then followed the age of the Reformation, during which Europe was divided into various sects, each continually employed in arming itself against every other; yet hostility to Islam was the common feature of all of them.

This in turn was followed by an age when religious feeling started to subside, but the hostility to Islam continued unabated. One of the clearest proofs of this is that French philosopher and poet, Voltaire, was one of the bitterest critics of Christianity and of the Church in the eighteenth century; yet, he was at the same time violently hostile to Islam and to its Messenger. A few score years later came the age in which Western scholars commenced to study foreign learning and to regard it with a measure of sympathy.

All matters connected with Islam the traditional dislike began to creep in under a form of partisan spirit which was not conducive to academic study. Thus, the gulf which history had dug between Europe and the Islamic world remained still unbridged. Dislike of Islam thus became a fundamental part of European thinking; and the fact that the first Orientalists of the modern age were Christian missionaries who were working in Muslim territory meant that the picture which they formed of the teachings and the history of Islam was distorted; for it was founded on an axiomatic conception that Europeans were superior to 'idolaters'.

Despite the fact that Oriental studies have now been liberated from missionary influence, this intellectual bias had persisted, although any mistaken view can no longer claim the excuse of ill-informed religious zeal. Hence, the attacks made by Orientalists upon Islam betray an inherited characteristic, and a peculiarity of nature; they are based on an impression created by the Crusades, and shaped by all the mental influences of these on the early Europeans. But it will immediately be asked:

> How does it happen that an ancient antipathy such as this, which was originally religious in its basis, and which in the period of its birth owed its inception to the spiritual mastery of the Christian Church, can persist in Europe in an age when religious convictions are no more than a matter of antiquarian interest?

There is never anything surprising in such a situation; for it is well known to psychology that men may lose all the religious beliefs which they held in their youth, and at the same time retain some of their personal idiosyncrasies, even those which formerly centered upon the very religious beliefs which they have now discarded. It is these idiosyncrasies which provide the intellectual motivation for every act of such men. This is the state which obtains in Europe regarding Islam.

Despite the fact that the religious convictions which gave rise to European hostility to Islam have now lost their power and been replaced by a more materialistic form of life, yet the ancient antipathy itself still remains as a vital element to pour a secret poison into the European mind. So far as the strength of this antipathy is concerned, it undoubtedly varies from one individual to another, but that it exists is indisputable. The spirit of the Crusades, though perhaps in a milder form, still hangs over Europe: and that civilization in its dealings with the Islamic world still occupies a position which bears clear traces of the early Crusader spirit."

European imperial interests can never forget that the spirit of Islam is firmly opposed to the spread of imperialism. Such an opposition must either be crushed or at least diverted. No weight need be attached to the contention of gullible or mercenary writers that religion is of no concern to Europeans, that the source of European power is not religious, and that the only thing about the Muslim world which Europe fears is its material power. Fundamentally, religion is a spiritual power which is always effective for the provision of material powers.

Islam is essentially different from Christianity; it encourages the fostering of material powers, it enjoins self-defence and defensive war, and it warns the weaklings who tamely submit that theirs will be an evil fate in this world and in the next.

"Prepare for them as much as you can in the way offerees and cavalry, with which you may overcome Allah's enemies and your own."

"Do not take unbelievers for your friends in preference to Believers."

"So let those fight in the way of Allah who would exchange the life of this world for that of the next."

"Do not grow weary or grieve now that you have the upper hand, if you are true Believers..., etc."

Spiritual and Material Powers : Islam is at once a spiritual power and an incentive to material power; it is at once a form of opposition in itself, and an incentive to a still more forcible opposition. Therefore, European imperialism cannot but be hostile to such a religion. The only difference lies in the fact that the form of that hostility varies according to the imperialistic methods of each nation, and according to local conditions. Thus, for example, France declared open war on Islam in the Western Arab world, under the name of "Protecting the Barbars," or some such phrase. But England took a more devious and tortuous road to the same end in Egypt, that of education.

Its aim was to encourage the growth of a general frame of mind which would despise the bases of Islamic life, and even of Eastern life. When this was accomplished there would be a generation educated into this frame of mind, ready to go out into the schools and educational offices to imbue the coming generations with the same ideas.

These would set a fashion in manners and customs which

would ultimately lead to the permanent establishment of the desired frame of mind, and would emphasize the difference between the basic elements of Islamic education and the policies of the Education Ministry. Thus, England could dispense with open hostilities as a means of opposition to religious convictions. And this objective was actually ascribed by a large and influential party to a desire to establish a pan-Egyptian mentality. In the Southern Sudan, again, there was no call for such guile; the position there was simply that which we have already described in speaking of the Christian missionaries and the Muslim merchants.

Thus, each imperialist state has proceeded by one means or another to oppose and to throttle Islam since the last century, and even before that. And that they still proceed to do essentially the same thing in concert is obvious from the position taken up by the United Nations on the question of Indonesia and Holland, on that of Kashmir, India and Pakistan, and on that of Hyderabad, India and the Nizam. Finally the same thing is supremely evident in the position of the United Nations on Palestine.

There are those who hold that it is the financial influence of the Jews in the United States and elsewhere which has governed the policy of the West. There are those who say that it is English ambition and Anglo-Saxon guile which are responsible for the present position. And there are those who believe that it is the antipathy between East and West which is responsible. All these opinions overlook one vital element in the question, to which all other elements are subordinate, the Crusader spirit which runs in the blood of all occidentals.

It is this which colours all their thinking, which is responsible for their imperialistic fear of the spirit of Islam, and for their efforts to crush Arab strength. For the instincts and the interests of all occidentals are bound up together in the crushing of that strength. This is the common factor which links together Communist Russia and Plutocratic America.

The truly remarkable thing is that the spirit of Islam has survived all these attacks which have been launched against it from the earliest period of its life right up to the present. It has persisted, in spite of sudden assaults and the effect which these have had on its life; it had lasted out, in spite of the modern conquest by Western civilization with its material and educational weapons, from which some Muslims have borrowed the means of breaking down and destroying Islam at the direction of imperialistic powers.

Despite all these things, the spirit of Islam has remained essentially sound, and its inner force had left clear imprints on the course of human life in the broadest sense. Islam has left its marks on the forms and objectives of civil government throughout fourteenth centuries to the present day. There is no political or military institution in the world that owes something to Islam; and this has been true even in those ages when the Muslim world has been weak and divided, when it has seen its spiritual, social, and economic life disturbed.

But the period of obscurity and weakness is now at an end, and the tide of Islam has commenced to rise. In East and West alike the Arab world is gaining unity, and two great Islamic blocs have made an appearance in Pakistan and Indonesia. These are portents which cannot be overlooked, significant of the underlying vitality of Islam. They are significant also of the massive resources of Islam, sufficient to bring about a complete renewal of Islamic life. Such a renewal need not be based merely on wishful thinking or on good fortune; rather it may be based on actual concrete facts which are apparent to the sight.

I personally, quite apart from the religious faith, have an absolute belief in the possibility of a renewal of Islamic life within the Muslim world. I believe in the soundness of Islam as a worldwide, rather than a local, system for the future. I have no desire to take refuge in vain speculation, but I do believe this to be not only possible, but even easy.

Not that there will not be various and vast difficulties; there will also be great tasks which must be accomplished before the complete renewal of Islamic life can take place with any facility within Muslim society. The assessment of these vast obstacles, and the inspiration to undertake the tasks involved is something which is necessitated by any true understanding of the immensity of the goal at which we are aiming, and of the weight of responsibility awaiting any man who aims at that goal. It is something which is necessitated also by an understanding of the importance of public opinion in such vast undertakings.

But, it is not enough for any one man to issue a ringing call for hope to become actuality, and expectation reality. The results and the consequences must be assessed, and the man who exhorts others must equally offer to them the same vast effort which he demands of them.

In the very nature of the case, the wide divergence between existing political theory and the spirit of Islam, which has arisen over a long period and has hence become deep-seated, will make it a matter of some difficulty to return to a theory which is truly based on that spirit. For the machinery of the state and of society, the foundations of life in all its aspects, the spiritual and intellectual background are all so built up on specific bases that they are difficult to change without the application of vast energy over a long time. And the longer the time, the greater the difficulty, and the greater the need for yet vaster and longer enduring effort.

The time factor is linked up with another consideration in the present age. We do not live only in this world, but we cannot live in isolation from it. Thus, our interests and our needs are interwoven. The with this present world, which is governed by a certain form of civilization, involving an outlook completely contradictory to that of Islam. This we shall see later. In one respect, this fact will slow down our progress along the path of renewing the true Islamic form of life, and in another respect, it will lay additional responsibilities upon us.

The importance of this last consideration is enhanced by the fact that this Western world with which our interests are interwoven is at the present moment stronger than we; we do not have today the control over it, or the strength equal to its strength, that we had in the first age of Islam. At the same time, it is hostile to us, and in particular hostile to our religion. Therefore, it will not permit us to produce a new Islamic system, or to renew a truly Islamic form of life, however great the effort we put forth. This result we could hope for only if we had control of the Western world, if our strength were comparable to its, or if it were honest with us and with our religion to which we seek to return.

But all this does not mean that return to the Islamic system is impossible. All that it means is that this is a great and difficult task, requiring unremitting effort. Above all it demands courage to believe in it, boldness to face the inevitable results, patience to endure the hard work demanded, and faith to believe that this is necessary for Islamic society and for mankind as a whole. It demands the fostering of a new mentality, whose task will not be simply to elevate the existing state of things, but rather to produce a new and perfect state.

This is our task. We have already seen the foundations on which the system must be built; thus, we can now balance the profits which we shall enjoy if we return to it against the labours and sacrifices which we must make in order to realize it. When our faith in these profits reaches the point at which they outweigh the sacrifices, then let us settle the matter, make up our kinds, and leave the result with Allah.

Perhaps one valuable aspect of the present situation might be pointed out here. The great Western civilization has led the world into two global wars within a quarter of a century; after the second of these it has led it to a complete division into two blocs, an eastern and a western, and to the constant threat of a third war.

It has brought about a state of hostility in every quarter, it has produced starvation and destitution and adversity throughout three parts of the world. It should be pointed out also that the social fabric of the whole world today is in that state of insecurity and instability where it must look for new foundations and search for some spiritual means of restoring to man his faith in the principles of humanity.

We must not, however, read more than is legitimate into this readiness of the Western world to accept the foundations of our Islamic civilization; this is another matter. Although it may be, it noted that such a man as Bernard Shaw says that the West had already started to turn in this direction, and even prophesied that it well come to it eventually, in these words:

> "I forecast that the religion of Muhammad will be accepted in Europe in the near future, for it has already started to gain some acceptance. The priests of the Middle Ages insisted on portraying Islam in the darkest colours, either out of ignorance, or from criminal bigotry; but they were led to excess by their hatred of Muhammad and his religion; indeed they held him to be the anti-Christ. For myself I find it preferable to call Muhammad the saviour of mankind, and I believe that if such a man were given authority over the modern world, he would succeed in solving its problems and giving it peace and happiness. And how great is the world's need of these things."

Western Perspective : There were some impartial thinkers in the nineteenth century who discovered how much value there is in the religion of Muhammad. Among them were Carlyle, Goethe, and Gibbon. From this fact, there has arisen a salutary change in the attitude of Europe towards Islam.

Thus, Europe has seen a great advance in the past years of the twentieth century, and has even started to respect the faith of Muhammad.

It may be that in the century that lies ahead, Europe will make further progress, and will acknowledge the contribution of this faith towards a solution of its problems. Many among may own nation and among all European nations already belong to the religion of Muhammad, a fact which enables us to say that the conversion of Europe to Islam has already begun. But so far as we can see Shaw's prophecy is still no more than a prophecy—if, indeed, it is not intended to drug the senses of Muslims and to make them content to wait idly for Europe to embrace their faith. But, however, this may be, we must at least wait until time has proved such a statement, for two principal reasons:

1. There is this deep-seated and inherited hostility to Islam in the very European nature itself. This is at present augmented by the opposition of imperialistic interests to the very existence of our faith, as being an obstacle in their path.
2. European culture is rooted in material foundations, and the influence of intellectual and spiritual interests are very weak; such has been the case from the time of Roman civilization to the present day. This matter requires detailed consideration, and a full treatment, rather than merely a brief mention. So, we must here make an extended study of this important question: Is it possible for Islamic and Western civilizations to work together in partnership? And if so, then what are the limits of that partnership?

We have already asserted at the beginning of this book that Europe was never at any time truly Christian, because by its very nature its people had to fight over their meagre territories. Thus, the tolerant principles of Christianity could gain no footing in such a stubborn ground. In addition to this, Christianity is essentially an asceticism, a refusal to live, or to take an interest in, a practical worldly life. To these two factors we must now add a third, to which we have already made a passing reference.

This factor was the existence of the Roman Empire, and its position to thwart the path of Christianity, together with the permanent influence of that empire on the bases of European civilization even today. And that despite the infusion of Christianity which the Roman Empire received in its last days.

We may quote here some passages from Islam at the Cross-roads, which we find completely satisfactory: The doctrine on which the Roman Empire was founded was to destroy by force, or to exploit other people for the sole benefit of the mother country. In order to indulge this privileged body the Romans saw nothing wrong in their violence and nothing humiliating in their oppression.

The famous Roman justice was a justice for Romans only. It is apparent that such a tendency as this is possible only on the basis of a materialistic ideal, which is wholly devoted to wordly life and civilization—though it may be an ideal promoted and shaped by a philosophical taste.

In any case it was far removed from any appreciation of spiritual values. The Romans did not really understand religion; their traditional Gods were only variant forms of the Greek myths which, as being mere shades, were never believed to have any connection with social affairs, and which were never permitted to interfere in any way with the real business of life. Their duty was to speak in metre through the agency of their attendant priests, when questions were asked of them; but no one ever expected them to enunciate laws for the guidance of mankind. Such was the soil in which modern Western civilization grew up, though during the period of its growth it undoubtedly came under many other influences. Thus, in the very nature of the case, it changed and thereby modified the legacy which it had received from Rome in more than one way. Nevertheless the fact remains that all that is truly great in the modern West, whether of life or nature, owes its origin to Roman civilization. Hence, since, the intellectual and social environment of ancient Rome was always secular rather than religious—and that no exhypothesis, but in actual fact—so the same environment persists in the modern West.

The European mind has neither possible argument against the complete futility of religion nor will it ever admit the need for such an argument. For modern European thinking in general leaves the absolute outside its scheme of practical considerations— although— it does tolerate religion, and even at times may assert that it is a social virtue. Western civilization does not irrevocably disown God, but it can see no place and no significance for Him in its present intellectual system. It has made a virtue out of a philosophical inability on the part of man, that is to say, out of his inability to take a comprehensive view of the whole field of life.

European, modern Europe tends to attach the greatest practical importance to the values deriving from the experimental sciences, or at least from those sciences from which may be expected some perceptible influence of human social relationships. And because the question of the existence of God does not fall into either of these categories, the European mind tends to drop the concept of God out of the sphere of practical considerations. A question emerges here:

> "How is this tendency to be reconciled with Christian thought? Is not Christianity a faith founded on the Absolute, as is Islam? And is it not ostensibly the spiritual background of Western civilization? There is no doubt that all these things are true. But there could not be any greater mistake than to imagine that Western civilization is the outcome of Christianity. The true philosophical basis of the Western system is to be sought in the ancient Roman view of life as a

> matter of advantage, quite independent of absolute values."

It is a view which can be summarized thus: Because we have no specific knowledge, either in the way of practical experience, or in that of proof, about the fundamentals of human life, or about its destiny after physical death; therefore, it is best for us to confine our powers to those material and mental fields which are accessible to us, rather than let ourselves to be tied down to metaphysical and moral questions arising from claims which can have no intellectual proofs.

Such an argument as this which is characteristic of modern Western civilization, will certainly not find acceptance in Christian thought, as it will not in Islam or in any other religion, simply because it is essentially religious. Thus, to try to establish a casual relationship between Christianity and modern Western civilization, is a gross historical error.

Christianity may indeed have played a very small part in the rise of intellectual materialism which today dominates modern Western civilization, but the truth is that the growth of this spirit had been the product of Europe's prolonged struggle, against the Christian Church, and against its supervision of life. In its general aspect Christianity today is a purely spiritual thing, as was the case with the Roman deities, which were neither permitted nor expected to exert any real influence on society.

No doubt there are in the West individuals who are still prepared to judge and to think on a religious basis, prepared to fight a last ditch action to reconcile their beliefs with the spirit of their civilization; but they cannot be more than isolated cases. To Europe as a whole it is a matter of indifference whether the political system is 'democratic or fascist, plutocratic or bolshevist, technical or intellectual.'

Europe knows but one necessary religion—the worship of material prosperity; the only belief that it holds is that there is but one goal in life—the making of that life easier and easier. It is, as the definition has it in significant terms, an escape from the tyranny of nature.' The shrines of such a culture are huge factories and cinemas, chemical laboratories and dance-halls and power stations. The priests of such a worship are bankers and mathematicians, cinema stars and scientists and aviators.

The inevitable result of this state of affairs is that man strives to gain power a pleasure; this brings into being quarrelsome societies, all armed to the teeth and intent on mutual destruction whenever their conflicting interests come into active opposition. On the intellectual side, the upshot has been the evolution of a humanism with a moral philosophy confined to purely scientific questions, in which the highest criterion of good or evil is whether or not any given thing represents material progress.

The sum and substance of all this is that the present-day European conscience is not ready to accept the spirit of Islam, or to seek in it a solution of human problems. But even so, it is not impossible that even this may take place after a number of other changes and developments in the West, and after the Islamic world itself has entered upon a clearly defined and independent renewal of Islamic life. In this, the West may find philosophical realities and practical truths which will attract its attention and balance its thinking. But it is my personal belief that many generations must elapse before the West will be able to appreciate the spirit of Islam in any real sense.

Again, the substance of this argument is that the mode of the Muslim doctrine that work must serve moral ends, cannot be reconciled with the mode of the modern Western doctrine that morals must serve some material advantage. We must reckon with this fact, and hence we must work to establish a sound form of Islamic life; this cannot be achieved by the importation of elements borrowed from abroad, since such elements will not fit into the texture of our native beliefs.

The Muslim world will have to admit defeat on the first occasion on which it seeks to renew its own life by borrowing Western ways of thought, life and custom. Such an experiment can only result in the suffocation of that very form of life which it seeks to revive; for from the very first step the Muslim world will be departing from its own true and natural path.

This path involves a belief based on Islam that the moral element is fundamental to the structure of life; it regards work as a means to moral ends, and it will not make material advantage the highest aim of morals. We have already seen in an earlier chapter of this book that Islam satisfies all the highest aims of life, among them the moral consciousness. We have also seen that Islam's supreme virtue is that it preserves the unity of life, and that it makes no distinction between the means and the ends. It will not lend its authority to any idea that there is an opposition between material and spiritual in the substance of life or in the nature of the universe or of mankind; rather it emphasized that the whole of life is a unity which must make an orderly progress towards the highest objectives.

Islam, then, enunciates for men a complete theory of life. This theory is always liable to growth by development or by adaptation; it is not open to change or to adulteration, either in its fundamentals or in its general aims. Therefore, in order that this complete theory may bear its full natural fruits, it is necessary to make a complete application of it. Otherwise, even the slightest change in its fundamentals or its aims will produce a disorder, because it will no longer be in conformity with the Islamic conception of life.

The continual growth of this universal theory by development or by adaptation is a natural product of the nature of Islam; it is encouraged by Islam, the institutions of which are adapted to recognize it. Analogy, interpretation, and the wide powers entrusted to the head of the state—all these are living methods of ensuring growth through development and adaptation, in order to keep pace with life and to meet its needs as they emerge. But there is one thing which must be kept in mind: these developments must not pass out with the roots of the fundamental Islamic theory, nor must they be allowed to serve any foreign aim; they must not betray the spirit of Islam or give allegiance to any other spirit in preference to it.

The criterion by which we may accept or reject any development is first to compare it with the basic theory and the general spirit of Islam. Anything that is in agreement with this theory and this spirit we may accept, and anything which is contrary to these we must reject. Thus, we may profit by all the fruits of human labour within the bounds of our basic philosophy of the universe, man and life; we need raise no barriers between ourselves and human endeavour, nor need we stand in isolation from the continuous business of living.

Above all we must be firmly convinced of the value of faith and enthusiasm; we have a scheme of life greater than any possessed by the followers of any religion or school or civilization which has yet been born. And that is to say the least of it.

No renaissance of Islamic life can be affected purely by law or statute, or by the establishment of a social system on the basis of the Islamic philosophy. Such a step is only one of the two pillars on which Islam must always stand in its construction of life. The other is the production of a state of mind imbued with the Islamic theory of life, to give permanence to external forces leading to this form of life, and to give coherence to all the social, religious and civil legislations.

Social justice is an integral part of this Islamic life. It cannot be realized unless this form of life is first realized, and it cannot have any guaranteed permanence unless this form of life is built up on solid foundations. It is similar in this to all other social systems; it must have the support of public belief and confidence in its merits. Failing this, its foundations will be purely spiritual, and its establishment will depend on the force of religious and social legislation; these are too weak to sustain it, in which case it may easily miscarry.

Hence, Islamic legislation is more akin to ecclesiastical ordinance because it depends on religious belief. Thus, we must always keep in mind the necessity for a renaissance of our religious faith; we must cleanse it of all accretions, such as alterations and interpretations and ambiguities; only thus can it be a support for the necessary social legislation which will establish a sound form of Islamic life. This form of life will depend upon legislation and exhortation, those twin fundamental methods of Islam towards the achievement of all aims.

We must, then, establish our Islamic theory in individuals and societies, at the same time as we set up the Islamic legislation to regulate life. And the natural method of establishing that philosophy is by education.

But how can we possibly induce Islamic theory by education? For educational methods and modes of thought are essentially Western and essentially inimical to the Islamic philosophy itself; first, because they stand on a materialistic basis which is contrary to the Islamic theory of life; and second, because opposition to Islam is a fundamental part of their nature, no matter whether such opposition is manifest or concealed in various forms.

As we have already maintained, we shall advertise our defeat the first time that we adopt a Western theory of life as the means of reviving our Islamic theory. So, primarily, we must avoid the ways of Western thought; rather we must choose the ways of native Islamic thought, in order to ensure pure results.

The import of these words is not that we should adopt a position of isolationism in regard to thought, education, and science; all these are a common heritage of all the peoples of the world, in which we among the foremost have a fundamental part. We shall continue to take our rightful share in the furtherance of these things, even if it should become apparent that we are far removed from the influence which they exert. For the only true and permanent form of cooperation is that between all the nations of the Earth.

Isolation from human life, then, is not our aim; rather what we seek is to build up a characteristically Islamic theory of life, and to renew that form of life now, when it is apparent even to some of the more enlightened occidentals that the philosophy of materialistic Western civilization is a danger to the continued existence of man.

It breeds in human nature a ceaseless anxiety, a perpetual rivalry, a continual strife, and a weakening of human ties to the breaking point. And this is spite of all the triumphs of science which could have tended to human happiness and peace and content, had it not been that the bases of the Western philosophy of life were purely materialistic and hence unsuitable to men along the path to perfection.

As long as our aim is the building up of this Islamic theory along these lines, we must make a distinction between things which we may profitably accept, and those which we may profitably reject, out of Western society. Only thus may we complete the building of an Islamic society out of sound materials which will produce a structure secure against cooperation and opposition alike, against both borrowing and giving.

From another point of view we must ensure to the theory of life which we establish a safeguard in the form of a period of fostering...fostering, that is, in our own minds rather than in its own essence. For Islamic life in itself is a strong and definite thing when in does not stand in awe of any other Western form. Rather, it is we who need to be fostered and nurtured, as we are living on a strange diet hence we must be on our guard while we are engaged in the establishment of our new system.

In the case of the pure sciences and their applied results of all kinds, we must not hesitate to utilize all things in the sphere of material life; our use of them should be unhampered and unconditional, unhesitating and unimpeded.

Similarly, we must be careful to derive the fullest profit from other things also; from philosophy, which is the intellectual treatment of the universe and life; from literature which is the emotional treatment of these things; from history, which is a factual treatment, and from legislation, which is a treatment of the relationships between individuals and societies.

It will do us no harm to make use of the pure sciences in all the spheres of life; but on the other hand, it will do us harm to account these as the sum total of life; for such a view involves a philosophy which is not ours. It tends to establish a conception of the universe and of life which is at variance with the Islamic conception of those things; ultimately, it would led us along a path which is not that of Islam. It is this path which has produced the present ailments of mankind, and which is responsible for their present troubles.

It is sometimes objected that even if this be so, the pure sciences themselves cannot be held responsible, because essentially they cannot be divorced from the method of Western thought. The experimental method rests on the basis of a definite philosophy which is neither intellectual nor spiritual; if this had never established itself in favour, science would never have followed the course which lately it has taken.

In the same way, science can never remain in isolation from philosophy, nor can it be content to be influenced by philosophy without in turn influencing it. For philosophy is benefited by the experimental results of science, and is influenced by it in aim and method.

Thus, a study of pure science involves a study of philosophy, which is influenced by that science, and which in turn exerts an influence on it. All this is over and above the fact that the applied results of science must influence all material life, methods of gaining a living, and the division of wealth. All this will in due time produce new forms of society based on a new philosophy, or at least based on a theory of life which must be influenced by these developments in the course of life.

All this is very true. But what must be there is no possibility of living in isolation from science and its products, though the harm that it does may be greater than the good. There is no such thing in this life as an unmixed blessing or an unalloyed evil. Thus, Islam does not oppose science, or the utilization of science; there is nothing contrary to the spirit of Islam in culling the fruits of science from all the sources of the world.

But while we may acknowledge the universal influences of philosophy and culture, history and law, together with all their consequences in the way of educational methods and modes of thought and logic, we must set all of this in its proper place on a spiritual Islamic foundation. We must hold to the guiding principle that all the results and material consequences of science do not essentially affect our universal philosophy of life and custom.

When we mention educational methods we might well bear in mind here that these are indivisible and inseparable from the general philosophy of the community. Thus, when we borrow Western methods of education, systems of training and curricula, we borrow also a general scheme of philosophy and a mode of thought which underlies these methods and systems and curricula, whether we like it or not.

There is a belief that these are questions of pure 'pedagogy', and therefore universal and identical throughout all countries. This is a naive and shortsighted belief, encouraged by the delusion of the psychologists, who give an undue weight to their own subject; despite the difference between psychology and philosophy, such men believe that they can master their own subject, and through it can answer the philosophical questions of education also.

That claim is one thing, but the actual fact is quite another. Psychology may perhaps be a pure science to be studied in the laboratory. But the treatment of its results and the use to which these are put, such as educational techniques and curricula—all these things are still influenced by the general philosophy of life, still accept the dictation of that philosophy, and still form an integral part of it.

Moreover, the very fact that psychology is ruled by the laboratory is one of the influences exerted by experimental philosophy, or by the experimental method. It is this same method which in later years has governed all materialistic Western thought. The only type of independence which psychology can expect from the philosophy which is its mentor is that superficial independence which cannot influence the final result.

For an example, we may look to the American curriculum, their methods of education and instruction, these are more akin to vocational training than to any system of thorough and systematic study; they have as their objective the promotion of technical skill based on theoretical principles. The reason for this tendency is to be sought in the philosophy of pragmatism, founded by Charles Pierce in 1878 which was advanced by William James and applied by John Dewey, the modern educational philosopher. This school of thought represents a reversal of the accepted terms of thought and study: bare ideas and theoretical principles are abandoned, as is the study of things according to their logical class and nature. According to Pragmatism, all study should be confined to the practical effects and result of objects.

According to Charles Pierce of Pragmatism the idea is no more than a secondary product of some act or activity; it is not in itself a reality. For example, I may have the 'idea' of the horn of an automobile passing in the street; this 'idea' gains no meaning by my study of its nature, its origin, and the method of its production. It may be a reality or it may be a figment of imagination; it may be produced by the ear and the nervous system, or it may be produced by the horn, whether, the automobile is turning right or left, and whether a path must be cleared for the vehicle and its driver. It means only:

> "I am about to change the direction of my vehicle and to proceed in a different direction. Hence, Pragmatism argues that the idea is secondary to the act, or the product of certain conditioning circumstances. This is the first step along the path of Pragmatism in which all the remaining steps must follow."

It has been the rise of this theory or this method of thought which has produced the educational techniques of America. It has been responsible for a teaching curriculum and a system which will encourage the mind to take this view of things and to rationalize life along this line. Also, it is this which has given American life its most characteristic mark, which has directed it towards technical production, and which has to a large extent diverted it from academic and theoretical education.

Accordingly, we must reckon with this general philosophy of life; if we borrow educational techniques, teaching systems, and curricula, this philosophy underlines all of them. This philosophy shapes and forms them, assisted by the results of pure psychology. Such an influence is inevitable, though this same science in its methods and in its results is itself influenced by that very philosophy.

From the theoretical point of view, then, our method of establishing an independent Islamic scheme of thought is to proceed readily but cautiously in the matter of borrowing such a philosophy along with its concomitants, such as educational techniques, teaching systems and curricula, literature, history and law. But we shall deal now with all these subjects together.

Universe and Mankind : So far as the study of philosophy is concerned, we have already indicated the universal theory of Islam on the universe, life and mankind, this is essentially different from the nature of other universal philosophies which have originated in the West from the days of the Greeks to the present. This is not the place to discuss this difference, and it will suffice to recognize merely that there does exist a radical divergence.

A petition of peculiar importance was once addressed to the Azhar University concerning a matter which was not favourably regarded in this quarter. It requested that study be directed to this universal Islamic theory of life and that a full and clear treatment of it be given in modern terms and applications; also that it be compared with other schools of philosophy. But the Azhar, instead of responding to this petition, continued to teach in its Faculty of Theology what it called the errors of Islamic philosophy, taken from the writings of Ibn-Sina and Ibn-Rushd.

This is, of course, a reversion to Greek philosophy, which has no real connection with the universal philosophy of Islam. Thus, in effect, the petition sent to the governors of the Azhar was neglected, and a spiritual and intellectual defeat was acknowledged in our primary seat of learning, a defeat for the Islamic theory of life.

If, then, we are to establish a sound Islamic theory of the universe, life and mankind, it is essential that Western philosophies and their moral corollaries should not be studied at all in our secondary schools, and that they should be studied in the university only after at least two years in the department of philosophy. And by the very nature of the case they should not be studied in the Azhar colleges until the very end of the course. In every centre of study such Western philosophies should be preceded by a course in pure Islamic thought, as distinct from the so-called "Islamic philosophy," in order to emphasize the true Islamic viewpoint.

Thus, the minds and thoughts of the students will assimilate the native bases of the spirit of Islam, together with its ideas on the universe, life and mankind, good and evil, work and reward, and all the other philosophic aspects of pure Islamic belief. This having been assured, we may in the later years of university study proceed to give some account of the other philosophies; these would include Greek philosophy and its opposition to Islamic, modern European and American philosophy; these should be compared in every case with Islamic philosophy.

In this way, we can ensure that the student's mind and conscience will not be too much influenced; we can ensure also a minimum influence on student's ideas and thoughts, because by then they will be equipped for critical appreciation. They will have the requisite knowledge to reject all that does not agree with the fundamental modes of thought of a Muslim people. Under these circumstances their new knowledge will not harm, but will rather benefit students; for it will be purely academic knowledge, largely independent of any influence on their conscience or on their conception and understanding of life and its requirements.

We have already given one example of pragmatism in its view of things. But in this example, there was no indication of the dangers inherent in that philosophy or in its method; so we must now follow out this philosophy in its further results, in order to note the dangerous influences of its intellectual system on many a nation which follows such modern of thought.

Most people believe in God. This is an idea which logically may be either false or true. Intellectual theory says:

> "If God really exists, then His existence must be logically demonstrable. Pragmatism on the other hand attacks the problem from a different angle, and lays the emphasis on a different aspect. In its view the truth of the idea of God does not depend on logical

> necessity; it depends solely on the profit of this idea to our well-ordered life, in our daily activity and on our experiences. If the idea tends to produce a profit in life, then it is sound and therefore true. Hence, God does exist. Apart from this test, pragmatism claims, in the first place we cannot judge this idea; and in the second place we cannot trust our own judgement."

The Islamic line of thought differs to a greater or lesser extent from that of pure intellectual theory, insofar as it does not entrust the whole question to human logic alone, but relies also upon revelation. But it is in complete opposition to pragmatism; for when we follow out its logic to a conclusion we find that the idea of God must disappear if the outward benefits of material life are not forthcoming.

The idea of God loses its existence because it cannot control its instruments and set the machinery in motion. In consequence, material profit becomes the sole criterion, not only of the acceptance or the rejection of things, but also of existence or non-existence. This implies a state of affairs in which man loses all nobility, where he is neither more nor less than an instrument.

Policies in this world cannot be divorced from such philosophies. Thus perhaps, we are not far from the truth when we say that the policy of the United States on the Palestine question and its stand in the United Nations on the question of Egypt were merely the results of its intellectual background of pragmatism— in conjunction, of course, with other factors.

The idea of right and justice had little effective place in materialistic American life; and hence it had little chance of permanent acknowledgment in international policies. This idea is perhaps the most satisfactory comment on these puzzling policies. What we do not want is to establish such an intellectual background as this, in our Islamic society. We must therefore be cautious about the study of Western philosophy until we have first established in adolescent minds a firm, strong, and clear pattern of thought which is founded on the universal Islamic theory.

Similarly, we must be cautious about borrowing educational techniques, curricula, and systems of teaching; for all of these are ruled by the general field of philosophy in their native lands; they subserve the aims which that philosophy assigns to them, whether immediate or remote.

Moral Philosophy : Literature is the emotional response to life. It issues from the same well-spring whence flow in any culture all the philosophies, the religious beliefs, the experiments and the influences. Literature is the most important factor in the establishment of a moral philosophy of life, and in the production of any specific influence on the human mind. Hence, we must exercise care in the choice of Western literature which we make available to our youth, alike in their Arabic and their foreign studies.

It is not necessary to take this as meaning that our youth are to be prohibited from reading European literature; what we have in mind here is simply a process of choice and selection. For in this literature, there are elements, the spirit of which is at one with the spirit of Islam. By this, we do not mean that such books 'encourage goodness and reprobate wickedness' for literature is no preacher to exhort and to direct. Rather, we mean that such books have a view of life which is spiritual and moral, rather than materialistic, and that they acknowledge the spiritual values of life.

This type of literature agrees in spirit with the general teachings of our Islamic theory; it can therefore do no harm to the moral consciousness of our youth, nor can it upset their emotional and mental development at a dangerous stage. This dangerous stage lasts at least until the third year of university work, if not until the time of graduation.

There is no harm, but rather great benefit, in having private reading including all types of the literatures of the world, without restraint or exception. But the prime aim of a process of choice and selection is to safeguard the period of adolescence from being debilitated and led astray.

History is a branch of literature; but it is one which has its own characteristics, and which therefore had also its peculiar dangers. For history is a presentation of the events of life, and it is necessarily influenced by the materialistic background of the West. Even if it is by intellectual theory that it is influenced, it will still ignore the spiritual powers and their effect on the course of events, together with the spiritual explanation of facts. It will give its own interpretations, designed to establish a philosophy of life independent of the spirit and unconnected with moral aims. Here, it is opposed to Islamic theory.

Beyond this, historians, who have been for the most part Europeans, have made the history of Europe the focal point of world history. In view of the nature of man this is excusable, and we have borne it with patience as a characteristically Western and European delusion. Yet, if our youth are to study history in this spirit and by this method, then they will finish with two false beliefs:

1. That spiritual factors have no influence on the course of events in time, or at least that any such influence is very weak.
2. That Europe is the mistress of historical events, and that the influence of the East and of Islam is exiguous.

Both these ideas have harmful and dangerous results; they establish a false general idea of life, of the world, and of events, and they endanger our patriotic pride and our pride in Islam, which is so necessary in face of the sweeping pride of Europe. In order to guard our youth from this evil we must take the two following steps:

1. We must begin by putting general world history, as Islam views it, in perspective, in the form of events and happenings. We must not be concerned solely with the

European point of view in this present dangerous fashion. In such a history we must give Europe its rightful place and no more, and we must emphasize the part played in world history by the East in general, and by Islam in particular.

2. We must change the present curriculum of history teaching in our schools and colleges. We must start by teaching primarily the history of Islam throughout the Muslim world, and by expounding it from the Islamic point of view. It is not enough to teach our children the history of Islam as written by Western authors, or as expounded by Western philosophies. When their minds are filled with the history of their own countries, then we can give them the world history as written by ourselves, to form the next stage of study. And when they have completed that, then we can give them in successive stages the remainder of the developments of history.

The study of law is similarly influenced by the Western point of view, by Western philosophy, history, law, and society. For law is a reflection of society, or is produced by it; and society is the offspring of all these factors.

In order to build up a sound Islamic doctrine, we must teach Islamic law in a broad general way before beginning to teach any specific legal system. The teaching of Islamic law must be firmly in the control of Muslim professors, and the Western point of view must not be allowed to obtrude, except in the later stages. Similarly, the study of law in general must not be opened up till that same later stage.

It is one of the requirements of Islamic life that the religious law shall occupy a paramount position; and that very fact will make necessary such a study of Islamic law as we have indicated. The great necessity which faces our professors of Islamic law in this field is to follow the authoritative path traced out by the

Imams and their students at the time of the first growth of Islamic law.

When we have disposed of this theoretical question of the objective, we are still confronted by that of the specific constitutional enactments which will ensure a sound form of Islamic life and which will guarantee social justice to all. In this question, it is not possible to take a stand purely on the form of the original Islamic life; rather we must utilize all possible and permissible means which fall within the general principles and the broad foundations of Islam. Nor must we be afraid to use also all the discoveries which man has made in the way of social legislation and systems, so long as the principles of these do not run counter to the principles of Islam, and so long as they are not opposed to its theory of life and mankind.

We must include these in our legislation so long as they conduce to the true welfare of society, or so long as they ward off any impending evil. In the two principles of 'public interest' and 'blocking of means' we have two clear Islamic principles which give wide powers to the temporal ruler to ensure the general welfare at all times and in all places. Before we go on to deal with the application of these two principles it might be well to quote a short passage in explanation of them.

Public Interest: Any welfare measure which has no specific detailed authority to support it is known as a measure of public interest. The question of whether or not it is a root of jurisprudence is a matter of dispute among the jurisconsults. Al-Qarafi has argued that all the jurisconsults have used it or have admitted it as a proof at one time or another, even though in lecturing most of them deny it the status of a root. He says in regard to this point:

> "Other people loudly deny the validity of public interest. But when the case is closely examined, they are found to refer to the word in its absolute sense. They do not trouble to take any account of the evidence

offered by the reference of the term in its synonyms and contexts; they hold that it means merely convenience, and that such is the sole meaning of the phrase, public interest."

No matter whether this claim is true or false, it is certain that the validity of any measure of welfare which lacks a specific validating authority is a matter on which the *Ulama* may well disagree. And even if public interest is not one of the accepted roots of jurisprudence, at least it had the status of a custom, as Al-Qarafi indicates. The opinions of the *Ulama* in this matter can be divided into four main views, as follows:

1. The Shafites and those who share their opinions do not believe in any form of public interest whose validity is unsupported by legal evidence; for they only admit legal precedents and the treatment of these by analogy, based on the existence of a solid connection between the root and its derivatives, that is to say, between a case governed by a precedent and another analogous to it. If we follow Al-Qarafi we must admit that it is strange that they should deny public interest while they admit analogy.
2. The Hanafites and others of similar opinions maintain the principles of preference and analogy, but their interpretation of preference is sometimes almost indistinguishable from public interest. A fair estimate would say that in their system they make a greater use of interest than do the Shafites, But even so, the extent to which they do use it is negligible, and hence we cannot say that this principle is one of the roots of their system; not, at least, on any grounds of the use which they make of it in itself.
3. There are those who attach an excessive importance to public interest, even to the point of making it stronger than precedent in their dealings with cases; they regard it as a form of precedent, or rather, as a form of

consensus. Thus where the *Ulama* are agreed on a point turning on precedent, but some aspect of that point runs counter to public interest, then the validity of the latter is the stronger. This applies also to specific cases, as Al-Tufi has maintained.

4. There are those who hold a middle course, which is the soundest of all. Here, validity is granted to public interest, but it is not derived from precedent, which is held to be entirely different. To this view most of the Malikite rites adhere.

Malik held that public interest was an independent root of the system of jurisprudence, but that it was a derived, rather than an original root; and that so, for the following reasons:

1. The Companions of Allah's Messenger found that questions arose after his death which had not been apparent during his lifetime. Thus, they collected the noble Quran in book form. This had not been done in the time of the Messenger, but now such a collection was in the public interest; for they feared that the Quran might be forgotten because of the deaths of those who had memorized it. Umar saw such men dying in numbers during the Wars of Apostasy, and, fearing that through their death the Quran might pass from memory, he advised Abu-Bakr to have it collected in book form to this the Companions gladly assented.
2. After the death of Allah's Messenger his Companions agreed that the punishment for wine-drinking should be eighty lashes. Their reason for this was the public interest or general inference; for they saw that drinking tended to produce lying and the slandering of chaste women because of the wild talk in which drinkers indulged.
3. The orthodox Caliphs agreed upon imposing conscription on craftsmen, although the root principle

was that the exercise of their craft was a matter of good faith. But it was found that unless they were conscripted they would neglect the care of the people's belongings and wealth. There was great need of craftsmen, and therefore, it was in the public interest to conscript them, that they might perform the duties which they had. Thus Ali, when he prescribed the conscription, said: 'The people's interests cannot be served otherwise.'

4. Umar ibn-al-Khattab used to claim half of the wealth of those governor whom he suspected of having increased their resources by extortion. This also was a form of public interest, because to his mind it was in the interests of the governors to prevent them capitalizing on their power to amass money and heap up illegal plunder.
5. It is told of Ali that he poured out on the ground milk which had been adulterated with water, as a lesson to the man who had done it. This act also was akin to public interest, to show that people were not to adulterate goods.
6. There is tradition that Umar put a whole community to death for the murder of one man, for which they had been jointly responsible. This he did because the public interest demanded it. There was no precedent for the case, but the public interest demanded that the case be considered as one of premeditated murder of a sacrosanct individual. To let the murder pass unavenged would have been to deny the root principle of 'an eye for an eye', while to choose one out of the many who had a hand in the business would have made the whole matter ridiculous. For the man chosen would know that in his case it was not a case of retaliation. Or if it were said that this was an anonymous murder, a killing without a killer, on the grounds that every single individual could not be said to be the murderer, then

> the guilty party was the community itself. The whole of a community can commit a murder in exactly the same way as an individual criminal. And murder can be charged against a community just as it can against a single person, and the members of the community stand in the same relation to the act of murder as does an individual. Hence, the community furthers the public interest when it prevents bloodshed and guards communal life."

Role of the Imams : Another general aspect of public interest is the power which is granted to the Imam to levy upon the rich whatever toll he thinks that the circumstance warrants. This he can do when the public treasury is empty, or when the army has extraordinary needs, while there are no funds to meet those needs. Toll may be levied until the treasury is replenished, or until the needs are sufficiently met.

Further, the Imam has the duty of instituting this levy at times of bountiful harvest and plentiful crops, so that the rich will not be overburdened by the fact that it is they alone who pay it. The public interest here lies in the fact that if a just Imam did not do this, his power would be in vain, and wealthy establishments would provide an incentive to civil war, and to attacks by envious persons. It is sometimes said that the Imam, instead of enforcing the provisions of the levy, borrows money for the public treasury. To this Al-Shatibi retorted that:

> "Borrowing in times of need is allowed only when the treasury has the prospect of more revenue. Otherwise, or alternatively when the revenue is too small to be sufficient, then recourse must be had to the principle of a levy."

A means is that which leads to an end, and to 'block the means' is to remove it. The sense of the phrase is that anything which conduces to a forbidden end is itself forbidden, while anything conducive to a desirable end is itself desirable. Thus, for example, adultery is forbidden, and, therefore, to admire the charms of a strange woman is also forbidden, as being a means towards adultery.

On the other side, attendance at prayers is compulsory, and therefore an effort to attend prayers is also compulsory, as is leaving one's business to make that effort. To make the pilgrimage is compulsory; therefore an effort to visit the Sacred House and to perform the other rites of pilgrimage is also compulsory.

The fundamental reason for the validity of 'blocking the means' is a realization of the repercussions and final results of all actions. If they are conducive to those public interests which constitute the aims and objectives of the dealings of man with man, then they are as desirable as those aims themselves. But if they are not equally desirable, or if their results might be evil, then they are forbidden just as evil is forbidden, even though the means may be somewhat less objectionable.

In considering the results of actions, the matter of interest is not the purpose or the objective of the agent; rather, it is the result and outcome of his action. The individual will be rewarded or punished for his intention in the next world; but in this world, it is according to its result and outcome that an action is good or bad, desirable or undesirable. For this world must take its stand on the welfare of mankind, on judgement and justice, and these things require a scrutiny of results and outcomes rather than of estimable aims and worthy intentions. A man who out of a sincere love for the worthy intentions and for the worship of Allah reviles idols has gained the approval of Allah by the formulation of his purpose; and yet, he has forbidden such reviling in cases where it would result in the rage of the idolaters, who would then revile Allah the Great, Himself. So, His exalted words run:

> "And do not revile those who invoke deities other than Allah, lest in response they revile Allah without knowledge." In this noble prohibition, regard it had

> to be the actual consequences, rather than to the commendable religious aim. Hence, it appears that in cases which tend towards crime or evil, the veto is directed not towards the aim itself, which is sincere, but towards the consequences which will arise; thus an act may be forbidden because of its consequences, even though Allah may be aware that the intention underlying it is sincere.

Sometimes also a man may seek an evil end through a legal act, in which case he is guilty in his own conscience and in the sight of Allah. But no man may take measures against him, nor may any legal penalties be invoked upon him. Such is the case of man who cuts the price of his goods in order to injure a business rival. This is undoubtedly a legal act; yet, it is a means towards a crime, that on injuring another.

This crime is the man's object, but in spite of that his action cannot be punished by the power of the law, nor does it fall under any penalty which the law of the land can impose. His action, from the point of view of intention, is a means to evil, but externally it is a means to public and private benefit. Undoubtedly the seller benefits by selling, by the circulation of his goods, and by the goodwill which he gains; equally certainly the public benefits by the cut in price, by which a general lowering of prices is encouraged.

The principle of blocking the means had regard not only to individual aims and intentions, as we have seen, but also to the encouragement of public welfare and to the prevention of public evil. Thus, it must take account of the consequences along with the intention, or even of the consequences alone.

The principle of 'means' is firmly established in the Quran and the Sunna. In the former, there is the verse: "And do not revile those who invoke Gods other than Allah, lest in response they revile Allah without knowledge." Of this it is related that the idolaters said that they were content to have their Gods reviled if they in turn could revile Muhammad's God. Thus again: "O you who believe, do not say Raina; say Unzurna and hearken. This was because the Muslims used the former word with good intention, but the Jews took it as implying a derogatory sense to the Prophet."

In the Sunna there are many stories of the Prophet and many decisions of his Companions. Among them is that of his refusal to kill the hypocrites, lest the unbelievers should have a pretext for saying that Muhammad killed his Companions.

There is also the story that the Prophet forbade a man who had loaned money to accept a gift from the debtor, unless the gift was counted as part repayment of the loan. The reason was simply that the gift was a means of postponing payment, and was therefore a form of interest. For the lender would get his money back and extra also in the form of the gift. We have also the account of the Prophet's having forbidden that men's hands should be cut off in time of war; the purpose was to stop this practice leading to an illegal treatment of fighting men which would inevitably ensue.

Similarly, laws should not be intermitted in times of war, lest freedom become licence; the two are closely related. And there is the account of the earliest Believers, both Emigrants and Helpers, having on their death-beds appointed their divorced wives as their heirs; this they did because there was a suspicion of a plot to debar such wives from inheriting. It was not even certain that such a plot existed, but divorce was a 'means' which might have produced injustices.

Again, the Prophet forbade monopolies, saying: 'Only sinners hold monopolies.' For a monopoly is a means to oppress the people in all things which are considered to be essential. But there is no law against a monopoly in any article which cannot injure the people by being withheld, such as cosmetics and the life; for these things do not come under the heading of necessities.

The Prophet also forbade any man who had given alms to buy them back, even though, he might see them displayed for sale in the market. Thus, he sought to check the means to recover what had been given to Allah, even by purchase. Thus, anyone who gives alms is forbidden to repossess them by purchase, and is yet more stringently forbidden to repossess them by other means. To permit repossession by purchase might be a means of cheating the poor; the rich out of his wealth would give alms to the poor, and might then buy them back from him at less than their value. The poor man, on the other hand, would see some profit to himself, and thus his conscience would not oppose the sale.

Thus, there are many indications of this principle, deriving from the Messenger and his Companions. Ibn-Qiyam has collected some ninety such examples from actual occurrences, in all of which the principle of blocking the means is clearly illustrated.

"Means are counted to be half of the legal principles of Islam."

These two principles, that of public interest and that of blocking the means, both run back to a common root, that of ensuring the welfare of society. They are integrally connected with the established laws of Islam and with its general purposes. It is these two principles which can guide us towards the legislation necessary to ensure a sound form of Islamic life and to include in its scope a comprehensive social justice.

This principle must be our concern in a general work dealing with social justice in Islam; yet, it is desirable to mention some of the things which Islam is able to ensure in this sphere for the present and the future. We must also deal with the legislation necessary to produce these things, so that it may be used as a pattern for analogous treatment in other cases. We cannot deal with all possible developments but these may be safely left to the dictation of circumstances times and conditions.

Legal Structure

This tax was a compulsory duty in Islam, levied on all possessions according to a sliding scale of one-tenth, one-twentieth, and one-fortieth. In all cases, it represented a very small fraction, and hence, it is but natural that the question should arise: How could such a small sum be of assistance to all the Muslim poor? To answer this question we must consider the following facts:

1. The small amount of capital on which the tax had to be paid made the greater part of the community liable to it. The exemption value for the poor-tax was fixed at six pounds, which meant that practically all the population had to pay the tax; thus the income from it was relatively great.
2. Disbursements from the tax money were confined to specifically limited classes of people. For their livelihood the great majority had to rely on work, which has always been reckoned by Islam to be the primary source of a living.
3. Most important of all, the livelihood of the very poor did not depend solely upon this source of income. There were also the vast sums acquired as booty during the war days, sums which lasted for more than half a century. In this booty all the fighting men shared, and most of them were of the poor classes. They received four-fifths of the booty, while the other fifth was turned into a charitable foundation for the benefit of all classes of necessitous persons, relatives, orphans, the destitute, and the wayfarer. And when Umar resolved not to take the booty away from the conquered countries, but to leave it for the benefit of the native peoples, he instituted the land-tax in its place, as this later on was sufficient to provide for all the poor.

Today, the last primary source of revenue is no longer

available, and the poor-tax in itself is not sufficient. Therefore, we must consider alternative sources to take the place of booty and plunder, in order to provide an ample living for the generality of men.

Before we consider new sources we must first exhaust the poor-tax as a source in itself. It is a compulsory duty, and it must be paid if the community is justifiably to be described as Islamic. For the payment of the poor-tax is a spiritual duty as well as financial one. Again, we must consider the source of the poor-tax as including all types of property, some of which are not at present included because they were not familiar in the early days of Islam.

That is to say, we must bear in mind those forms of wealth which are liable to the poor-tax but which are not mentioned in the Quran except generally in the verse:

> "O you who have believed, expend of the goods which you have acquired, and of that which We have provided for you from the Earth. And do not propose any evil in thus expending it; for you got it yourselves only by connivance."

The fact that the poor-tax was prescribed as a duty only upon such types of property as were familiar in the time of the Prophet does not prevent its being prescribed today as a duty on all that is known as Property or wealth, and on all that produces an income. It may not be of difference that such things may not be the kind on which the tax was originally imposed.

Similarly, we can control the outlets for the tax money, just as Umar exercised the same control when he stopped payments designed to convert unbelievers. It must not be given in any form of money to those who are eligible for it; rather it must be given to them in the basic form of goods or services, or it must be used to buy for them some part of their basic necessities. The source of their livelihood must be fixed and unconnected with any kind of temporary or haphazard charity; for these things are not in accord with the needs of modern life.

But in any case such detailed considerations have no place in this book. The scope of our thinking here is the broad field of the promotion of social justice and equity, as the Muslim world gives its attention to a renaissance of the true Islamic life.

Mutual Responsibility of Society : The Prophet said: "Any household which suffers a man to remain hungry among them is outside the protection of Allah, the Blessed and the Exalted." In this brief sentence, he emphasized the principle of mutual responsibility in society, a principle which most of us must recognize from the precedents and the examples provided by our study of the Quran. This principle was authoritatively imposed on both the individual and the social conscience. Today the law must again enforce it as an essential root of Islam. This means that the law can enforce that which Umar intended to enforce:

> "If I had known earlier what I now know, I would have taken the excess of their wealth from the rich and given it to the poor."

Thus, the law can impose taxes, the only limit of which is the establishment of equality in the social sphere, the removal of crime and oppression from the community in general, and the ample provision of food and drink, clothing and housing, medical treatment and skill for every single individual in the country. It does not matter how much tax is placed upon capital so long as the latter is not thereby made incapable of work and of reasonable increase; this condition must be observed because the steady turning of the wheels of labour brings other benefits which cannot be overlooked.

Thus, the law can put into the hands of the poor with perfect justification a stretch of funded property which they may use without paying any basic rent, or at a nominal rent, that they may from it obtain a means of life. For this constitutes a source of livelihood and is the only means of work within their power. By this act the law will fulfil the Messenger's words:"

> "Anyone of you may permit to his brother the use of his land as gift, without exacting for it any agreed rent."

The law may also with justification fix the wage of the factory or the farm worker at a stipulated proportion of the production or of the harvest. The lowest limit of this wage must be a competence to cover food and drink and clothing, and medicine and medical care to a certain extent. The standard is to be taken as that of a moderate living, determined by the proportion of the inhabitants of the country to its general wealth.

General Taxation : Every individual in the Muslim community has the duty of taking a share in the general expenses of the state according to his ability. We have already noticed the opinion of the Imam Malik on what may be done when the treasury is empty, or when the needs of the army are increased; the law has the power according to need to levy a toll on the wealth of the rich. Similar to the needs of the army are the other needs of the state, such as improvements in public services, irrigation of waste lands, the education of the people, and the medical treatment of the sick.

All these things are communal duties which must be met and satisfied just as much as the needs of the army; they must be preserved as strongly as frontiers and defence posts must be guarded. This is particularly true today when wars make demands on all the resources and services of the belligerent nations. In modern war, everyone may be said to be in the army, and thus should be capable of taking responsibility in time of peace.

Public Resources : Monopolies on the necessities of life are forbidden by Islam. A monopoly on food is forbidden, for example, since Islam has always asserted the communal ownership of water, pasturage, and fire, as being the primary needs of life. But the needs of life are not unchangeable, varying as they do from age to age. Consequently, the preservation of this general Islamic principle demands what is known today as the nationalization of natural resources.

It is essential not to have in the hands of private individuals or companies the resources of water, light, heat, electricity, coal and oil, or the resources of public transport and public food supplying, and other such things. For private ownership gives the power of monopoly, imposes upon the general public he will of the monopolists, and permits them to indulge in that disgraceful exploitation which we witness today.

The head of the state has the power to make all these things state-owned, and to fix prices and costs of them so that they can get it at equitable rates without excessive prices. By these means the Islamic aims for the checking of monopolies can be realized.

Public Interest and the Blocking of Means : Everything which tends to advance the public welfare or to retard oppression of the public is a duty laid upon the law, and everything which tends towards a prohibited end is itself prohibited. The application of these established principles of Islam lays on the law today following duties:

1. The taking of excessive wealth out of the hands of bloated capitalists. The fact that such excessive wealth is in their possession tends towards a number of crimes. In the first place, it tends to produce that luxury which is forbidden by Islam. Luxury is a relative matter, which can be defined only in terms of the general condition in each age and country. The permanent rule is that luxury shall not increase beyond the mean struck by the national wealth in proportion to the population. One result of luxury is the iniquitous rise in prices which springs from the fact that one section of the

populace has an unlimited power to buy, while the goods available for sale are not equal to the demand. Another result is the rise of social vices, springing from the fact that some people possess more money than they need; to dispose this, they look for illegal outlets and seek sensual and corrupt pleasures; through these, their morals and their standards are degraded, and on the other hand their victims are the needy men and women who always exist in an unbalanced society.

2 The removal of extreme, poverty, because it results in the way of crime and evil. These results include a great number of social evils which can only exist in surroundings of privation and destitution, theft, infamy, and moral degradation, a general atmosphere of corruption. This is over and above the vast differences which are set between those who have and those who have not, the hatreds and the social disturbances which the law must prevent before they occur by removing their causes. If it be asked how this extreme poverty is to be removed, it is by the ample provision of work for every able-bodied man, and by the provision of an adequate wage, by social security for all who are disabled, and by speedy relief. This is the method in general outline; the specific applications are easy once the general aim is established.

3. The struggle against disease and ignorance: Because of their evil effect on the individual and the community these weaken the general strength of the community and afford a footing to its enemies. This condition is forbidden, as is any factor which leads to it. Nothing can oppose disease and ignorance successfully except a rise in living standards and in general wealth; but the laws of charity and such other things are only a palliative to soothe the sore, not to heal it. The real treatment is that every individual should be possessed of private

means for medical and educational purposes. Or alternatively that medical care and education should be provided free to every individual in the country on a common basis and to a common level. The rich must not be able, by money, to get more than the poor in schools or hospitals.

Legacies : When there are present at the division of the estate relatives, orphans and poor people, give them a provision out of it and speak to them fair. Thus runs the Quranic precept. It clearly means that out of every estate there must be a share for relatives, orphans and the poor. The law has the power of disposal according to the nature of the case; it may change the beneficiaries, or it may leave them unchanged. So, Umar did in the case of paying out money to convert others to Islam. The law also has the power to apply the regulations according to the needs of the estate or according to those of the community.

We must remember that the meaning of being 'present' can legitimately be extended to cover virtual presence, 'that is to say, existence. In every community, there are orphans and poor, and there is no necessity for them to be present in person when an estate is being divided; they are already present in time and space. So by the power of the law all duties must be enforced which are not enforced by the power of conscience.

Mutual Help and Usury : Islam rooted out usury, and fought it in all its forms and appearances; hence, it is impossible for any form of Islamic life to exist on an economic basis which includes the principles of usury. We have already discussed the causes which made Islam unable to countenance usury, but they may be summed up by saying that it is the negation of the spirit of mutual help and friendliness. If usury obtains, then it is to the benefit of the capitalist who can thus increase his wealth without working and without the risk of loss.

The national economy must be set on a basis of mutual help rather than of usury. All the faults which can be alleged against the later system have been summed up to justify its rejection by Maulana Muhammad Ali in his book, *Islam and the New World Order*, from which we may quote the following passage:

> "It is objected that to forbid interest on money will hinder business and commercial transactions, and will hinder the accomplishment of important domestic projects. We may grant the truth of this, but on the other side we have the far greater advantage that to proscribe interest will prevent world wars, which can only end in misery, and which are kindled and inflamed only by loans and debts governed by interest. And if we examine the facts of the case, we shall find that from the very first, trade followed its natural course and spread over more and more widely! Wider limits were brought within the Islamic sphere. So that today the Islamic states are still among the greatest of the old-established countries of the civilized world."

This prohibition of usury cannot in any sense be reconciled with the conditions of the new world which materialistic Western civilization is bringing into being. The social system most required is that practical system which Islam today has in mind, which was successfully applied in practice by, at its inception, centuries ago. The As for the capital sums, without which business cannot be carried on, there was little difference between the gains which they made under the Islamic system and those which they made by ordinary lending; for the Islamic system was in effect of partnership between capital and labour. Such a partnership is not impossible, for the Islamic system holds that capital and labour should share together in all profit and loss; whereas the result of paying a steady rate of interest is that, capital makes a continual profit, even when labour had to work at a loss.

It is sometimes objected that the partnership of capital and labour in both profits and losses is not practicable, because it means that regular accounts have to be kept, since this is one of the necessities of trade; and further, because trading records have to be available for the assessing of taxes which have to be paid. But all the share-issuing companies which take part in trading on a large scale have to keep accounts.

Indeed this partnership system is more to the public advantage than that of giving all the dividends to capital; for it is the latter system which produces most of the evils of capitalism, and which is the source of the oppression of the workers. And the loans which are floated by governments or companies to carry out immense projects such as railroads or canals or such things have done no more than prove this point.

But since the system of state banking depends on the principle of mutual help, which is approved by the Islamic social system, it must be of great benefit to mankind.

This is a general statement, the particular details of which are too lengthy for a book dealing with general ideas. At the same time, there can be no harm in giving an example as a guide to the general objective which we have in mind. Suppose, the state decrees the abolition of interest on funds in banks, companies, public enterprises, and private loans, what will happen then?

What will happen will be that capitalists will find themselves unable to increase their wealth except by two general methods. First, they may put it to some profitable use themselves in manufacture or trade or agriculture. Or second, they may put it to a profitable and helpful use by investing it in share-issuing companies, where the share values may rise or fall. Both these methods are sanctioned by Islam, and neither of them will work the slightest injury to economic life.

It is sometimes feared that the rich will refrain from depositing their money in the banks, which generally finance the large public projects. This is an imaginary danger which gains currency among us because we are familiar only with European methods of using money.

In Europe, the primary natural impulse is to make money increase; this can be accomplished only by using it for some means of exploitation, and so, this natural impulse is a guarantee that money will not be kept out of circulation. But when he desired to take in handsome large project to justify what is known as the great ear of production, we have the power to create legislation covering various kinds of industry; this legislation enacts that no new enterprise may be set up except on the basis of capital over such and such a sum. On that capital sums flow in to take up shares and to become liable to profit and loss on the market.

Thus, there is no more need for banks, except for the issuing of currency. If other banks wish to make a profit, then they must only with permission-in some profit seeking enterprise, where the shares are liable to fluctuation in the open market. But the system will not stop the flow of capital, either domestic or foreign; for the greater proportion of capital wealth is not deposited in banks, but is put out to profit in enterprises.

At for insurance companies, it may be that their basis is Islamic, inasmuch as the funds which are deposited with them are liable to profit and loss, to fall or rise. Funds deposited in these companies are put to work in profit-seeking enterprises, subject to fluctuation. Everytime a beneficiary receives more than he has paid in, the amount of the company's loss is deducted from the remainder of the depositors in proportion to the funds which they have invested. Thus insurance companies' members form a body united for mutual help; in effect they pay out of their own pockets to support any unfortunate one of their number, when need arises.

They have a form of security from which they can benefit in time, of hardship or need. This can be applied also to savings banks and similar institutions, all of which rest on the basis of mutual help in one way or another, and from which funds are employed in profit- seeking enterprises, always liable to fluctuation. Such institutions have no fixed rate of interest, and hence our economic system here can be free from the taint of usury; hence also all capital is compelled to work as the only method of achieving profit and increase.

Gambling : Gambling is a dishonest practice, both in act and in spirit, for it represents an effort to make money without working. In addition, it produces enmity and hatred among its adherents, and gives rise to laxity and insecurity in the fabric of society. There are many forms of gambling, of which lotteries are but one. It is not any spirit of charity which prompts people to buy lottery tickets, not is it any desire to assist works of healing and charity. It is merely the desire to gain more money without working. This is at once practically and spiritually dishonest, as we have said; it hinders and retards the feelings of mercy. There is no need to mention the disgraceful foreign race-meetings which draw their immense crowds; this is merely the outcome of luxury, and the corrupting result of luxury loving natures with their aversion to virtue and their love of vice, with their avarice except when money is lavished on sensual pleasures and coarse enjoyment.

We must halt the practice of gambling altogether, with its green tables, its tempting lottery tickets, and its late hours. Islamic life had need of none of these things, and Islam will never admit that relations between man and man should ever stand on such a basis, or that charity should spring from such impure desires.

Prostitution : Prostitution is the product of spiritual degradation and material destitution, sometimes together and sometimes separately. Islam prohibits illegal sexual intercourse in all its forms, and the most degraded of these is prostitution. Lewdness is the poison characteristic of an unbalanced community, for the two factors which produce prostitution are excessive wealth and humiliating necessity. It was once said:

> "A well-born woman cannot feed from her own breasts because she is hungry; but she may do so if she is in danger of death."

We must not expose people on the one hand to the trials of need, and on the other to the temptations of wealth and other things, and then expect them to be models of self-control and virtue. The principle of blocking the means, demands that the law gives attention to check this thing at its root. The laws affecting prostitution must be established without delay.

Alcohol : The nature of these laws needs no discussion. Alcohol is undeniably forbidden, and the Islamic community can never countenance its use. It is closely related to prostitution in most cases, and is especially allied to it socially; similarly, it is related to luxury and to the destitution which arises from luxury. For luxury produces a spiritual weakness and a need for inhibiting thought and vital activity by means of some intoxicant. Whereas the life, the work, and the watchfulness which Islam prescribes can never be reconciled with alcohol or with any other drug.

Islam forms a plastic social system, capable of adaptation to all times and all circumstances; it is preserved by its general spiritual principles. Its duty is to ensure a form of life which will be virtuous, sound, productive, and strong; to ensure a comprehensive social justice based on all the foundations of human nature, and aiming at giving every man his due. But it must never stand in the way of fruitful individualism, nor must it permit individualism to become a harmful egotism.

The Islamic theory of life is the finest that the world has known because it brings together the material and the spiritual elements of life, making out of them a unity directed towards the highest standards and aimed at patterns which can be actually achieved. It does not envisage objectives which are woven only of the imagination.

But the perplexed and disturbed world, fearful and cautious, can only be brought to Islam and to peace, can only be given complete security and justice, when it returns to this perfect social system, under the will of Allah.

Where Experiment Failed?

After taking stock of the failure of the national constitutions and international charters in protecting the fundamental rights of man, we now come to the basic question: Why could not man so far succeed in finding out a satisfactory arrangement for the protection of his rights, and why this problem has defied thought, intellect and understanding of man so far?

The Quran furnishes a definite and decisive answer to this. It tells that there is only one cause of all this corruption. You have changed the Sovereign, and the tin-gods you have fashioned for yourself as the centre of all your obedience and loyalties have you in their clutches and are denying you your rights. The Quran says that the first covenant of man was made with his Creator and the real Ruler of this universe. And according to this covenant recognizing God as the Sovereign every one had individually taken an oath of allegiance to Him alone and none else besides Him. Nor shall any partners be assigned to Him whether it be in His Person, attributes or authority. This oath of allegiance and bearing witness to His Sovereignty was the basis of man being made the vicegerent of God, the true Sovereign, and his being sent in His Realm with a way of life prescribed for him.

Here he had to run all his individual and collective affairs according to this code of conduct as also according to the guidance received from Him through His Messengers and His Revelations from time to time. In this covenant, which was renewed and reminded of from time to time and which was presented to mankind in its most perfect and complete form through the last Prophet, Muhammad (Salam) and for ever made immune against perversion, so that it may serve for the guidance of mankind to the end of days, the absolute rights and powers of the Sovereign. His kingdom which knows of no frontiers, the true nature of His man's relationship with Him and His servant—the position of man in the world, the goal of his life, the means of attaining this goal, the norms of success and failure, the mutual relationship between man and man, the sphere of the activities of individual and collective life, the powers of those entrusted with the collective affairs of men in this kingdom of God, the limits and conditions of obedience, accountability for each and every deed of his before the Sovereign in the Hereafter and according to the record of his conduct here in this world, the reward or punishment, every thing is given in such detail that in their light the right and straight path of life has been made quite evident.

Now whoever takes to the straightpath, also called the path of rectitude by the Quran, is successful in this life as well in the next, to be rewarded with eternal bliss; and whoever, leaving this path, takes to another path of his own liking and chalked out by himself, is doomed to failure here in this life and liable for eternal torment in the next.

The whole Quran was revealed to point out this "Straight Path" and the "Path of Rectitude", The Psalms of David, Torah and Bible were all revealed to make clear this path. Right from the first man and prophet of God, Adam, to the last Prophet Muhammad (Salam) all the prophets come only with this message: "Servants of God! Do not make the servants of God your god. You are passing your life under the only Sovereign Whose unlimited, eternal and all pervading authority and rule extends over every little particle of this universe. Other than Him you have no Lord and Cherisher, no Absolute Ruler, no Master and no Sustainer. Going through the Quran we find that all the prophets had the one and only mission —to end the sovereignty of the tyrants of their time, Pharaoh, Nimrods and others and redeeming the servants of God from abject slavery to them, bring them back to the service and obedience of the wisest of judges."

Before taking stock in some detail of the effects on human life of living up to the terms of this covenant and also of turning away from it, let us see what that first covenant was which the servants of God made with their Lord.

> When thy Lord drew forth the children of Adam—from their loins—their descendants, and made them testify concerning themselves, (saying): "Am I not your Lord (Who cherishes and sustains you)?" They said : "Yea ! We do testify!" (This) lest you should say on the Day of Judgement: "Of this we were never mindful" or lest you should say: "Our fathers before us may have taken false gods, but we are (their) descendants after them: wilt thou then destroy us for the deeds of men who were futile."
>
> Al Quran VII: 172-173.

The Covenant : Long before commencement of the life of man on earth, was this covenant made, and has certain very prominent points for our consideration:

1. Accepting Allah as one's only Cherisher and Lord.
2. All the men from the time without beginning to the end of days taking oath of allegiance to God individually and their being witness to that oath.
3. Promise on oath to abstain from polytheism or taking any other god instead of God or ascribing partners to the one and only God.
4. Closing the door for putting forth the creed and practices of forefathers as an excuse for polytheism.
5. Accountability for each and every deed of this world in the next.

Allah also made arrangements for continual reminders and renewal of the commitment after this first ever covenant of His servants, lest digressing from the straight path of guidance, they may not fall into the abyss of lowness and disgrace by becoming the slaves of any one else other than Allah. The covenant made with men collectively, was made individually also with the prophets who were sent for the ratification and as a reminder of their first covenant, although they were among those participating in the first covenant as the progeny of Adam.

But to make them realise the high position and the great responsibilities of that position, the Lord and Cherisher of the Heavens and the Earth took an oath of allegiance from them individually:

> Behold! God took the covenant of the Prophets' saying: "I give you a Book and Wisdom; then comes to you an apostle, confirming what is with you: do ye believe in him and render him help". God said: "Do ye agree and take this My covenant as binding on you?" They said: "We agree". He said: "Then bear witness, and I am with you among the witnesses." If any turn back after this, they are perverted transgressors.
>
> Al Quran III:82.

These covenants of the position of vicegerency and that of prophet-hood were renewed time and again. Allah renewed this covenant with every prophet and every Ummah separately:

> And remember We took from the prophets their covenant: from Nuh, Ibrahim, Moses and Jesus, the son of Mary: We took from them a solemn covenant that (God) may question the (custodians) of Truth, concerning the Truth they (were charged with): And He has prepared for the unbelievers a grievous Penalty.
>
> Al Quran XXXIIL-7-8

The covenants made with the prophets did not only include acceptance of Allah as the Sovereign and exclusion of others from servitude meant for Allah alone, but they were also asked to take an oath of allegiance to Allah that they would proclaim the faith of Allah over all other religions and redeem them from the rebels who have taken to the path of disobedience and rebellion, and in the realm of Allah have carved out a kingdom for themselves, and made the servants of Allah their own slaves, and depriving them of the freedom conferred on them by Allah, have tried to make them subservient to themselves. Reminding the prophets of their mission, the Quran says:

> The same religion has He established for you as that which He enjoined on Nuh—the which We have sent by inspiration to thee—and that which We enjoined on Ibrahim, Moses and Jesus: camely, that ye should remain steadfast in Religion and make no divisions therein: Al Quran XLII:13.

The Ummah, literally a group, a community or a nation, in Islamic terminology, a group or community organised on the basis of revelation and the teachings and preachings of an apostle or prophet of God for whose guidance the prophets had been sent, were also asked to take an oath of allegiance and were reminded of their covenants. Addressing the children of Israel it was said:

> God did aforetime take a firm covenant from the children of Israel, and We appointed twelve captains among them. And God said: "I am with you if ye (but) establish regular prayers, practise regular charity (give Zakat regularly), believe in My apostles, honour and assist them, and loan to God a beautiful loan, verily I will wipe out from you evils, and admit you to Gardens with rivers flowing beneath; but if any of you, after this, resisteth faith, he hath truly wandered from the path of rectitude. Al Quran V: 13.

At another place the same covenant has been recalled to mind thus:

> And remember a covenant from the children of Israel (to this effect): worship none but God; treat with kindness your parents and kindred, and orphans and those in need; speak fair to people: be stead fast in prayer; and Practise regular charity (give Zakat regularly). Then did ye turn back, except a few among you, and you back-slide (even now). And remember We took your covenant (to this effect): shed no blood amongst you, nor turn out your own people from

> your homes: and this ye solemnly ratified, and to this ye can bear witness. Al Quran II : 82-84.

In these verses we find not only acceptance of Allah as one's Lord and Cherisher, but the whole code of conduct for which the covenant had been made. These verses also reveal that all the prophets of Allah have been coming with the same message. These injunctions for establishing prayers and paying the Zakat is not just poor-due or alms or charity as translated by some translators of the Quran. Of the two types of worships, one involving physical effort, like prayer and fasting, and the other spending out of the God-given bounties, in His way. Zakat falls in the second category.

It is just as obligatory as prayers, and not optional as the words alms or charity suggest. A believer not paying Zakat in spite of capacity to do so, is a transgressor. But one denying its obligatory nature is no more a believer unless and until he repents and mends his mode of thought spending in the way of Allah, kind treatment to parents, kindreds, orphans and those in need, speaking only the truth, respect for human life and abstaining from making people the targets of oppression and tyranny, have not been given to the followers of Muhammad (Salam) alone but all the Ummah of the past had been given the same injunctions, and Allah has taken the covenant of all peoples to abide by the same code of conduct for life for the establishments of human society on moral principles.

The children of Israel have also been reminded of their covenants with Allah in Quran 11: 93, 95, III: 187 and IV: 154-155.

Let us now have a look at the following remarks of the Quran about the followers of Jesus Christ:

> From those who call themselves Christians, We did take a covenant, but they forgot the part of the Message that was sent to them. Al Quran V : 14

After relating the account of the covenants taken from the

Ummah of the past, breach of trust and its fatal consequences, the Quran addresses the Ummah of the Last Prophet thus:

> And call in remembrance the favour of God unto you, and His covenant, which He ratified with you, when ye said "We hear and we obey": and fear God, for God knoweth well the secrets of your hearts.
>
> Al Quran V:7

Alongwith reminding the Ummahs separately of the responsibilities of their covenants, Allah, drawing their attention to their first ever covenant, addresses the entire mankind thus:

> Did I not enjoin on you, O ye children of Adam, that you should not worship Satan; for that he was to you an avowed enemy? and that ye should worship Me, for this was the straight path?
>
> Al Quran XXXVI:60-61

The Quran, along with making mankind realize the responsibilities of their covenant, puts before them very clearly the consequences of living up to it and also those of its contravention, so that they may not remain labouring under the misapprehension, that there is going to be no accountability and punishment for their breach of trust, nor be dispirited with the erroneous idea that making good his promise was not going to benefit him. Allah, giving glad tidings of a great reward to the keepers of the trust and warning to the defaulters against a painful torment, Himself makes a covenant with His servants:

> Nay—those that keep their plighted faith and act a right,—verily God loves those who act a right. As for those who sell the faith they owe to God and their own plighted word for a small price, they shall have no portion in the Hereafter. Al Quran III : 76-77

> Those who break God's covenant after it is ratified, and who sunder what God has ordered to be joined,

> and do mischief on earth: these cause loss (only) to themselves. Al Quran II: 27

The same thing has been said in verse 25 of Surah Rad (XIII) in a slightly different manner. Pointing out the difference between those keeping their pledge and those breaking the vow and the reason for the different treatments meted out to them, Allah says:

> Is then one who doth know that which hath been revealed unto thee from thy Lord is the Truth, like one who is blind? It is those who are endued with understanding that receive admonition; Those who fulfil the covenant of God and fail not in their plighted word. Al Quran XIII : 19-20

These verses of the Quran reveal that right from Adam to the last individual of his off spring, every one of us, under the first ever covenant and then its renewal individually through every Prophet, is strongly bound in this covenant with his Greater and Master that he would not take any one else as his Lord and Cherisher and shall not bow down his head before any one in subservience other than Him. He shall not recognise any one as his absolute ruler and shall shape his individual and collective life according to the guidance and injunctions received from his Sovereign through the prophets raised by Him, received finally in their most perfect form through Muhammad, His last Prophet, made immune against all perversion and distortion. If ever a mortal among them rises to proclaim himself as their god, his claim shall be thrown back into his face; and he shall receive the treatment that rebels deserve. He himself will obey his Lord and Cherisher and call others too to it. Not in any single affair of his life he will act but in accordance with the injunction of Allah, conveyed through His prophet and obey only those in authority obeying Allah and His prophet and he will completely abstain from polytheistic practices.

After this elucidation of the First Ever covenant and its

renewal let us now see what are the effects of recognising Allah as the sole Sovereign or rejecting His Sovereignty, on man's life, and how through the decision of man on one or the other side, the distance between the Truth and Falsehood goes on increasing until they are poles apart, and how man basically enjoying the status of the vicegerent of Allah and the noblest entity in this universe, next only to his Lord, losing all his high status and position falls into the abysmal depths of lowness and disgrace.

He, the Lone Sovereign : Under the covenant of Allah, taking Him alone as the Sovereign, and to stick to it as His obedient servant, the following inference automatically emerges.

1. The state has come into existence not through any social contract but as the natural corollary of the covenant between man and his Greater and Master.
2. According to this covenant, there is only one Lord and Cherisher and all the rest are His servants.

To command is for none but God: Al Quran XII-54

It is for Him alone to create and to govern ?
Al Quran VII:40

3. There is no partner in His authority (Sovereignty), nor any equal.

He has no partner in (His) dominion:
Al Quran XVII-III

Nor does He share His command with any person whomsoever. Al Quran XVIIL.26

Do not turn to any one except Allah for help. There is no god other than Allah. Al Quran XXVIII:88

4. His authority is eternal and all pervasive. Not a single particle in the entire universe is beyond His control.

To Him belongs what is in the heavens and on earth and all between them and all beneath the soil.
Al Quran XX-7

To Him belongs every being that is in the heavens and on earth: all are subservient to Him.

Al Quran XXX.-26

5. This world of ours and the entire universe beyond it is one kingdom or State.

Blessed be He in Whose hands is Dominion; and He over all things hath power; Al Quran LXVII

His Throne doth extend over the heavens and the earth. Al Quran 11:255

6. Man is the vicegerent of Allah on earth and as such after his Creator, he is the noblest and most dignified entity in the universe.

It is He Who hath made you (His) Vicegerent on earth. Al Quran VI: 165

We have honoured the sons of Adam; provided them with transport on land and sea: given them for sustenance things good and pure; and conferred on them special favours above a great part of Our creation.

Al Quran XVIL70

7. The logical result of there being one single authority (Sovereign) and one single kingdom (State) is the unity of mankind. As the citizens of a single state and the subjects of One Sovereign, all men are equal. All differences and distinctions of colour, race, language and territory are baseless.

O mankind! We created you from a single (pair) of a male and a female, and made you into nations and tribes, that ye may know each other (not that ye may despise each other). Al Quran XLIX;13

8. The natural concomitant of the unity of mankind was that the whole offspring of Adam must have been given the same code of conduct for their life. The Quran says:

The Religion before God is only Islam (Submission to His Will); Al Quran III; 9

Faith, from Day One : This is not the religion represented by Muhammad alone. All the prophets of Allah through the ages had been calling humanity to this faith, and they were all Muslims (Submitting to the Will of Allah).

9. A single code of conduct for life provided man the basis for the building up of the same individual and collective character. In spite of the differences of natural capacities, trends, and leanings, the different natures of the obligations and responsibilities, the unity of the goal and the similarity of basic sentiments and factors of the building of character gave man the same hue as regards his thought and action, which Allah Himself termed 'Colour from Allah.'

> (We take our) colour from Allah, and who is better than Allah at colouring. We are His worshippers.
>
> Al Quran 11:138.

10. This code of conduct for man's life is based on the highest moral and spiritual values. Therefore it completely ends the clashers interests, existence of classes, and antagonism and conflicts between individual and collective life and establishes among men perfect harmony of thought and a strong relationship of practical cooperation. It also strikes at the roots of snatch and grab, plunder, exploitation and greed and creates in man the spirit of mutual sympathy and sacrifice. And in this way putting an end to the possibility of grouping together of classes based on material interests, brings into existence a classless society. Morality is the spirit and foundation-stone of this code of conduct for human life. The Quran puts forth this morality as the greatest attribute of the Prophet:

> And thou (standest) on an exalted standard of character. Al Quran LXVIll:4

> You have indeed in the apostle of God a beautiful pattern (of conduct) Al Quran XXXIII:21

11. In this code of conduct, field for competition and vying with one another has been provided so that the spirit of striving and action and the natural desire of man to go ahead of others may help in the manifestation of his individual capabilities and the development of his personality. But this spirit of competition had been cleansed of such motives of getting material comforts and fulfilment of personal ends and aspirations in a manner which creates enmity between man and man, push him down to the lowest level of beasts. Here, there is competition but in "Taqwa" or fear of (the displeasure of) Allah which aims at the purity of soul, the moral elevation and inculcate the quality of obedience to the commandments of Allah with all one's heart and soul and the total submission of one's personality. Here, greatness does not mean a person possessing more wealth than others, living in high and magnificent mansions and enjoying luxuries denied to millions of men like him. Rather real greatness lies in his record of good deeds and obedience to Allah which may elevate his position in the sight of Allah and he may be entitled to better reward than others.

The most honoured of you in the sight of God is (he who is) the most righteous of you.

Al Quran XI-IX: 13.

This is the criteria of superiority established by Allah. According to this standard a person can excel others only in the field of virtue and piety. No other standard of honour and superiority carries any weight with Allah.

12. The code of conduct for man's life is not merely a lifeless collection of beautiful principles. There is a powerful sanction behind it. And it is this sanction that is its real spirit. The Sovereign says:

Then shall any one who has done an atom's weight

> of good see it! And any one who has done an atom's weight of evil shall see it. Al Quran XCIX:7-8

> Verily We have warned you of a Penalty near, the day when man will see (the Deeds) which his hands have sent forth. Al Quran LXXVU1:40

This concept of the accountability in the Hereafter introduces an element of responsibility in his life and protects him from becoming refractory and instead of following the dictates of his own will and the strong urges of his innerself, he keeps before himself the will and pleasure of his Master: his Lord and Cherisher.

13. In this kingdom of God there is perfect rule of law. The duty of his servants is to follow this law in their own lives, and in their capacity as the vicegerents on earth it is their duty to enforce it also. None of them, not even any prophet of Allah has any right to make the slightest change in this law by way of amendment, cancellation, deletion or addition.

The way an ordinary person follows it in his life, a prophet has also to do the same. There are no privileged personages here and no body is above the law. Such a concept of the rule of law is not to be found any where except in the faith of Allah:

> We have sent down to thee the Book in truth, that thou mightest judge between men, as guided by God. Al Quran I.V:105

> Say: "It is not for me, of my own accord, to change it: 1 follow naught but what is revealed unto me: if I were to disobey my Lord, I should myself fear the penalty of a Great Day (to come). Al Quran X: 15

14. Like the eternal, untransferable and irrevocable, sovereignty, the fundamental rights conferred on man by Him are eternal and irrevocable. No body has a right to change or curtail them. These well protected and definite rights establish a firm relationship between the

> individual and the state, and instead of mutual bickerings and strife, make them each other's helper and guardian. The Divine laws do not change every day. In those spheres (of life) in which He has given man freedom (of choice) no one has any rights to meddle with it. And where He has given definite commandments, no one has any right of legislation in that sphere.

> The word of thy Lord doth find its fulfilment in truth and in justice: None can change His words:
>
> Al Quran VI: 115

> No change (let there be) in the work (wrought) by God: that is the standard Religion.
>
> Al Quran XXX:30

> No change will thou find in the practice approved, of God. Al Quran XXXIIL 62.

> There is none that can alter the word and Decrees of God. Al Quran VI:34.

That means, the code of conduct for life of man conferred by Allah is a permanent constitution, not an iota of which can be changed until the end of days.

Pondering over the consequences of abiding by the covenant of Allah one must invariably conclude that in taking this covenant, Allah has been most beneficent and gracious to man. This covenant is really the Magna Carta of freedom through which the sovereignty of man over man has been put to an end. Allah abhors it that man whom. He gave such a beautiful shape (And has given you shape and made your shapes beautiful Al Quran XL:64), and created man in the best of moulds, (We have indeed created man in the best of moulds, Al Quran XCV:4), who has been endowed with the wealth of knowledge (And He taught Adam the names of all things; Al Quran 11:31) unto whose service were pressed all the objects in the universe (Seest thou not that God has made subject to you men all that is on the earth, and the ships that sail through the sea by His command—Al Quran XXIL65), and breathing into him His own spirit, made him worthy of the obeisance of the angels (Breathed into him of My spirit, fall ye down in obeisance unto him. Al Quran XV:29), he should degrade himself by serving other men like himself and fall down in obeisance to other creatures (much lower than himself), thus divesting himself of the honour and greatness conferred on him by Allah, should go down the abysmal depths of degradation and lowliness. He repeatedly brings home to man, in man's own interest that in the creed of the unity of Allah there is honour, superiority, dignity and eminence. Slightest digression from this creed ultimately leads to perdition and destruction. That is why the entire stress of the Quran is centred on two points, the unity of Allah and the position of roan as servant of Allah. It elucidates the point in different contexts and forbids him to bow down to any person or thing. He says:

1. Verily those whom ye call upon besides God are servants like unto you: Al Quran VII: 194
2. Such is God your Lord: to Hirn belongs all Dominion. And those ye invoke besides Him have not the least power. Al Quran XXXV: 13
3. If there were in the heavens and the earth, other gods besides God, there would have been confusion in both! Al Quran XXI:22
4. Nor is there any god along with Him: (if there were many gods) behold, each god would have taken away what he had created, and some would have lorded it over others! Al Quran XXJII:91
5. Say: if there had been other gods, with Him,—as they say, behold, they would have sought out a way to the Lord of the Throne! Al Quran XVIL42
6. God puts forth a Parable—a man belonging to many partners at variance with each other, and a man

> belonging entirely to one master: are those who equal in comparison? Al Quran XXXIV . 29

To clarify the position of all other claimants to the position of Lord and Cherisher and to rid man of the awe with which they seem to inspire him, the Quran has adopted a unique method to bring home the truth:

> O men! Here is a parable set forth! Listen to it! Those on whom besides God, ye call, cannot create even a fly, if they all met together for the purposes! And if the fly should snatch away anything from them, they would have no power to release it from the fly. Feeble are those who petition and those whom they petition!

Can we imagine that the servant of Allah could be enslaved by any power in the world however great? Is there any other sovereign who could bow his head before himself?

The one act of obeisance (to the Lord) which weights heavy upon thee rids man from bowing down at so many other door steps.

After having had a glimpse of the human society coming into existence as a logical result of recognising Allah as our Sovereign, let us now proceed to take stock of the effects and (evil) consequences of rejecting Him as the only Sovereign and turning away from fulfilling the demands of man's covenant with his Lord and Cherisher, which are before us in a very definite and material form.

1. When man refused to recognise the covenant of Allah immediately the problem cropped up where to seek the sanction for his own rights, the entity of the state and the authority of the rulers. Under which legal documents, the relations of the individual and the state should be determined? This dire need made them invent an imaginary covenant under the name of social contract.
2. The real covenant had made man take an oath of

allegiance to recognise his Creator and Master as his Lord and Cherisher. The hypothetical covenant compelled man to take men like himself as gods and bow down to them, and in this way started the lording of man over man.

3. In the true covenant the Sovereign was one entity. The false covenant brought into existence sovereigns without number who had to be vested with all the rights and powers of the real Sovereign, and man had to put on his own neck the yoke of the gods he had carved out for himself.
4. The unity of authority had given birth to unity of the state. Now the multiplicity of the authority (sovereignty) has divided the world into hundreds of small states and humanity has been badly scattered.
5. Allah's authority is all -pervasive and eternal. When sovereigns with transient and limited authority came into existence and they tried to make their sovereignty eternal and their powers unlimited, oppression and mischief came in their wake. These gods carved out by man himself fell out among themselves, and their quarrels and fights, greed for conquest, lasciviousness. and exploitation destroyed the peace and tranquility of mankind.
6. Man as the vicegerent on earth enjoyed the highest position of greatness and dignity in this world and was the choicest creation. He had now become the lowest of the creatures of earth in the realm of men passing as gods. He had no value as a human being. Some sovereign enjoyed the spectacle of his being torn to pieces and devoured by the carnivorous blasts, some others overeigns consigned him to the flames and yet others made him the fuel of gas chambers. Some one had him broken on the rock or had him crushed in a press; others rode on thrones borne by him, as a beast

of burden, on his shoulders. Then there were those who pilloried him or put iron collar round his neck like a dog and drove him in herds like cattle to be sold in slave markets. Some sovereigns attempted his wholesale annihilation by dropping atom bombs on him and some others drowned him in oceans. And even now they are competing with one another which of them can kill how many more men per second. In short, these sovereigns, fashioned by man himself, made life miserable for him. Neither his life nor property nor his dignity and honour are safe at their hands. He has got himself entangled in the meshes of a net of torture and is finding it impossible to get out of it.

7. All men had been made equal in status as men by Allah. Now colour, race, territory, tongue and other distinctions have grouped them into various nations and then the every day growing national interests and their protection took the shape of a regular philosophy that gave rise to the curse of nationalism which brought the small and weak nations under the yoke of the powerful ones.

   It was from the womb of this nationalism that Hitler's Nazism, Mussolini's Fascism and American and British imperialism took birth as its offshoots, and first they took the rest of the world into the grip of their colonialism and then the clash of interest led to the two world wars throwing humanity into the hell of misery, destruction and death.

8. All the children of Adam had received the same code of conduct for life from Allah. Now when men decided to formulate a way of life for himself, so many strange, contradictory and disproportionate philosophies, theories and concepts emerged before him that he was bewildered. Not one of them was such as could be acceptable to the entire humanity since they bore stamps

of particular interests and particular geographical and historical background, particular atmosphere and above all the stamps of limited knowledge and intellect. The multiplicity of these theories and concepts so much confused man that, with all his intellect, he totally lost sight of the Straight Path of Life.

Plato and Hebal's Idealism, John Stuart Mill's Individualism, Benthan's Utilitarianism and from Marx's Communism down to Godwin and Kropotkins Anarchism, hundreds of ideologies with particularities of time and places, and their interpretations by thousands, bewildered man and confining him to various intellectual and political circles, not only cut off from one another but antagonised them.

9. Since the code of conduct for man's life formulated by himself was not based on a common goal and moral values, there was no possibility left of any uniformity of character. Every petty sovereign, with a view to serve his particular national interest, under a peculiar system of training, moulded the citizens into a mould of character that they may prove good citizens for their own country, but outside the boundaries of their country, for the rest of the world, they may play the role of dacoits, plunderers, murderers and goondas. It was thus that there was no basis left between man and man for universal brotherhood. All of them became enemies of one another's life and property, honour and dignity, country, race, country's resources and government and authority. The separation of the centres of beliefs and thought, aims and objectives, tendencies and leanings and obedience and loyalty , separated them all, one from the other, and converted the entire world into a place of contradictions, differences, tensions and enmity.

10. The code of conduct for man's life conferred on him by

Allah was based on the highest moral teachings. Man rebelling against Allah and putting aside the morals, made the material interest the basis of his efforts. This attitude of every one looking to his own interests created enmity among men living in the same country. Instead of sacrifice and sympathy and cooperation and well-wishing among them, tendencies of selfishness and man-baiting were aroused. It was this self interest that on the one hand created aggressive loot and pillage and on the other classes came into being for organized defence. And then the cold and hot war among these classes, made man bloodthirsty thus destroying the peace and tranquility of the world. This class war became an organized philosophy according to which cutting the throats of men belonging to the opposite group came to be a virtuous act, and to get killed in this way was regarded martyrdom.

11. According to the Divine code of conduct for man's life the real field of competition was *taqwa* or fear of (the displeasure of) Allah. But this was now replaced by the struggle for an abundance of luxury goods and satisfaction of the carnal urges and proving them further excitants. This field of competition changed every person into a slave of his cravings and created in him a craze for amassing wealth by fair means or foul. All the barrier of approved and prohibited were removed, and the criterion of greatness came to be the abundance of luxury goods. This trend of thought putting man on the path of selfishness and sensuality made him a wolf for the other individuals of the society.

12. The common frailty of all the systems or the ways of life designed by man is this that there is no sanction behind their moral principles. Firstly, they do not attach the importance to morality which it enjoys in the Divine way of life. And if at all some moral principles are

decided upon for a civilized social life they prove lifeless and defunct, since there was no power to compel man to abide by them. Turning away from the belief in the life Hereafter, man became used to irresponsible attitude in life. He made the life of this world the be-all and end-all of man's destiny, and totally obvious of any accountability in connection with the deeds here in the earthly existence, he became refractory. If at all he followed some moral principles in his collective life for the "collective interests" he reserved his rights to keep the individual life totally free from the hold of these principles, and in this sphere of his life came down to the animal level.

13. In the kingdom of God there was rule of law, but in the kingdom established by man the will of the ruler became the law. The Will of the true Sovereign manifested itself in the form of a permanent and eternal constitution, whose applicability was pervasive and beyond the limits of time and space. But the will of the sovereign carved out by man himself is always wavering-now this way and the next moment some other way. Its applicability is limited to a specific period and a particular region. It is subject to amendments day in and day out, and with every change of the sovereign which are so frequent it changes too. That is why the concept of the "rule of law" in the constitution framed by man is a fraud.

14. The rights conferred on man by Allah were permanent and untransferable. But the transient nature of the constitution framed by man made the fundamental laws, under this constitution, also transient and changeable, and made them a regular subject of wrangling and struggle between the individual and the state. Now these rights have to be fought for by the individuals before they can have them. But the single

> kick of a dictator smashes them like glass bangles. These are those serious and destructive consequences man has to face in this life for the crime of breaking off with the true Sovereign as His servant and making men like himself his sovereigns. He had declared his independence to escape the checks put on him by the Divine Law and to live independently in His Realm a life free from all restrictions. But did he really come by his cherished freedom and independence? Did he get a chance to live a life of his own choice? Or was it just the opposite in as much as leaving One God, he had to crown men like himself with sovereignty, bow himself down at their feet, to surrender all his freedoms, fundamental rights, and his dignity and greatness due to the highest status as the vicegerent of Allah on earth, and submit his life and property and honour, his resources and mental and physical powers to be used by them. And in his abject servility to them, he got nothing from them but the worst subjugation, degradation infamy and grief and despair.

Which of the gods carved out by man himself has not raised the slogan: "Who is superior to Us in strength?"—Al Quran XLI: 15 and "I am your Lord most High/'—Al Quran LXXIX: 24 and not tyrannized and oppressed his own and aliens and not ruined thousands of homes for an odd fancy of his?

The fact is that man was not created for sovereignty and rule. His mission in life is service to Allah and not to take upon himself the role of God. His Creator has deeply ingrained slavery, devotion and service to Allah in his nature.

> I have only created Jins and men, that they may serve Me. Al Quran LI: 56

Here in this verse service and devotion do not mean only prayer, fasting and praising God, but along with these forms of service, devotion also includes this that Jins and men have not been created for the worship, obedience and subservience to any one other than Allah. They are not to bow down to or obey and follow the laws of any one else; not to regard any body as one who can make or mar their destiny and not to pray or petition any one other than Allah. In all matters pertaining to life, perfect obedience to one God and to carry out His orders alone is service to Him.

Man has been endowed with all the qualities of the head and the heart and all the physical powers to meet the demands of this service. To overlook this position of his as the servant of Allah, is to rebel against himself, his nature and it invariably results in his proclamation of his own divinity or bowing down in devotion to some false god. As soon as man proceeds on this course of rebellion, tyranny and mischief also find their way in his deeds. Since Allah has created all men with the same nature some one of them becoming the ruler and others being the ruled, both are against their nature. Sovereignty, be that of a king or a dictator as individuals, of the citizens of a State or the people of the world as a whole, tyranny must raise its head, since the sovereignty of man in every individual or collective form, brings into existence a sovereign that is incapable of taking the place of the true Sovereign, which is at the root of all mischief on earth.

The cause of this mischief is that Allah due to His self-sustained entity, His immortal position, His Power of creation, His capacity as Lord and Cherisher of the worlds, and other unlimited and peerless attributes of His, is the (true) Sovereign, His authority is not borrowed or a gift from any one but a part of His entity; His authority emanates from His Own self and not from any one else; He Himself is independent of every thing and every prop. He does not take any thing from any body, but His Own bestowal and endowment extend to every tiny particle of the universe; one and all are needy and depend on His bounties for sustenance, but He is free from want and is independent. So the high position of sovereignty becomes Him alone. But whoever, other than He comes up with the claim of sovereignty, cannot boast of any one of these attributes. Considering all his powers, capabilities, his knowledge and perception, his sentiments and feelings, his necessities and urges and the natural limitations of his authority and intention, he is just like other men. Now the question is that with all these human frailties, how he is to impress other people with his superiority and supremacy: how he is to make a show of his sovereignty and rule, and how to compel others to submit to his subjugation and obediences.

There is one and only one way of doing it. And that is, to make or at least show himself big, he should snatch and grab from those living in his sphere of authority, the power to rule, rights and privileges, wealth and property, rank and dignity, and take into his possession all the resources and means of meeting the needs of right from the protection of his own life to that of his seat of authority. And once he is in possession of these powers and resources, he is to rally and organise them and use them for grabbing more of such powers and resources. And when the limited resources of his own country do not suffice to meet his needs and ambition, he is to attack his neighbours and snatch and grab their resources and man-power. And he is to be constantly engaged in the struggle to extend his sphere of influence and meeting other rivals on the same path (of expansionism), should go on annihilating them or be himself annihilated in a clash with them.

There is no other course open to him, since he himself, according to the example furnished by the Quran, is incapable of making a fly or recover something snatched by the fly from him. All his affairs are conducted with the power and resources grabbed by him from others. And as the powers and resources, through usurpation, accumulate with him, there is a proportionate increase in his despotism, his awe-inspiring majesty and grandeur, the expanse and height of his mansions, the abundance of the articles of luxury, and the sphere of his authority, and exactly in the same (inverse) proportion, those in the clutches of his powerful authority go on getting deprived of their liberties, their rights, their means of sustenance, their liberties and their honour and dignity.

In most countries of the world this kind of rule prevails. The world strategy of the super-powers too is taking this course. Wherever and whenever man, getting loose from the service of Allah has taken up the rein of rule over the fellow man in his own hands, the result has always been tyranny and oppression-constant tyranny. There is no concept of man's sovereignty without oppression and tyranny.

This malady can neither be remedied through any constitution framed by man nor through any change in the system of government on the concept of man's sovereignty. The only way to get rid of it is that man should in all humility recognize the right of God's Sovereignty and come down to his true position of the servant of God. He should neither try to take on the role of a god, nor allow any one else to dominate over him as a god.

2

Liberal Values

The secular civilizations have been instrumental in eroding the noble feelings, righteous emotions and moral values of the human race, but even greater destruction has been wrought by the doctrine of social evolution. This doctrine took its birth from materialism. It was fostered by the utilitarian outlook and man's conquest of time and space which lent maturity to it. The doctrine was developed by Kant, Fischter, Hebal, Karl Marx and several other philosophers. With the rise of this theory, wrong took the shape of right and evil became good. Bloodshed, savagery and exploitation of the weak came to be regarded as the highest moral virtues of humanity.

The present chapter cannot admit of a detailed discussion on the subject. I shall, therefore, confine myself to a brief examination of the ideas which have gone into the making of this doctrine. We take up Hebal first, for although the doctrine of social evolution has been extant in the world for several centuries, it was Hebal who with profound conviction and full force of logic presented it to the world as a well-knit system of philosophy.

It is rather a marvel for the student of historiography that this astute German philosopher emphatically refutes Kantian system, yet strives with even greater force and energy to affirm the Kantian theory. He infuses logic into the dull philosophy of Kant and carries the philosophy started by the 'iconoclast' of reason to its final conclusion.'

Avoiding technical intricacies of philosophy, we may explain that in Hebal's view, the evolution of human civilization follows this process: the appearance of contradictions, their conflict and fusion. Each period of human history is a unit and a whole. In a given period, all phases of human life, economic, political, cultural, moral, intellectual and religious ideals are at a particular level. They are all closely interrelated, and they all reflect the age in which they exist. When at the behest of the "Absolute Spirit," the history of mankind advances some steps further, some antithetic ideas, tendencies and doctrines rise from within the body of politics of that age.

An intense conflict between the thesis and antithesis ensues which rages for some time. At last both come to terms. Weak elements on both sides are eliminated and thesis and antithesis merge to from a unity which consists of strong and pure elements of both side. Thus, a completely new system of thought and practice emerges, which in due course of time meets the same fate as its successor. Thus, human civilization continues to advance by this evolutionary process.

In his own terminology, Hebal calls it the Dialectical Process of History. According to this theory, a given period of history is a battleground in which a logical debate and conflict is constantly going on and it is the force of this conflict that propels mankind to further progress. First a thesis appears and then an antithesis arises to challenge the thesis. After a prolonged conflict between the two, the 'Absolute Spirit' brings about a reconciliation between them. Thus, a new entity comes into being which in every respect is better and more comprehensive than its predecessors, for, it contains all the best elements of the preceding entities. Hence each step takes mankind to further advance. This is the Hebalian philosophy of social evolution.

Marx borrowed his philosophical framework from Hebal, but filled in details from his own intuition. He discarded the concept of soul and held that material causes or economic factors were the prime force in the process of historical evolution. Whereas Hebal regards ideas as the most effective power, in Marxian theory, the decisive factor is the material environment and even in this environment the real factors of importance are the means of production.

Hebal thinks that the conflict between thesis and antithesis occurs in the realm of ideas. Marx believes that the main battle-ground of life is the economic sphere and that it is in this sphere that the destiny of mankind is decided. Economics is the pre-eminent factor in human life and the superstructure of morality, religious doctrines, culture, arts and sciences is erected on the foundation of the economic system. The contours of intellectual and political life in a given period are determined by the various means of economic production in that period. According to Marx, the process of social evolution takes the following course:

> "To begin with a change in the means of economic production takes place, which directly affects the distribution of means of life and the modes of ownership of property. Consequently, all the values of life undergo a change, and a new system comes into existence."

At this stage, a conflict between the new and the old system in the sense of Hebalian dialectics takes place which ends eventually in conciliation and both systems merge to create an entirely new system which contains only the best elements of the preceding systems. Evidently, the emergent system is in every respect superior to former systems. This then is the Marxian view of the process of social evolution.

The third philosopher whose viewpoint lent force to the doctrine of social evolution was Darwin. According to him, all living creatures have a natural tendency towards unlimited growth, development and changing their physical form. But the evolution of various creatures is not determined by any constructive process initiated by providence, but is the result of a destructive process.

The evolution of living creatures does not occur without mutual conflict, famine and death. Darwin reposed implicit faith in Malthusian theory of population and inferred from it that since the number of living creatures multiplies at a faster rate due to availability of food and other necessities for existence, hence each creature is constrained to fight constantly against other creatures in order to preserve his own existence.

In Darwin's view, life is a battleground where at all moments and in every direction the strong are engaged in eliminating the weak in an overall struggle for existence. Only the fittest survive in this struggle and it is really they who deserve all that is best in life. Those who perish in this callous struggle receive a just punishment for their infirmity. In short, this earth, and the means of life on it sustain only those who are the strongest.

There is no room on earth for the weak and the sooner they liquidate their infirm existence from this universe the better. Thus under compulsion of circumstances the process of evolution is initiated and through a constant course of conflict produces higher forms of life. Man too, climbs the high rung of humanity through this complex struggle. Those who emerge victorious from the struggle of existence are pure and the universe belongs to them only.

The theory of social evolution which emerges from a combined view of the doctrines of these philosophers contains the following major principles:

(i) The evolution of life takes place through conflict.

(ii) Human progress is the consequence of this conflict.

(iii) Only the strongest have the right to live and develop in this universe.

(iv) Success by whatever means it may be achieved is the main object of existence.

For the moment, I do not intend to point out the intellectual flaws in this doctrine. What I wish to emphasize is that this philosophy instead of humanizing man has actually transformed him into a brute and rather than making this world a heaven of peace, it has changed it into a veritable hell.

The Philosophy : The first impact of the philosophy of social evolution is that man has come to regard material progress as the highest achievement of life, whereas upon a careful consideration it will be found that material development only aids the consciousness of man; it has no creative power of its own. Actually, spiritual power is the prime mover of human consciousness.

It is at this point that the exponents of doctrine of social evolution have committed the greatest blunder. When social evolution means only material development, it necessarily follows that different sections and classes of people should cast morality to the winds and launch a frenzied struggle against each other for expropriating the material means of life, for if they refrained from the struggle, they would perish. This philosophy has produced a permanent fear complex among the people. This savage competitive spirit has enveloped individuals as well as nations, and everyone is scared of the other. This permanent fear complex has developed the vilest qualities among human beings, such as, for instance, selfishness, callousness, avarice, bigotry, faithfulness, corruption and falsehood.

Modern psychologists have established the fact that human actions calculated to make a show of strength spring from a fear complex. Hence ostentations, display of military strength, assertion of superior authority and a craving of power without responsibility are various forms of the same fear complex.

Secondly, this philosophy has plunged the future of

humanity into darkness. A philosophy which explains the creation of human ego in terms of time and place can provide man with the knowledge of laws and boundaries of this universe, but cannot liberate man from its cruel fetters. It is for this reason that modern man daily grows pessimistic about his future. The well-known Italian philosopher Croce comments on this problem as follows:

> "The shadow of pessimism covers from time to time the life of the individual and similarly the life of societies; and doubts, fears and despair over the future belongs to all eras of history. But in the years through which Europe is living, that shadow has become wider and darker, philosophers, or people who call themselves philosophers, have become prophets and describe to us, under the guise of philosophical and historical reality, the steep incline, we shall perforce descend...when, as frequently happens, we conceive it as a tangle offerees which act outside us and according to their own laws, we have, with the nightmare of these forces, the feelings of helplessness, since, if they are outside us, there is no way of getting among them and of dominating or regulating them. There is nothing left to do then but to speculate, seeking in the external world other forces which may oppose, defeat or check them, and to put our hope in these. But it is uncertain hope, always fearful, because it depends on others and not on us, and, whether fearful or hopeful, we feel ourselves in the clutches of others."

Thirdly, because this doctrine is founded on the idea that the evolution of man takes place through conflict between hostile forces, hence instead of promoting cooperation among human beings, it has aroused in them a fierce sense of jealousy and competition. This doctrine inculcates in the minds of the people that prosperity and progress in life depend on total commitment to the struggle for worldly gains.

Consequently, it has transformed man into a callous and insensitive creature. This doctrine holds it perfectly natural for the strong to enrich himself at the expense of the weak, by doing so, he proves that only the fittest have the right to survive. Conversely, the weak deservedly suffer persecution and are rightly downtrodden by the strong. Not only has this doctrine turned human beings into savage tyrants, but it has also furnished a rational basis for capitalism and imperialism by endorsing that might is invariably right. Fighting has been a part of human history since long, but before now men considered fighting as evil, though at times a necessary one. This doctrine has baptized war as a definite blessing. In the past, people looked upon a tyrant as an evil-doer.

Today, they laud him as a just man. Max Eastman's comment on the materialistic interpretation of history is, in fact, truly applicable to the whole doctrine of social evolution. He remarks:

> "Notwithstanding their high-sounding claims to humanism, the Marxists have become haughty and violent under the influence of this doctrine. The basic assumption of the doctrine is that man attains evolutionary progress through a process of severe and violent conflict. Good and evil in this doctrine are merely names for two material forces and man achieves glory only through a collision between these two forces. "A French author Boris Soyrarine comments:
>
> "All respect for humanity has been erased from our hearts. Life has lost its real worth and use. At the present time, one has the spirit to eliminate the savagery of the tyrants. Actually, brutishness has reached its zenith."

Referring to the Darwinian theory of evolution another writer Kenneth Walker in his book, *Meaning and Purpose* states that the glories of war described by Trietsechke and Bernhardie is the fruit of the analysis of Darwin's theory of evolution.

In England, which according to the saying of Napoleon is more a land of shopkeepers than of armies, the theory of selection has provided a justification for the worst economic competition and a criminal inelegance on the part of the workers.

Again, this philosophy of life has imparted conviction to the people that movement and conflict of every sort, provided it is materially successful, ensures human evolution. This theory impelled man to worship power and force rather than truth and justice. Man devoted his intellect and skill to the exploration of those means by which he could augment his power and strength.

Aggressive colonialism and oppressive imperialism are mischiefs borne out of this theory. This doctrine represents the darkest period of human history as the most luminous. A famous critic of the Hebalian philosophy, Croce rightly declares that this theory provides instigation for everything, be it conservatism, revolution or restoration.

Similarly, another critic remarks that this doctrine has provided the Marxist writers with an opportunity to justify their stand in every matter. This notion is the major cause of tyranny and oppression in the modern age.

Finally, this theory taught men to repudiate the social significance of religion and morality. It preached that men should exclusively and relentlessly absorb themselves in the struggle for their survival, stability and the grasping of strength and power, wherefrom they may be obtained.

If religion and morality prove useful in achieving this purpose, they should be adopted. If, on the other hand, success is ensured by their repudiation, they should be instantly cast aside. The popularity achieved by the precepts of that high priest of deception, Machiavelli, during the last four centuries has been largely owing to this false doctrine. The following words of Dr. Funk and Goebels represent a true definition of this theory.

"The sole purpose of all power and strength is to secure the capitation of the enemy by all means, fair or foul. Our movement is perfectly free from moral restraints prescribed by religion. Every act performed for the purpose of dismantling the citadel of colonialism is a moral act."

This, then, is a brief analysis of the components of western civilization and their impact on human life. Modern man is immersed indeed by anxiety. He is at a loss to know why in spite of all the progress in art and sciences and abundance of material provisions, he is still unhappy. The earth yields millions of tons of grain every year, yet, its inhabitants suffer from hunger and privation. Innumerable fountains of knowledge are gushing forth, yet man is still wallowing in ignorance.

In point of fact, the groping for a millennium during the last three or four centuries has led men far astray from their goal. In a New Year message on 1st January, 1935, Iqbal referred to this failure of the secular civilization in the following words:

> "The modern age prides itself in its progress in knowledge and its matchless scientific developments. No doubt, the pride is justified. Today, space and time are being annihilated and man is achieving amazing successes in unveiling the secrets of Nature and harnessing its forces to his own service."

In spite of all these developments, the tyranny of imperialism struts abroad, covering its face under the masks of democracy, nationalism, communism, fascism and heaven knows what else besides. Under these masks, in every corner of the earth, the spirit of freedom and the dignity of man are begin trampled underfoot in a way to which not even the darkest period of human history presents a parallel. He sums up the modern man, equipped with power but lacking in vision, in these striking and beautiful verses:

> Love is denied to him and intellect bites him like a serpent,

He has failed to subordinate intellect to love!

He has succeeded in tracing the course of the stars.
But failed to make his way through the labyrinth of
his own ideas!

He has got so entangled in the maze of his knowledge,

That to this day he does not know profit from loss.

He ensnared the rays of the sun,

But failed to illuminate the dark night of his life.

Having analysed the ingredients of secular civilization, we shall examine the contemporary social movements which have risen under the patronage of this civilization. Although, these movements bear diverse titles, the spirit which animates them is born of the same mother civilization.

Civil Society in Medina : Having seen the state of Nature and the social and governmental contracts in Medina, we now turn to the civil society. Here, we shall try to see how the individualism of the state of nature which was replaced by the acceptance of Islam by a community of Muslims soon gave way to an organic conception, that is, the individuals who had accepted Islam were yet individual Muslims of Aus and Khazraj, and they had not yet begun to think in terms of a common community and before the coming of the Prophet Muhammad (Peace be on him,) the community of Muslims was like the joint stock company of Locke.

It was like a bundle of sticks which is tied up by a common rope, but every stick keeps up its identity separate. The only common bond of the people of Medina was no doubt acceptance of Islam, but as yet they had not forgotten their individuality. The whole conception, yet, was arithmetical: it was in no sense organic.

It was, therefore, the first task of the Prophet to unite these scattered elements in an organic whole, and to this task he at once turned his attention. Says Wellhausen:

> "The first Arabic community with sovereign powers was established by Muhammad in the city of Medina, not upon the basis of blood which naturally leads to diversity, but upon that of religion which is equally binding on all." Margoliouth also affirms the same thing when he says:

> "In the new community all tribal differences were to be sunk, and the theory of the platonic republic, according to which the members of the community should share pains and pleasures to the same extent as the members of one body, is attributed to the Prophet."

Thus, the first care of the Prophet in Medina was to build a mosque, for which he bought a plot of land, though every man offered his land and house free of any charge for the purpose, but the Prophet did not accept them. In the construction of the mosque all worked with the greatest enthusiasm the more so because the Prophet himself was working with them, and they chanted with loud and cheerful voices as they bore along their burdens:

> O Lord! There is no joy but the joy of futurity.

> O Lord! Have mercy upon the Citizens and the Refugees.

In this way, the elected President of Medina gave practical proof of the fact that he was but the first citizen and the Prophet showed that he was only like an ordinary mortal, and because he was the representative of God, he has to prove and justify himself as the "First Muslim" as the first servant of God. Thus, for the first time in the history of Medina (and even of all Arabia) the people began to meet on a footing of absolute equality in the mosque five times a day.

A new community had grown up out of heterogeneous and individualistic elements, and as the above couplet has shown, the tribal differentiation of Aus and Khazraj was done away with, for the Citizens of Median began to be called Ansar or helpers, and the people who had migrated and settled from Mecca with the Prophet were called Muhajirin or Refugees.

Covenant of Brotherhood : But still, in the beginning, a greater attachment in the Muslim spirit of brotherhood was necessary between the Ansar and the Muhajirin for the latter were still no more than mere guests of the Ansar as they had forsaken everything of their own—house, wealth and other property at Mecca for the sake of God and their faith. They were, therefore, entirely ill-provided and ill-provisioned.

The Prophet at once created a new Tie of Brotherhood (aqd-i-Muwaqqat) between the Ansar and the Muhajirin. 'Become brethren every two and two of you,' such ran the command of the Prophet; and he himself 'set the example by taking Ali', or as others say Uthman, for his brother. Accordingly, each of the refugees selected one of the citizens as his brother. The bond was of the closest description, and involved not only special devotion to each other's interests in the persons thus associated, but in the case of death, the 'brother' inherited the property of the deceased."

This covenant or contract lasted only up to the Battle of Badr after which inheritance was allowed to be based on the law of consanguinity as laid down in the Holy Quran. This contract of brotherhood makes it definitely clear that while the contract of Locke was meant for the preservation of property, the Islamic contract was based on the idea of the sacrifice of property and this sacrifice was done with the greatest sincerity.

Contract with Jews : After, thus, providing for the two urgent needs of the hour, the Prophet turned his attention to the condition of Medina itself, where another elements could not be ignored. These were the Jews of the three tribes Banu Nadir, Banu Quraiza and Banu Qainua who were not prepared to accept Islam. They came to the Prophet and said:

"We have come to make a treaty of peace with thee,

> to the effect that we shall be neither for nor against thee, that we shall aid no one against thee; nor injure any who aids thee; on condition that thou injures neither us nor our friends until we learn what becomes of thy affairs and of those of they people."
>
> The Prophet, complied with their request on condition that they would afford aid to no one against him; nor against any of his companions, neither by word, arms, or cattle, neither openly nor secretly.

This must be pointed out that in spite of all efforts to win over the Jews, they could not be reconciled and from the very beginning were always bent on mischief. Even the Quran refers to their adverse activities in a clear manner, for what they could not tolerate was the unification of Aus and Khazraj into one community under the leadership of the Prophet. One Shammas bin Qais (a Jew) set a mischief monger in a meeting of Aus and Khazraj with instructions that he should recall the events of the Battle of Buath. As soon as couplets regarding that battle began to be recited, the extinguished fire of hostility and ravage was rekindled and it took no time to move from verbal hot exchange of words to actual fight and hostility. When the Prophet, on hearing of what was going on, at once appeared on the scene and addressed them to fear God and not to go back to the state of ignorance out of which God had taken them out.

On hearing this, they threw away their implements of war and began to weep and embrace each other. Thus was the unity of the Islamic community maintained in the firm grip of the rope or Covenant of God. They took God to witness that, in case they should fail to keep this agreement and covenant His Lordship would be at liberty to shed their blood, to confiscate their property as well as to capture their wives and children.

A treaty was written for each tribe. Thus, the Prophet associated the Jews in a contract or 'Treaty of Mutual Obligation drawn up in writing between the Refugees and the Believers of Medina on the one hand and the Jews on the other, confirming the latter in the practice of their religion and in the secure possession of their property.'

Traditional Support

This agreement was, therefore, the First Charter of Religious Toleration in the history of man's political development. It has been preserved in full by Ibn Hazari and is a lengthy document. It begins thus: 'In the name of God, the Compassionate, the Merciful. It is a Covenant (Ahad-Nama) of Muhammad the Prophet of God, on behalf of the believers of Quraish and Yethreb (Medina) and those that are under them and those that may join them and strive with them for the faith. Verily, they form a community apart from the rest of mankind.

Thus, the opening words definitely tell us that the Muslims were now a community and the Holy Quran refers to this unity in these words:

> 'Surely, this your community is one community and I am Your Lord, Therefore be careful (of your duty) to me." 23:52.

Wellhausen has expressed this aspect thus:

> "The Community, at the head of which God stands, and the Prophet as God's representative, has power to deliver the shedder of blood over to the avenger, and it is the duty of the community to see that this is done, and in this covenant, as we shall see noted below, it is specifically stated that if a man kills a Muslim wrongfully, the Muslims shall join as one man against him."

The other clauses of this covenant may now be given in brief, to make the above statements clear:

1. The Refugees and the Believers of Medina shall defray the price of bloodshed among themselves (respectively) and shall ransom honourably their prisoners.

2. Whoever is rebellious or seeketh to spread enmity and sedition, thee hand of every man shall be against him, even if he be a son.
3. No Muslim will kill a Muslim for an unbeliever and non-believer will be helped as against a Muslim. And verily, Allah's Protection is meant for one and all. The Believers are pledged to protect each other against all others.
4. Whosoever of the Jews followeth us, shall have aid and succour; they shall not be injured, not shall any enemy be aided against them.
5. No Unbeliever shall grant protection to thee people of Mecca, either in person or property, nor interpose between the Believers and them.
6. Whosoever killeth a Muslim wrongfully the Muslims shall join as one man against him.
7. The state of peace and war shall be common to all Muslims; no one among them shall have the right of concluding peace with, or declaring war, against the enemies of his co-religionists.
8. The Jews who attach themselves to our commonwealth shall be protected from all insults and vexations; they shall have an equal right with our people to our assistance and good offices.
9. The Jews shall contribute with the Muslims and join with them in defending Medina against a common enemy.
10. The Jews of the various branches of Auf, Najjar, Harith, Hisham, thalaba. Ans and all others domiciled in Medina shall form with the Muslims one composite nation, i.e. one people with the Believers.
11. The Jews will profess their religion as freely as the Muslim theirs.

12. The interior of Medina shall be sacred and inviolable for all those who join this covenant.
13. All true Muslims shall hold in abhorrence every man guilty of crime, injustice or disorder.
14. Controversies and disputes shall be referred for the decision of Allah and His Prophet.
15. None shall join the men of Mecca or their allies; for, verily, the engaging parties are bound together against every one that shall threaten Medina. War and peace shall be made in common. And verily! Allah is the protector of the righteous and the godly, and Muhammad is His Prophet.

Free Church of Free State : From this brief summary of the covenant, it is clear, that it does not merely assert the unity and oneness of the Muslim community, it even asserts the unity of the City State of Medina itself, for the Jews and the Unbelievers also have been considered to form one nation with the Muslims, and they had equal obligations in the defence and the maintenance of peace in Medina.

Moreover, the fact Medina was made inviolable makes it clear that the Divine Laws of Peace had now been promulgated with full force in a land of war, turmoil and anarchy. Lastly, the tolerance that was granted to the Jews for the first time established a 'Free Church in the Free State of Medina', and it was the first charter of freedom of conscience and of religious worship in the history of the world.

The Prophet, thus reconciled the various parties in the city and introduced law, order and peace among its various elements. The covenant with the Jews was the crowning contract in the edifice of contracts which established the City State of Medina. Thus, in the words of Amir Ali, "the contract constituted the Prophet as 'the chief Magistrate of the nation, as much by his prophetic mission as by a virtual compact between himself and the people." Dr. Hell regards this contract (ordinance) as a piece of fare statesmanship and of far-reaching importance" of rare statesmanship because it was the only way of reconciling the tribe and the best means of Meccans with the united support of the whole of Medina; and of far-reaching importance because it made the Prophet the sole guiding power in a land which had known no common superior. Nicholson thus estimates the significance of this event:

> "Ostensibly a cautious and tactful reform, it was in reality a revolution. Muhammad dared not strike openly at the independence of the tribes, but he destroyed it, in effect, by shifting the centre of power from the tribe to the community, and although the community included Jews and pagans as well as Muslims, he fully recognised what his opponents failed to foresee, that the Muslims were the active and must soon be the predominant partners in the newly founded State".

The City State of Medina was founded on the basis of various contracts, and 'Islam thus became what, in theory at least, it has always remained a political as well as a religious system.' The First contract was the contract with God and this was the acceptance of Islam which every Muslim has to individually utter the 'Kalima' of faith: there is no god but God and Muhammad is His Prophet. Then the Second Contract was a contract for the Protection of the Prophet—not only as God's representative on Earth but also as their own elected ruler.

The Third Contract was the confirmation of the Second Contract by the whole of the Muslim population of Medina; and the Fourth Contract with the Jews was not merely a charter of toleration for freedom of belief and conscience, it was also a contract for the creation of a composite nation or community for common defence and protection. The Republic of Medina (of which the elected President was the Prophet) was thus recognised 'organic even though the whole process of its creation was individualistic and therefore contractual.'

Religious Cover

It is a recognised principle of modern political philosophy that the theory of contract assumes a mechanical way of creating a state and it makes it a mere manufacture, but it is now universally held that the state is not contracted or made, it grows. And here, in the City State of Medina we have said that it is by contract that the state has been made 'organic' (and that too in a double sense); for it is primarily a Muslim state, the Muslim community was already one and every Muslim was an inseparable part of the whole, as it was the greatest sin to shed the blood of a brother Muslim; and if it was a common state of all the peoples of Medina, they were solemnly bound, 'under the protection of God which extends to one and all' to defend the common state against all foreign dangers, and internally too, its soil was made inviolable and free from all bloodshed. This was the Islamic City State of Medina made 'organic' by contracts and to this day both the ideas of contract and the unity of the community continue to be the central features of Muslim religious life.

The idea of contract was therefore, never a fiction in Islam. As has already been shown, the making of contract was a historical reality in Arabia. But in political philosophy, it is not only Kant who has called 'contract' an 'idea of reason', modern critics have tried to make it even unreal and unnecessary in those who are the real classical writers of this theory. They have tried to show that these writers—Hobbes, Spinoza, Locke and Rousseau—have expressed their political ideas. Through the medium of the contract, not because it was essential for their political philosophy, but because it was the prevalent mode of expressing political ideas in terms of contract. Thus, says Vaughan, "of the four philosophers in question, Locke comes nearest in principle of accepting the theory of contract."

But he rejects it in terms; and, even when in substance he seems nearest to it, he inserts so many limitations, he puts in so many hostile amendments, that, in the net result, he is much farther from it than, at first sight we might be tempted to imagine. Of the remaining three, one Spinoza accepts it in words but in fact, takes away with one hand what he professes to give with the other. The two that are adjudged as one in the interest of absolutism and the other in that of the sovereign people reject it root and branch.

According to Vaughan, Locke was only a half-hearted social contract writer. But Jood has absolved Locke also of this irrelevancy absolutely in these words: "But the social contract theory, in the form in which Locke maintained it requires us to suppose that the abolition of Government involves man's relapse into a personal condition would admittedly be a condition of peaceable and socially disposed persons, and it would not be the same as the condition introduced by society, since it is the establishment of government which puts an end to this condition and establishes the condition of society. Such, at least are the contentions of the social contract theory as Locke states it.

It is difficult in the light of these contentions to see how society could survive the abolition of government; yet that it does so, is precisely what Locke, in making his distinction between society and government, maintains. This social contract theory is however, no sense essentional to Locke's political philosophy. Thus, critics have freed all the four political philosophers from being social contract witers, even though they have been the classical writers of this theory. This means that critics have made them what they had never thought about their own writings.

Contractual Organicity : In the Islamic conception of the State, as we have already seen, the 'contract' (social and governmental) is a reality just as much as the conception of the community is organic. "The Islamic State may, therefore, fittingly be called a 'contractual organism" in the words of Fouillee, a modern French writer. The defect of the contract theory is that it makes the state a plaything of individual caprice even though it emphasises the 'consent' as the basis of the state; the defect of the organic theory is that though it emphasises the interdependence of the individual and the community, it entirely belittles individuality and the individual is made unreal. Both these defects are not to be found in the Islamic state.

A Muslim has to individually make a contract with God; but at the same time, he is an inspirable part of his community of which he is an equal member. Thus, the individual in the Islamic state is both individuality and his dependence upon the community. This explains the full significance of the conception of contractual organicity in Islam.

Abolition of Slavery : Aristotle maintains that slavery is based on nature, and that certain races are intended to be subject. Whether this be true or not, it would be useless to hope for the abolition of slavery in Muhammadan countries under present conditions. Whether the Prophet of Islam could have abolished slavery altogether among his followers is very doubtful and his prescriptions regarding the just and humane treatment of this unfortunate class, taken all in all, are praiseworthy.

On the other hand, there is nothing whatsoever in Islam that tends to the abolition of this curse. As Muir has well said, "Rather, while lightening, he riveted the fetter. There is no obligation whatever on a Muslims to release his slaves."

Acquisition of Slaves : "The greatest of all divisions, that between a free man and lave, appears as soon as the barbaric warrior spares the life of his enemy when he has him down, and brings him home to drudge for him and till the soil." The two main causes of slavery are want and war, and of these two it may be said that the acquisition of slaves was chiefly connected with warfare. (In Sura 47 Muhammad commands his followers thus, i.e. verse 4.f.):

"When ye encounter the Unbelievers, strike off their heads; until ye have made a great slaughter among them; then bind (the remainder) in fetters. And after this give (the later) either a free dismissal or exact a ransom, until the war shall have laid down its arms."

The usual expression for female slaves in the Quran as we have already seen is that which your right hands possess. Muhammad says nothing in the Quran regarding the purchase of slaves. According to Islamic law, a slave is:

1. a person taken captive in war, or carried off by force from a foreign hostile country, and being at the time of capture an Unbeliever.
2. the child of a female slave whose father is (a) a slave, or (b) is not the owner of the mother of the child, or (c) is the owner of the mother, but who does not acknowledge himself to be the father.
3. a person acquired by purchase.

War and slavery, as one would expect, is also closely bound together in the Old Testament. In Num, chap. 31, the Children ol Israel are commanded to wage a war of vengeance against the Medianites. And in verse 7, ff, we read:

> " And they warred against Medinian, as the Lord commanded Moss, and they slew every male... (9) And the Children ol Israel took captive the women of Median and their little ones, etc."

As far as strangers were concerned, the Israelites were allowed to buy, sell, or transfer their male an female slaves. So, we read in Lev. 25, 44 ff.:

> "And as for thy bondmen, and thy bondmaids, which thou shalt have; of the nations that are round about your, of them shall ye buy bondmen and bondmaids. (45) Moreover, the children of the strangers families that are with you, which they have begotten in your land; and they shall be your possession (46) And ye shall make them an inheritance for your children after

> you. to hold for a possession, of them shall ye take your bondmen for ever."

As among the Muhammadans slaves consist partly of children of female slaves, and partly also of those that are acquired, so in the Old Testament we have the two expressions:

> "He that is born in the house, and he that is bought with money."

This shows us that among the Israelites as among the Muhammadans, the number of slaves might be multiplied by birth. This, of course, is true of all peoples who trade in slaves; since the slaves are the "possession" of their masters, their children also belong to them.

A further agreement between the Muhammadan and Old Testament laws consists in the limitation of slaves to foreigners. In Lev. 25, 39.ff.we read:

> "And if thy brother be waxen poor with thee, and sell himself upto thee; thou shalt not make him to serve as a bond servant: (40) as a hired servant, and as a sojourner, he shall be with thee; he shall serve with thee unto the year of jubilee: (41) then shall he go out from thee, he and his children with him. (42). They shall not be sold as a slave is sold."

> And so with the Muhammadans, who are strictly forbidden to take believers as slaves, thee Muhammadan like the Israelite is to regard his fellow-believer as a brother.

Among the Babylonians, however, it was otherwise. Slaves were recruited both from within and without. If a son, whether natural or adopted, sinned against his parents, his father could see him as a slave. And likewise the husband had the right to dispose of a quarrelsome wife for money. Also the captured enemy naturally took the position of a slave, especially did the white (light complexioned) slaves from Gutium and Shubarti at that time appear to be much desired.

Treatment with Slaves : We have already seen how the Prophet in the Quran insists upon the just and humane treatment of the widow and orphan. And a like treatment is demanded by him also for slaves; and that in accordance with his teaching that all men belong to God, and are therefore in a certain sense alike. So, we read in Sura 16,73:

> "God hath caused some to excel others in worldly possession; Yet those thus excel do not give of their wealth unto those whom their right hands possess (their slaves) so that both may have an equal share thereof. Do they, therefore, deny the beneficence of God.?" Also Sura 4, 40:
>
> "Honour God, and associate none with nil" and show kindness unto parents, relations, orphans, the poor, the neighbour who is of kin to you, and he who is not, and to your trusted friends, and the traveller and to those whom your right hands possess for God loveth not the arrogant and the proud."

In the year before his death, the Prophet, during a farewell pilgrimage at Mina, delivered an address to his followers, in which, among several other injunctions, we find the following:

> "And your slaves! See that ye feed them with such food as ye eat yourselves, and clothe them with the like clothing as ye wear yourselves; and if they commit a fault which ye are included not to forgive, sell them; for they are the servants of the Lord, and are not to be tormented.'
>
> If Muhammad could not abolish slavery, he has certainly done what he could to secure for slaves a humane treatment. And if present-day Muhammadans disregard his injunctions, it is not fair to hold the Prophet himself responsible for it. Also, as already observed, it must not be forgotten that the legislation of the Quran was enacted for a seventh-century people.

The position and treatment of slaves among the ancients in different lands naturally differed in accordance with the character of the various people, as well as the character of the slaves themselves, that is whether they be foreign or inland born. And there was also a difference of treatment by the same people at different times.

But if the enactments of the Prophet were only faithfully observed by his followers, the treatment of slaves in Muhammadan countries would in all cases compare very favourably with what it was among the ancients. Also the treatment of slaves, as enacted in Muhammadan law, taken all in all, can only be regarded as just.

As we have already seen in the case of adultery, female slaves were held to be less guilty than free women, and consequently their punishment was to be less severe. And especially did the law enact that they should be sufficiently supported, and not made to suffer.

On the other hand, it must be remembered that slaves, like any other property, were transferable. A Muhammadan has the right to sell his concubine, as long as he has no child by her. And even if he has a child by her, he can always deny the paternity (although this does not often happen). And in any cases, the slave would have to continue to serve him, and be his concubine, that is unless he, when she has born a son to him, presents her with her freedom by way of compensation.

Emancipation of Slaves : The founder of Islam not only insisted upon the humane treatment of slaves, but also that it should be made possible for them to secure their freedom, when they have shown themselves worthy of it by their conduct. Accordingly, the emancipation of slaves among the Muhammadans must be regarded as a meritorious act. Sura 24, 33 reads:

"And those of your slaves who desire a deed of

> manumission, write it for them, if ye have a good opinion of them, and give them of the wealth of God, which he has given you."

The manner in which this emancipation is brought about in Muhammadan countries varies. Sometimes complete and immediate emancipation is granted to a slave gratuitously, or for a monetary compensation to be paid later. This is done by means of a written document, or by a verbal declaration in the presence of two witnesses; or again by the master presenting the slave with the certificate of sale obtained from the former master. Also, in conformity with the Prophet's demand in Sura 24, 33.

Future emancipation is sometimes agreed upon to be granted on the fulfillment of certain conditions; or more frequently, upon the death of the owner. In the latter case the owner cannot sell the slave with whom the agreement has been made. Also, as the owner cannot alienate by will more than one-third of the whole property that he leaves, the law ordains that, if the value of the said slave exceeds that portion, the slave must obtain, and pay to the owner's heirs the additional sum. We shall see further on that for certain offence, such as manslaughter, etc., the freeing of a captive is reckoned in part-punishment.

It is not impossible that Muhammad (PBUH) to some extent, at any rate, was acquainted with the Old Testament enactments concerning the emancipation of slaves. While, however, the Old Testament deals only with the emancipation of Israelite slaves, who has become bondmen through debt, Muhammad speaks of the emancipation of all slaves.

Ideological Support

We have now seen the state of Nature as it prevailed before the advent of Prophet Muhammad (Peace be on him!) and we already briefly touched upon the excellence of the laws of peace that transformed that country of war, anarchy and moral degradation into one of unity, harmony and moral excellence. Now we will try to see how that contract was made which brought about the civil society in which the laws of the sword were replaced by the articles of peace.

We will begin with a brief sketch of the life of the Prophet for he was the moving spirit which restored the laws of reason from oblivion and brought light in a country of darkness and sin. The Prophet was born at Mecca as a posthumous child in 570 A.D. and was bred and brought up by his grandfather who entrusted him to the care of Halima, a nurse of the clan of the Banu Sad. From his fourth year, he began to accompany the sons of Halima when they went out to graze their cattle.

When he was only six years old his mother died and he was left without any protection. His uncle Abu Talib then became his guardian. In his thirteenth year, he went to Syria for trade (with his uncle) and in his 20th year occurred the notorious Sacrilegious War (Harb-al-Fijar), so-called because it was waged during the sacred month of Dzulqu 'd. It was fought out between the Quraish (the Prophet also belonged to this clan) and the Banu Kinana on the one side, and the Banu Qais bin Ghailan on the other.

In this war, the Prophet did not take any part save that of gathering up the arrows discharged by the enemy and handing them over to his uncles.

Beginning of Social Contracts : After four years of fighting, peace was restored and as there was no government worth the name at Mecca, the descendants of Hashim and the families of Zuhra and Taim formed an association known as the 'Hilfal-Fudul' and agreed to stand by the oppressed and get justice done for them. Ibn Sad thus notes the character of this contract:

> "This contract was better and superior to all such previous pledges."

It was initiated by Zubayr bin 'Abdul-Muttalib and he

called upon others to pledge. The Banu Hashim, the Banu Zuhra and the Banu Taim gathered in the house of 'Abdullah bin Judan for purposes of agreement. They first met on a common dinner and then they organized the meeting. In the presence of God, they made a contract among themselves that they would fight on behalf of the oppressed against the aggressors up to the time the latter agreed to pay compensation to the former. Ibn Hisham puts this affair in this way:

> "All unanimously agreed on oath in the city of Mecca whether the oppressed be a traveller or be one of the residents, they would force the oppressor to pay compensation."

The Prophet was also present at the time of this contract and he said:

> "If further such contracts be made for the cause of the oppressed and 'I be called, I would certainly respond."

But other clans did not join this contract and they remained in the state of hostility in which they were passing their lives.

The Prophet as Amin : The Prophet's gentle-sweet disposition, his austerity of conduct, the severe purity of his life, his scrupulous refinement, his ever-ready helpfulness towards the poor and the weak, his noble sense of honour, his unflinching fidelity, his stern sense of duty had won him among his compatriots the high and enviable designation of Al-Amin the trustworthy.

In his twenty-fifth year, he married Hadrat Khadija who was much influenced by his honesty, virtue and the nobility of the soul.

In his thirty-fifth year, the Quraish decided to build the Kaaba which was now in a shattered condition, but they began to quarrel on the fixing of the 'Black Stone.' 'The Prophet at once Jook a sheet of cloth and asked four men of the four divisions of the Qur:aish to hold each corner and the Black

Stone was placed in the middle of the cloth. When it had been raised to the proper height, it was affixed by the Prophet himself. This settled a quarrel which might have again brought in a state of war as Hobbes pictured it. Says Tabari:

> "When the time came of affixing the Black Stone, every one desired to place it at the Spot. On this basis, all of them began to get out of the limits of patience and, one oath, became ready for war and bloodshed. The Banu 'Abdud-Dar went to the extent, according to the Arab custom of swearing on such hard occasions that they filled a cup with pure fresh blood and following the practice of the Arabia of ignorance they dipped their hands and of those of the clans of the Banu' Adi bin Kab into this cup of blood thus signifying with steadfastness their readiness for bloodshed and war."

Because of his God-fearing nature, the Prophet used to retire to the Cave of Hira and there offered prayers to the Almighty—the only 'Light of Nature.' It was here in his fortieth year, that the mantle of Prophethood fell upon him and he received the "Light". His wife'—Hadrat Khadija—at once accepted the Light of Islam and she was followed by Abu Bakr, 'Ali Zaid and a number of other followers such as 'Uthman bin' Affan so that the number of his followers in no time reached forty. This began to perturb the heathen Quraish and there was no meeting in which the growing power of Islam was not discussed.

The Muslims dared not offer prayers openly for fear of growing opposition. However, for three years the Prophet preached his religion of peace secretly. But when he began to do it publicly, the Quraish at once felt infuriated and they approached his uncle Abu Talib to refrain the Prophet from reviling their Gods and condemning idolatry. When Abu Talib advised the Prophet to refrain from such activities, he received the prompt reply:

> "If these people would place the sun on my right hand and the moon on the left, even then I would not give up my work until God fulfils it or I die in its pursuit.""

Islamic Theory : The Quraish found that the activities of the Muslims could not be abated, they decided on their heartless persecution and the Prophet was forced to advise them to leave for Abyssinia. Eighty-one Muslims thus said good-bye to their hearth and home simply because they had got the 'Light' which they could not forsake for an exchange of worldly life.

However, in spite of growing opposition, Islam went on gaining converts after converts and even Hamzah and Umar became Muslims. Muir writes:

> 'These conversions were a real triumph of Mahomet.' Hamzah and Umar both passed, with great bodily strength, and indomitable courage which added to social position, secured an important influence at Mecca. Muslims now began to offer public prayers at the Kaaba.

This open challenge alarmed the Quraish beyond imagination and all of them gathered together and all of them unanimously made a written contract under which they decided for a social boycott of the Hashimites agreeing that they would not marry their women nor give their own in marriage to them, nor buy aught from them; and that dealings with them of every kind should cease.

The written document was then hung in the Kaaba duly sealed. This contract or agreement has been called the 'Covenant of Tyranny' as distinguished from the earlier contract of the Hilfal Fudul. The former was a contract for the oppressed and the latter was made to oppress: the one was an instrument of human sympathy, the other an instrument of intolerance and cruelty.

For three years, the Hashimites were put to the greatest

trouble because of this boycott, but when, on the suggestion of the Prophet, that document of tyranny was examined, it was found out that it had been devoured by the insects (only in the name, of Allah! remained). Thus, the whole opposition was set at nought and the obligation of boycott was lost. The Covenant of Tyranny was annulled.

Contract between the Quraish and the Prophet **:** Soon after, however, the Prophet not only lost his wife—Hadrat Khadija—but also his uncle Abu Talib who had suffered so much because of his affection for his nephew (the Prophet).

Immediately before his death, another attempt was made by the Quraish to come to some agreement with the Prophet. Some of the well-known leaders went to Abu Talib and said that after his death quarrels and contentions would arise between the Quraish and Muhammad (peace be on him!) and therefore it was desirable that the Prophet should enter into a contract (a treaty of peace) with them for 'ceasing injuring their religion,' and on their part they would also 'let alone his'. Abu Talib at once sent for the Prophet and when he came he said:

> "My son, the nobles and chiefs of the Quraish have gathered here to make a contract (Muahada) with you and they agree to promote thy interests, and act according to thy behests, if thou will comply therewith".

The Prophet at once said:

> "My uncle! It is excellent. I request them to utter only one expression and the result of pronouncing this will be that they will reign over the whole of Arabia and the whole of Persia will accept their religion."

That expression is 'there is no god but God and Muhammad is His Prophet.' On hearing this, they clapped their hands and said:

> "O! Muhammad wishest thou to reduce our gods

> from one thousand to one." After this they arose and dispersed.

The passing away of Abu Talib emboldened the Quraish for further persecution and they even threw dust and dirt and even the intestines of goats and camels when the Prophet was busy in prayers, but he bore all this patiently. He then went to preach to the people of Taif but was not only hooted and treated in an unbecoming manner, he was also pelted with stones and pursued by a relentless rabble. In this way, he was forced to go back to Mecca.

Then the Prophet adopted the practise of preaching to the peoples of the suburbs of Mecca when they gathered for the performance of the Hajj but here too he was relentlessly opposed by the Quraish and made the target of calumny and ridicule. But the Prophet undaunted by adversity carried on his mission, and it is to this sublime attitude that Muir refers to in these words:

> "Mahomet thus holding his people at bay, waiting in the still expectation of victory; to outward appearance defenceless and with his little band as it were in the lion's mouth; yet trusting in His Almighty power Whose messenger he believed himself to be, resolute and unmoved, presents a spectacle of sublimity paralleled only by such scenes in the sacred records as that of the Prophet of Israel when he complained to his Master, 'I even I only am left."

However, it now became quite clear that the blind Arabs of the age of ignorance were not prepared to accept the Light of Allah and they were determined to live a life of darkness and error. They were wedded to their ancient customs and traditions and did not want to follow the laws of Nature as they were disclosed by the religion of peace—Islam. Hence, the first institution of civil society was not be on the land of Mecca: it was to be in a far, distant city—the city of Medina.

This contract of Aqaba practice of preaching to the people of the suburbs who came for the Hajj, after all, was crowned with success. The Prophet met six people of the Banu Khazraj from Yethrib (Medina) and they accepted Islam (that is, made a contract with God) and unanimously agreed to forsake the ways of their tribe; and when they went back 'there remained hardly a family in Medina in which mention was not made of the Prophet,' for they had already declared that on their return they would call their people to the principles of Islam.

Next year, during the same pilgrimage, twelve people came from Medina (of these seven were newcomers and five from those who had accepted Islam last year). They belonged to the two tribes that inhabited Medina—ten belonged to the Banu Khazraj and two to the Banu Aus. They met the Prophet near Aqaba and those who had not yet accepted Islam now accepted it and all of them pledged their faith to the Prophet in these words:

> "We will not worship any but God, we will not steal neither will we commit adultery, nor kill our children; we will not slander in any way, nor will we disobey the Prophet in anything that is right. The Prophet then said:
>
> "If you keep this covenant, Paradise will be your lot. But if you commit any sins excepting idolatry and infidelity your pardon or chastisement will depend on the will of God. This first contract or pledge is known as the 'Pledge of Women' as not embracing any stipulation to defend the Prophet, it was the only oath required of women. However, the twelve men went back to Medina as missionaries of Islam and with them the Prophet sent Musab to teach the Quran, that is, to call them to the religion of peace—Islam, and to the divine laws of Nature.

Thus, it is clear that the spread of Islam or of the religion of peace was now to occur in a far distant city of Medina. It would, therefore, be advisable to know the condition of Medina before Islam, for though we have already read the state of Nature as it prevailed in the whole of Arabia, we have not yet specifically stated the condition of Medina before the Light of Allah dispelled the all-pervading darkness.

From the first pledge of Aqaba and its provisions, it is evident that the worship of idols, stealing, adultery, infanticide and slandering were prevalent in the people Yathrib (Medina) also and hence they made a Covenant with the Prophet of God that henceforth, they would abstain from those practices. Thus socially and morally, this part of Arabia was as low in the scale of civilisation as any other part of that country.

Political Conditions in Prophet's Time: Politically, however, besides the Arab tribes, the Jews had settlements round about Medina and the Banu Nadir, the Banu Quraiza and the Banu Qainuqa were their chief tribal settlements. They had even taken possession of the old city of Yathrib (Medina) and 'had built for themselves strong castellated houses capable of resisting armed attack'.

In the 4th century, several Arab tribes had migrated from Yemen towards the north, and they had gained a footing in Medina, thus supplanting the Jewish control in that city. They were divided into two clans—the Aus and the Khazraj, and both of them had developed strong enmity against the Jews. But, according to the general condition of Arabia, they themselves could not live at peace and were in the beginning of the 6th. century in a state of 'chronic' enmity, if not actual warfare with one another. Only four or five years earlier, hostilities had reached a crisis between them. Each was reinforced by allies from other Arab tribes; the Jews were divided, the Quraiza and the Nadir siding with the Banu Aus, the Qainuqa with the Khazraj.

In the year 616 A.D., there was fought the great battle of

Buath. This battle, like the so-called hundred years' war of Europe was a culmination of hostilities which had been going on for the past hundred and twenty years. At first, the Aus were worsted, but later on 'they dispersed the Khazraj with great slaughter. The Banu Khazraj were humbled but not reconciled. No open engagement after this took place, but numerous assassinations gave token from time to time of hardly suppressed ill-blood. No one yet appeared bold enough to seize the reins of government; the citizens, both Arab and Jewish, lived in uncertainty and suspense'.

State of Nature : Thus, in Medina also there had been prevailing the State of Nature as Hobbes pictured it and in the words of Wellhausen it was a state of 'hideous anarchy' conjured up by bloody feuds, which prevailed in Medina before the coming of Muhammad...Life was then indeed impossible. But at the time of the first pledge of Uquba as has just been said, there was, what Muir terms, grave 'uncertainty and suspense.' This means that there was a sort of armed peace and 'enjoyment of life or property' was 'very uncertain and constantly exposed to the invasion of others.' Thus, everything was 'very unsafe, very insecure.'

Apparently, therefore, it seemed that there was peace, goodwill, mutual assistance and preservation because it was a state of equality—and of liberty of each individual; in fact, however, men had become tired of that suspense and uncertainty and they were ready to quit that condition, 'which, however free, was full of fears and continual dangers'. This meant that self-love and passion and heart of controversy easily turned that life of apparent peace into one of enmity, malice, violence and mutual destruction and revenge carried everybody too far. Thus confusion or disorder was the rule, and men living together in this State of Nature lacked:

1. A settled known law;
2. A known and indifferent judge with authority to

determine all differences according to established laws; and

3. The supreme power to maintain order again, in the words of Wellhausen, 'There are neither officers nor officials, neither jailors nor executioners. There is no magisterial authority, no sovereign power with a revenue of its own drawn from taxation and an independent administration by official organisation'.

The Laws of Nature : Hence, the necessity of an orderly government was keenly felt by the individuals of Medina. But how could unity be brought about for they could not accept the sovereignty of any individual from either tribe—the Aus or the Khazraj? Nor had they accepted the Jewish faith, though they had heard from them that a Prophet was soon to rise to establish the Kingdom of God again "to make a permanent peace."

Thus, when six of them went to the annual pilgrimage to Mecca, they met the much heard of Prophet himself and accepted Islam, that is, they made a contract with him in the acceptance of the formula that 'there is no god but God and Muhammad is His Prophet.'

These people, as we have already seen, then went back to Medina and next year, twelve people made a similar contract with God and His Prophet by accepting Islam—the religion of peace. Thus, on their return Islam began to be accepted by the different individuals of the state of Nature in Medina. This means that they also renounced the law of the sword that had always existed in that city and they at once accepted the divine laws of Nature as they were given out by Prophet Muhammad (Peace be on him!).

Thus, the state of Nature in Medina had no natural laws in Locke's sense which was understood and apprehended by every one's reason, though there were news that such laws were going to be promulgated soon by a new Prophet. From this comparison of Locke's State of Nature and of the condition of pre-Islamic Medina, it is evident that by recognising the laws of Nature in the state of Nature, Locke had given a moral tone, and therefore he had no justification left for the people to quit the state of Nature (as it was one of peace) and create a civil society which was in no sense an improvement upon it. It was without doubt a fall. In the words of Vaughan:

> "Neither materially, nor morally is there any marked barrier between his natural and his civil state. Neither materially nor morally, therefore, is there any sufficient motive for the individual to go to the cost and trouble of removing such slight fences as divide them. He already possesses, already owes allegiance to the 'law of Nature,' a law which, on Locke's showing is at least a very tolerable substitute not only for the law of the land, but also ever for the Gospel."

However, about the coming of the Prophet, the individuals of Medina had already heard and hence when he came, they individually agreed (contract of acceptance of Islam is always made by every individual) to accept the divine laws of Nature and quit that condition of insecurity and uncertainty.

According to Locke, when the people decide to quit the state of Nature each individual from amongst them unites with others for the preservation of life, liberty, and property, and thus by this social contract they create a community for peace, safety and the public good of one and all. Similarly, after the first contract of the Quran, we shall see now, the majority of the various tribesmen had already accepted Islam.

Thus, out of the scattered individuals of two hostile tribes of Aus and Khazraj, they were now becoming compacted as individuals of one community of Muslims. But still they were individuals as they had also remained in Locke even after the contract, for in spite of their commonality in Islam they could not yet tolerate the idea that they should be led in prayers by either an Ausite or a Khazrajite. Hence, Musab not only taught them the Quran:

> "He led the prayers and thus kept in abeyance the rivalry of the state of ignorance."

We have already said that after the first contract at Aqaba, the twelve Muslims with Musab went back to Medina as missionaries of Islam and when they began calling people to the religion of peace, so zealous was their propagation that 'the new faith spread rapidly from house to house and from tribe to tribe.' 'In spite of the jealousy of the tribe of Aus towards Khazraj, by the energy of the learned Musab, whom Muhammad sent to Medina as his forerunner and as reader of the Holy Quran, Islam soon obtained a firm foothold in the city, so that two years later his adherents could venture to invite the Prophet to visit them.' Thus says Muir:

> "The Jews looked on in amazement. The people whom for generations they had vainly endeavoured to convince of the errors of heathenism were now of their own accord casting their idols to the moles and to the bats, and professing belief in the one true God – the only Light of the Heaven and the Earth, or of all creation."

However, in the month of Hajj next year, Musab along with certain Muslims and the unbelievers of Medina again went to Mecca. Among the Muslims there were 73 men and two women (62 of the Banu Khazraj, 11 of the Banu Aus). The meeting with the Prophet was again arranged secretly at 'Aqaba' and there he reached at the appointed time with his uncle Abbas (who had not accepted Islam by that time). When all were seated, Abbas thus began addressing them:

> "You men of Banu Khazraj! You know it full well that Muhammad lives amongst us in honour and safety, and we are his protectors against his opponents. But he prefers to leave this city and seek protection with

you. If you see the consequences of what you are going to do and feel that you will be able to defend him against his enemies, then give the pledge; but if you doubt your ability, you must at once give up the idea, for up to this time Muhammad is under our protection and in that case, I fear, you may hand him over to his enemies." On this Bara' one of their leaders replied:

"We have listened to your words. Our resolution is unshaken: our lives are at the Prophet's service. It is now for him to speak, and take whatever promise he takes from us."

The Prophet then began by reciting the Holy Quran, and inviting all present to the service of God said:

"I want to take such a pledge from you that you protect me in the way you protect your wives and children". On this Bara got up and taking the Prophet by the hand pledged to defend him in the way they defended their wives and children, and then followed the noise from those present for individual 'baiaf (pledge) even at the cost of life and property.

The second contract made at 'Aqaba (the women pledging only in the words used in the first contract and the men in addition pledging for defence and protection of the Prophet) and their treaty (contract) was ratified by the people (of Medina), who unanimously embraced the religion of Islam. The Prophet appointed twelve leaders from amongst them (9 from Khazraj and 3 from Aus) and addressing them said:

"I appoint you as the sureties (Kafil) of your people just as the Apostles (Hawari) of Jesus were, and I am the Surety of you all."

***Another Version*:** Besides this, another version of this second contract also had been given by the Raudatus-Safa and that too is interesting from the point of view of the study of the contract theory. According to this version, Abbas had said to the assembly:

> "O ye tribe of Khazraj and of Aus, Muhammad is my nephew, and I love him most of all creatures. If you believe him, place faith in him, and if you desire to take him with you. I want to establish a covenant between you, so as to specify my mind and to preserve him from injury and harm during his exile, especially as the Jews, who are your neighbours, harbour, enmity towards him, and I fear their cunning devices against him."

On this Sad bin Zararah stood up and among many other things addressing the Prophet said:

> "We are a people aware of our dignity, and no one could rule or govern us except one of our number. How much less could a man do so who has been abandoned by his own tribe and from whom his own relatives have withdrawn their hand of protection? We have, nevertheless, in good faith, of our own free will, concluded to submit to thee...We assent to follow thee, we promise to, and make a Covenant with God, Who is thy and our Creator, and Whose power is above all powers, that we shall sacrifice our lives for thine and shall protect thy body in the same manner as we guard the bodies of our children and wives. We know that if we keep this Covenant we keep our faith towards Allah the Most High, and we will become partakers of eternal felicity, and that if we break this promise, we break our faith towards Allah the Most High, and will be of the number of the damned. O Apostle of Allah, these words of ours are true, so help us God." Then turning to Abbas, he said that they were ready to make any agreement or covenant he liked. On this the Prophet said:

> "The conditions of our Covenant with reference to the Creator are: that you worship Him alone and attribute to Him no companion; and with reference to myself, they are that you protect me in the same manner as your own lives, those of your children and women." The assembly then said:
>
> "O Apostle of Allah, we assent to what thou hast said." When the Covenant was established the Prophet then selected the twelve leaders already noted above.

The news of this pledge soon spread to Mecca and it made the Quraish furious. They made up their mind to vehemently persecute the Muslims. On this the prophet advised his followers in Mecca to emigrate to Medina, and within two months, they settled in their new abode, with their families. The Quraish were thus paralysed by a movement which though unnoticed and suddenly planned, made their several quarters deserted. They at once met in the Darul-Nandwa (Council Hall) and began to plan the imprisonment, the assassination or the expulsion of the Prophet. They ultimately agreed (made a contract among themselves) that a young man of each clan be selected and all of them should at once attack and kill the Prophet. It this way, no blood feud would be raised by the Hashimites as they would dare not oppose all the clans put together.

But before they could act on their decision, the Prophet had already left his place and had sought refuge with his bosom friend Abu Bakr in the Cave of Thaur. There, they lived for three days and then made off to Medina. This is known in Islam as Hijrat or flight and it is from this that the Muslim year begins.

After eight days of tiresome journey, the Prophet and his companion reached Quba safely where the people (of the Aus tribe) had been expecting him morning and night. As soon as he was sighted, a thrill of joy spread all over the city. The converts from all quarters flocked to Mahomet and made obeisance to him. He received them courteously and said:

> "Ye people! Show your joy by giving to your neighbours the salutation of peace, send portions to the poor, bind close the ties of kinsmanship, offer up prayer whilst others sleep. Thus shall Ye enter paradise in peace."After four days, the Prophet started for Medina and when he entered the city, he found tribes and families ready to honour him.

"As the people of Medina received Muhammad with joyous enthusiasm, his entrance into the town resembled that of a triumphant prince rather than a poor fugitive." Muir also thus draws the picture of the Prophet's reception:

> "The tribes and families of Medina came streaming forth, and view with one another is showing honour to their noble visitor. It was indeed a triumphal precession. Around the camels of Mahomet and his immediate followers, rode the chief men of the city clad in their best raiment in glittering armour."

The cavalcade pursued its way through the gardens and palm groves of the southern suburbs; and as it now threaded the streets of the city, the heart of Mahomet was gladdened by the incessant call from one another as they flocked around:

> "Alight here, O Prophet! We have abundance with us, means of defence and weapons and room. Abide with us." So urgent was the appeal that sometimes they seized hold of Al Qaswa's halter. Mahomet answered them courteously and kindly:

"The decision, he said, rests with the camel; make way for her; let her go free."

It was a master stroke of policy. His residence would be hallowed in the eyes of the people as selected supernaturally, while the jealousy which otherwise might arise from the quarter of one tribe being preferred to that of another would thus receive decisive check. However, the camel halted at an open yard and the Prophet stayed with Abu Ayyub whose house was the nearest. There, he stayed in the lower story for the convenience of those who used to visit him, and "dishes of choice viands, bread and meat, butter and milk, presently arrived from various houses and this hospitality was kept up daily so long as the Prophet resided in the house."

Consolidation of Medina as Political Capital : Thus was Medina conquered by the Prophet. As he himself said in a Tradition:

"All cities or districts were conquered by force, but
All Medina was conquered by the Quran"

And certainly, it was the Quran that conquered it. It was a conquest of heart rather than of territory, and the means was the willing consent of the people rather than the sword of the conqueror. And the contract, which gave this consent, had taken three steps in its fulfillment.

In the first, the laws of Islam which were the divine laws of Nature were explained and promulgated; in the second the representatives of the two chief tribes entered into a definite covenant of protecting the Prophet; and in the third, each citizen, nay every child of Medina welcomed the Prophet as their saviour.

Religiously considered, therefore, the Kingdom of God was thus established in a land of darkness and terror, and heathenism or idolatry vanished with the onslaught of the Light of Islam.

Socially and politically considered, the state of Nature with its state of war or, at least, of uncertainty and inconvenience was done away by the acceptance of the laws of Nature, and the contract with the Prophet at once transformed that state into one of civil society. Gibbon says:

"In the state of Nature every man has a right to defend,

> by force of arms, his person and his possession: to repel, or even to prevent, the violence of his enemies, and to extend his hostilities to a reasonable measure of satisfaction and retaliation. In the free society of the Arabs, the duties of subject and citizen imposed a feeble restraint; and Mahomet, in the exercise of a peaceful and benevolent mission had been despoiled and banished by the injustice of his countrymen. The choice of an independent people had exalted the fugitive of Mecca to the rank of a sovereign; and he was invested with the just prerogative of forming alliances and of waging offensive or defensive war."

Thus, if the city state of Medina was the Kingdom of God in one sense and the Prophet was the Vice regent of God in that divine kingdom, it was also in another sense a true state of the people created by the people themselves, and the Prophet was an elected sovereign of a sovereign people. To summarize the whole of our survey, we may now say that:

1. The state of Nature in Medina also was a state of war but immediately at the time of the first contract, there was apparent peace, and therefore, it most truly resembled Locke's picture of the state of Nature.
2. The laws of Nature—of Islam—brought the individuals together into a contract (with God); that is, they accepted Islam and hence a community of Muslims was created, though that community was not yet organic in nature.
3. The absence of a well-known authority or judge was then provided for by the second contract with the Prophet, and this contract was then ratified by the whole community. This was a government contract. The Prophet thus became an elected chief of a people and he appointed their own leaders to look after them.

Western Interpretation : After this, we may now compare the character of this second contract from the point of view of political philosophy. From what we see of the addresses of Abbas, Bara and the Prophet, it becomes quite clear, that while Bara' pledged to protect the Prophet with life and property, the Prophet himself (in the worldly sense) promised nothing. That is, the Prophet in the literal sense of the contract of give-and-take, was not a party to the contract and the contract was only one-sided. This means that after the contract, and after its ratification by the people of Medina they got pledged to protect their elected 'Sovereign' and they had agreed to obey him in everything.

From this point of view, it becomes clear that this second contract resembled the contract of Hobbes in which the sovereign had promised nothing and yet he was to be obeyed absolutely. There was to be no rebellion because it would again result in the state of Nature from which they had run out for the law and the religion of peace.

Would it then be too fantastic on my part, to again ask, if Hobbes (as well as other social-contract writers) had this condition of Arabia in view, and that they were only interpreting things and events which were already past history?

Besides this interpretation, there can be another interpretation of this second contract in the view of Locke, if we take into account another 'report' regarding the proceedings of that contract. When that contract was going to be made Abul Hashim (one of those present) said to the Prophet:

> "O Apostle of Allah, between us and the Jews there are treaties and alliances, but if we break them, and Allah the Most High grants the victory, thou wilt possibly rejoin thy tribe, and abandon us to our foes." His Lordship smiled and said:
>
> "Blood is blood, and destruction is destruction. You are mine and I am yours. I shall fight those who fight you, and make peace with those with whom you make peace."

It is clear, that if after the first contract at Aqaba, the Muslim community was created in Medina (this resembles the social contract of Locke), by the second contract a governmental contract was made by which the Prophet became the chief authority of the city-state of Medina. In one point more, the resemblance of the events in the second pledge can be made with those on which Locke's contract was based. It is argued that Locke wanted to justify the Glorious Revolution of England in which William and Mary had been called from Holland (by seven notables of London). The Prophet was also a non-party man in Medina and he was called by 73 men to their land and then their contract or pledge was kept up by the people.

This governmental contract in Medina resembles, no doubt, the second (governmental contract) in Locke, but critics do not agree as to the making of a second contract. Thus, Vaughan emphatically asserts (and I think he is right) that there is only one contract in Locke—the social contract which creates the community. He observes;

"It has often been said that Locke represents the relation between the community and the executive as one of contract: the original contract between King and people of the famous convention resolution of 1689."

This may not be very far removed from the spirit of his doctrine, but it is doubly wrong as to the latter. For, on the one hand, the appointment of the Executive is apparently conceived by him as belonging normally not to the community, but to the Legislature. And, on the other hand, what is far more important, he never once uses the term contract to describe the instrument from which the Executive derives its authority. It is always a trust, or a fiduciary trust.

Hence, if according to this argument there is only one contract in Locke, the two contracts in Medina bear resemblance to the two contracts in Milton and Althusius and other anti-monarchist writers, though the purpose of their contracts was not the same. But the social contract of Medina does not fully accord with the first or social contract of Althusius or of Milton for in them even the king was a party to the original contract (which is of course not true of Medina, for the Prophet was still in Mecca when the social contract was made in Medina). Hence, the two contracts of Medina wholly and fully accord with the framework (and not the spirit or purpose) of the contract theory as it was stated in Vindicia Contra Tyrannos which was formerly ascribed to Brutus or to Languet, but is now understood to be the work of Mornay (1579). Mornay in his book has two contracts:

1. The first contract is between God on the one side and the people and their ruler on the other side for maintenance of true religion. It was upheld by the state in return for the protection and favour of Almighty God.
2. The second contract is between ruler and subjects to preserve and protect the natural rights of subjects in return for their loyal support of the Prince.

The first of these contracts is true of the social contract of Medina also for the people whose representatives had already accepted Islam at the hands of the Prophet himself had now accepted Islam at the hands of Musab who was the representative of the Prophet at Medina. This was certainly a contract of the ruler and the people with God to maintain the right religion which was Islam.

The second contract was made by the Prophet with the peoples' representatives and when he reached Medina the whole Muslim community ratified the baiat' (pledge or contract) that had already been made and the Prophet declared, as has been already noted above, that he was heart and soul with the people of Medina for they had declared to support him in thick and thin and he was also prepared to fight with their enemies as his own enemy.

Thus, from the above account of the contracts at Medina, it is clear that the social contract theory is not a mere fiction: it is a historical reality and ancient Arabia was the scene of such contracts even in the making and the construction of the state itself. The contracts in Medina do explain not only the origin of civil society in contract but also of its government. Contract in Islam, therefore, is a reality and not a mere fiction or only a mere idea of reason.

3

Social Sanction

It is not possible to give the right analyses of the nature and methods of Islamic social justice until we have first examined the general lines of Islamic theory on the subject of the Universe, life, and mankind. Social justice is only a branch of the great science to which all Islamic studies must run back. The faith of Islam, which deals with the whole field of human life, does not treat the different aspects of the life in the mass, nor yet does it split up the field into a number of unrelated parts.

Islam has one universal theory which covers the Universe and life and humanity, a theory in which are integrated all the different questions. In this Islam sums up all its beliefs, its laws and statutes, and its modes of worship and of work. The treatment of all these matters emanates from this one universal and comprehensive theory, so that each question is not dealt with on an individual basis, nor is every problem with its needs treated in isolation from all other problems.

A knowledge of this universal theory is necessary to the faith of Islam, because it enables the student to understand its principles and beliefs and to relate the particular to the general. It empowers him to study with pleasure and with understanding its characteristics and its aims. While on the other hand, the fact that the basis is religious guarantees that the theory will be both coherent and comprehensive, and not compartmentalized.

No theory of life can be of profit unless it comprehends all the departments and all the aims of human life. So, the best method of studying Islam is to start by understanding its universal theory before going on to study its views on politics or economics or the relationship between communities and individuals. For such questions as these are but issues arising out of that universal theory and they cannot be truly or deeply understood except in the light of it.

The true Muslim philosophy is not to be sought in Ibn Sina' or Ibn-Rushid, such men as these who alone are known as the Muslim philosophers. For the philosophy which they teach is no more than a shadow of the Greek philosophy, and has no relation to the true Islamic philosophy. The faith of Islam has a native universal philosophy which is to be sought only in its own familiar authorities:

> "The Quran and the traditions, the life of its Prophet and his every day customs."

These are the authorities in which the student must go deep to find the universal Islamic theory from which come all the Muslim teachings and laws, its modes of worship and work. Islam as a faith has laid down the nature of the relation between the Creator and His creation, the nature of man's relation to the universe and to the world, and of man's relation to his own soul; it has laid down the relation between the individual and society, between different societies and mankind as a whole, and the relation between one nation and another.

All these teachings are the expression in different aspects of the one universal, comprehensive theory which relates to one another all the separate aspects all of which together is Islamic philosophy. The detailed study of this philosophy is no part of this present work. Here, we shall confine ourselves to the examination of one specific subject, to the full completion of which may Allah's help be vouchsafed. So, here we shall merely outline the main headings of the general scheme, in order to facilitate our study of social justice in Islam.

Creator and His Creation

Man lived for long ages without achieving a comprehensive theory of his Creator and the Universe, or of the Universe, life and mankind. That is to say, 'man had never reached the point of working out such a universal and comprehensive theory until the birth of Islam. The relation between the Creator and His creation is to be found in the power of the World, the Active Will from which all creation came."

There is no mediating power of any kind between the Creator and His creation, but from His universal and absolute Will proceed all existing things in due and proper order; and by that universal, absolute, and active Will all things are sustained, ordered, and energized. "He manages the affair, sets the signs in order." "He grasps the Heavens that they fall not upon the Earth, save by His permission." It is necessary for the sun not to overtake the moon, nor the night to outrun the day; but each in its circle they revolve." "Blessed be He in whose hand is the kingship; and He over all things hath power."

So all creation, issuing as it does from one absolute universal active Will forms an all-embracing unity in which each individual part is in harmonious order with the remainder. And thus, too, every form of existence embodies a principle which relates it to this perfect and comprehensive order. "He it is who hath created 'seven' Heavens, one above the other, thou canst not see any oversight in the creation of the Merciful? Look again; canst thou see any flaw? Look again and again, thy sight will turn back, dim and wearied out." "And He set up upon it mountain peaks above it, and blessed it, and arranged its various kinds of food in it." "He it is who hath created death and life to try you, to test which of you is the best in deeds." "Allah it is who sends the winds to stir up the clouds, and He spreads it in the Heavens as He wills, and breaks it up; so you see the rain coming out of the midst of it; and when He causes it to fall on which of His servants He wills, behold they rejoice."

Accordingly, it is obvious that all creation must have a fundamental connection with the creative purpose and that the Will from which all creation finally proceeds, and by which it is continually sustained and ordered, is related to creation itself; thus only can that Will give to creation a coherence and a completed meaning. Thus, then, all creation is a unity comprising different parts; it has a common origin, a common providence and purpose, because it was deliberately produced by a single, absolute, and comprehensive Will.

It was suitable, adapted, and ready for the appearance of life in the general sense, and for the appearance of man, the highest form of life, in particular. So, the universe cannot be hostile to life or to man; nor can 'Nature' in our modern phrase be held to be antagonistic to man, opposed to him, or striving against him.

Rather she is a friend whose purposes are one with those of life and of mankind. And the task of lifting beings is not to contend with Nature, for they have grown up in her bosom, and she and they together form a part of the single Universe which proceeds from the single will.

Basically, man lives in a purely friendly environment, among the powers of a friendly Universe. So Allah, when He created the Earth, set up upon it mountain peaks above it, and blessed it, and arranged its various kinds of food in it. "And He cast upon the Earth mountain peaks, lest it sway with you." "And the Earth—He established it for mankind." "He it is who hath laid the Earth low for you, so walk ye about in its regions, and eat of its provision." "He hath created for you what is in the earth, all of it." So, the Heavens with their stars are a part of creation; they are connected with the other parts, and everything that is in them and in the Earth is friendly, cooperative, and interrelated with all the remaining parts. "And He decked out the lower Heavens with lamps." "Did we not make the Earth a flat expanse, and the mountains as tent-pegs? We created you in pairs, and We appointed your sleep to be a rest. We made the night for a covering, and We made the day for a livelihood. We built about you seven firm Heavens, and We set a lamp ablazing. We sent down from the rain-clouds copious waters to bring forth grain, and vegetation, and luxurious gardens."

And further, the Creator does not place the living beings and men in this world, without giving them also His kindly care and constant attention, for His perfect Will is constant throughout all the world, constant, too, over every individual part of the Universe at all times. "There is no beast on the earth but its provision is a charge upon Allah he knows its lair and its resting place." "We have created man, and We know what he whispers to himself. We are nearer to him than his jugular vein." "Your Lord said, 'Call upon Me, and I shall answer you. '20 "And do not kill your children because of poverty; We shall provide for you and for them." And so on.

Because, then, the Universe is a unity emanating from a single Will; because man is himself a part of the World, dependent upon and related to all the other parts; and because individuals are as atoms, dependent upon and related to the world, therefore, they must have the same dependence upon, and relation of, one another. So, the Islamic belief is that humanity is an essential unity; its scattered elements must be brought together, its diversity must give place to uniformity, its variety of creeds must in the end be brought into one. For thus and only thus can man be made ready to be at one with the essential unity of creation. " O ye people. We have created you male and female, and We have made you races and tribes, that you might know one another."

There can be no permanent system in human life until this integration and unification has taken place. This step is a prerequisite for true and complete human life, so that the rule offeree may be done away once for all, and so that those who have wandered from the true path may be brought back to it. "The recompense of those who make war against Allah and His Messenger, exerting themselves to cause corruption in the Earth, is that they be killed or crucified, or that their hands and feet on opposite sides be cut off, or that they be banished from the land." "If two parties of the Believers fight, then make peace between them; if one of them oppresses the other, then fight the oppressing party until it returns to the affair of Allah; if it returns, then make a just peace between them, and act fairly." "And if Allah had not resisted one party of the people by means of others, the land would have grown corrupt."

Accordingly, the fundamental matter is this inter-dependence and solidarity of mankind, and whoever has lost sight of this principle must be brought back to it by any means. For the first great divine law of existence is to identify the desires of individuals and of societies; and such mutual responsibility among all is in the end the sole aid of our unified world and of its Creator.

When we come to consider man as a race and as an individual, there is the same comprehensive unity to be observed; man's faculties which are so diverse in appearance are essentially one in purpose. Thus in this respect also man is comparable to the world in its entirety, since its power too is a unity, though diverse in appearance.

Man lived through long ages without arriving at any comprehensive theory of human and universal powers; he continued to differentiate between spiritual and material powers, he denied one of these in order to strengthen the other, or he admitted the existence of both in a state of opposition and antagonism. He organized his life on the basis that such an opposition between these two types of power was natural, and that the superiority of one was only to be gained at the expense of the other. He held that such superiority on the one side and inferiority on the other was inevitable, because, as he believed, such opposition was inherent in the nature of the world and of man.

Christianity at time shows examples of this theory of opposition, because it was by such a theory that it was led to libertarianism on the one hand and austerity on the other, accordingly as these two alternated in its life. For Christianity the salvation of the soul is to be gained by humiliating the body, by punishing it, or even by destroying it, or at the least by neglecting it and turning away from indulgence.

In Christianity and in other similar faiths, this is the cardinal principle on which are built up their systems of belief to it can be traced their doctrines on life and its purpose, on the duties of the individual on the one hand and of society on the other, and on man and the different powers and abilities which attach to his existence.

Thus, the struggle between the two types of powers—spiritual and material—continued, with men continually uncertain and perplexed, and without any definite assurance as to the true solution. Then came Islam, bringing with it a new, comprehensive, and coherent theory in which there was neither this tension nor this opposition, neither hostility nor antagonism. Islam gave clarity to all powers and abilities, it gave an identity of purpose to all desires and inclinations and leanings, it gave a coherence to all men's efforts.

In all these, Islam saw one embracing unity which took in the Universe, the soul, and all human life. Its aim was to unite Earth and Heaven in one world; to join the present world and the world to come in one faith; to link spirit and body in one humanity; to correlate worship and work in one life. It sought to bring all these into one path—the path which led to Allah.

In the same way, the world is a unity, composed of things which are seen and otherwise sensually perceived, and of things which are unseen and imperceptible. Life is a unity, made up of material abilities and spiritual powers, between which no separation can ever be made without a resultant disorder and confusion. And similarly human personality is a unity of spiritual desires which rise toward Heaven, and bodily appetites which cling on Earth. No separation can be made between these aspects of personality, because Heaven and Earth are one, because in the world there is a unity of things, seen and things unseen, and because in religion there is a unity of this world and that to come, between daily life and worship.

But beyond all this, there does exist one eternal and unchanging power, which has no beginning and no comprehensible end. To it belongs the government of the world, of mankind, and of life. It is the power of Allah. The human individual in his transience seeks to attain to this power which eternally pervades life, and from it he seeks help in his misfortunes. He strives after it when he is in the mosque at prayer, lifting up his heart to Heaven, and he seeks it no less when he is abroad in the world, busily intent upon his livelihood. So, he seeks to deserve the future life, not only when he fasts and denies himself all manner of pleasurable indulgence, but also when he breaks his fast and enjoys all the good things of life—so long as he does either of these two things with his heart firmly directed towards Allah. And thus the life of the present world, with all its prayer and its work, all its luxuries and its privations, is the only way to the future world, with its Heaven and its hell, its punishment and its reward.

This surely is the true unity between the sundry parts of the Universe and their powers, between all the diverse abilities of life, between man and his soul, between his experiences and dreams. Such a unity it is which can set a lasting harmony between the world and human life, between life and living men, between society and the individual, and between man's spiritual desires and his appetites. In a word, it means a harmony between the world and the faith, between Earth and Heaven.

This harmony is not established in favour of the physical side of man, nor yet in favour of the spiritual side; rather it imparts to both of them an equal freedom, thus bringing both to a healthy position of well-being and growth. Similarly, this harmony is not established in the favour of the individual, or of society; nor in favour of one nation over another, nor in favour of one community over a people.

But each of these is held to have its own rights and its own responsibilities. For the individual and society, the people and the community, the nation and all other nations—all are bound by one law which has but one aim, namely, that the freedom of the individual and of society should be equally recognized without any mutual opposition; and that the nations, one and all, should work to gather for the growth and progress of human life and for its orientation towards the Creator of life.

Islam, then, is a faith of the unity of all the powers of the world; and beyond doubt it is a uniting faith. It stands for the unity of gods, and for the unity of all religions in the faith of Allah, and also for the unity of all the Prophets in their testimony to this one faith since the dawn of time.

"Verily this community of yours is one, and I am your Lord so worship Me."

So also Islam stands for the unity of worship and work, of faith and life, of spiritual and material realities, of economic and spiritual values, of the present world and the world to come, of Earth and Heaven.

From this pervasive unity there issue all the Islamic laws and ordinances, all its exhortations and rules, as well as its teachings on political and economic theory, on the balance of credits and debits, and on privileges and responsibilities. Thus in this fundamental principal of unity there are contained all the various rules of life.

While we are examining this universal theory which takes its rise from the nature of Islamic thought about the world and life and humanity, we may study also the fundamental outlines of social justice in Islam. Above all other things it is a comprehensive human justice, and not merely an economic justice; that is to say, it embraces all sides of life and all aspects of freedom. It is concerned alike with the mind and the body, with the heart and the conscience. The values with which this justice deals are not only economic values, nor are they merely material values in general; rather they are a mixture of moral and spiritual values together. Christianity looks at man only from the stand point of his spiritual desires and seeks to crush down the human instincts in order to encourage those desires.

On the other hand, Communism looks at man only from the stand point of his material needs; it looks not only at human nature, but also at the world and at life from a purely material point of view. But Islam looks at man as forming a unity whose spiritual desires cannot be separated from his bodily appetites, and whose moral needs cannot be divorced from his material needs. It looks at the world and at life with this all-embracing view which permits of no separation or division. In this fact lies the main divergence among Communism, Christianity, and Islam.

Thus, in the Islamic view, life consists of mercy, love, help, and a mutual responsibility between Muslims in particular, and between all human beings in general. Whereas in the Communist view, life is a continual strife and struggle between the classes, a struggle which must end in one class overcoming the other; at which point the Communist dream is realized. Hence, it is patent that Islam is the undying goodness of humanity, embodied in a living faith, working in the world; while Communism is the evil of human nature, limited to a single nation.

Individual and Society

There are, then, these two great facts: the absolute, just, and coherent unity of existence; and the general, mutual responsibility of individuals and societies. On these two facts

Islam bases its definition of social justice, having regard to the basis elements of the nature of man, yet not unmindful of human abilities. The Holy Quran says of man that "Verily, for the love of gain he is violent;" the "love of gain" belongs to his nature and to his native endowment. It says also, describing that greed which is of the nature and constitution of man, that "souls are close to avarice;" it is always near to them. So also there occurs in the Quran a wonderfully skillful description of this human trait say: "If it were you who had in your power the treasures of the mercy of my Lord, then you would keep a tight hold for fear of spending; for man is niggardly." But, he is certainly liberal with His mercy in every way; and so, from this liberality of Divine mercy and from that human meanness, it is apparent how great is the extent of avarice in the nature of man if he is left without discipline of exhortation.

Accordingly, when Islam comes to lay down its rules and laws, its counsels and controls, that natural " love of gain" is not overlooked, nor is that deep natural avarice forgotten; selfishness is rebuked, avarice is death with regulations and laws, and the duty laid on man is that of liberality. At the same time, Islam does not overlook the needs and the welfare of society, nor does it forget the great achievements of individuals in life and society in every age and among different nations.

There may sometimes occur that type of social oppression which is inconsistent with justice, when the greed and cupidity of the individual prey upon society; or that same oppression may also take the form of society preying upon the nature and ability of the individual. Such oppression in a sin, not against one individual alone, but against the whole principle of the community.

It is an encroachment upon the freedom of the individual whose natural rights are infringed; but its evil effects do not touch merely the welfare and rights of the one individual; they go beyond him to touch the welfare of the whole community, because it cannot profit to the full from his abilities.

So, the regulations lay down the rights of the community over the powers and abilities of the individual; they also establish limiting boundaries to the freedom, the desires, and the wants of the individual but they must also be ever mindful of the rights of the individual, to give him freedom in his desires and inclinations; and over all there must be the limits which the community must not overstep, and which the individual on his side must not transgress, nor must there be interference with great individual achievements, for life is a matter of mutual help and mutual responsibility according to Islam, and not a constant warfare, to be lived in a spirit of struggle and hostility. Thus, there must be freedom for individual and general abilities rather than repression, and a restrictive constraint. Everything that is not legally forbidden is perfectly permissible and everything that is not useless is of value.

The individual is to be encouraged by having every freedom in a life which reflects the Divine nature and which gives promise of the highest achievement. This breath of vision in the Islamic view of life, together with the fact it goes beyond merely economic values to those other values on which life depends – these things make the Islamic faith the more powerful to provide equitable justice in society, and to establish justice in the whole of the human sphere. It also frees Islam from the narrow interpretation of justice as understood by Communism. For justice to the Communist is an equality of wages, in order to prevent economic discrimination; but in recent days when theory has come into opposition with practice. Communism has found itself unable to achieve this equality. Justice in Islam is a human equality, envisaging the adjustment of all values, of which the economic is but one.

In the Islamic view values are so very composite that justice must include all of them; therefore Islam does not demand a compulsory economic equality in the narrow literal sense of the term. This is against nature, and conflicts with the essential fact, which is that of the differing native endowments of individuals. It arrests the development of outstanding ability, and makes it equal to lesser ability; it prevents those who have great gifts from using their gifts to their own advantage and to that of the community, and it discourages the community and the individual from producing such gifts.

There can be profit in disputing the fact that the natural endowments of individuals are not equal. And while we may not be able to see this in the case of mental and spiritual endowments as we can in the sphere of practical life—yet we cannot deny that some individuals are born with endowments of disposition, which as goodness, or perfection, or patience; while others are born with endowments of body, such as sickness, or debility, or weakness. Can we deny that others can earn their living by the pleasantness of their conversation, by their pleasing appearance, or by their agreeable nature; thus the gates of undertaking and accomplishment open before them, the same gates which remain closed in the face of others not similarly endowed.

Accordingly, to deny the existence of outstanding endowments of personality, intellect, and spirit, is a piece of nonsense which cannot explain the existing differences between individuals. So, we must reckon with all these endowments and to all of them we must give the opportunity to produce their greatest results; then from these results we may take that which appears to be of permanent profit to society, we must not close off the outlet for such endowments, or discourage them by making them equal in reward with lesser abilities; we must avoid shackling such gifts and stifling them, and thereby depriving of their fruits the community and the human race alike.

Islam does, of course, acknowledge a fundamental equality of all men, and a fundamental justice among all, but over and above that is leaves the door open for achievement of prominence through hard work, just as it lays in the balance values other than the economic. "Verily the noblest among you in Allah's eyes is the most pious." "Allah will raise up in degrees of honour those of you who believe, and to whom knowledge has been brought." "Wealth and children are an ornament to life in the world, but the things which endure, the works of righteousness are better in thy Lord's eyes—better for reward, and better for hope."

From this it is apparent that there are values other than the merely economic; with these values Islam reckons, and these it brings into relation with the idea of justice in society, since different individuals have different methods of gaining their livelihood. Islam admits the reasonable causes of these differences, as begin differences in strength and in endowment. It does not admit differences which depend on rank and station; such it absolutely denies on economic theory.

Islam, then, does not demand a literal equality of wealth, because the distribution of wealth depends on men's endowments, which are not uniform. Hence absolute justice demands that men's rewards be similarly different, and that some have more than others—so long as human justice is upheld by the provision of equal opportunity for all. Thus rank or upbringing, origin or class should not stand in the way of any individual, nor would anyone be fettered by the chains which shackle enterprise.

Justice must be upheld also by the inclusion of all kinds of values in the reckoning, and by the freedom of the human mind completely from the tyranny of the purely economic values, and by the relegation of these to their true and reasonable place. Economic values must not be given an intrinsically high standing, such as they enjoy in those human societies which lack a certainty of true values, or which give to them too slight an importance; in such conditions money alone becomes the supreme and fundamental value.

In Islam, money is not given this value; Islam refuses to admit that life can be reckoned in terms of a mouthful of bread, the appetite of the body, or a handful of money. Yet at the same time, it demands a competence for every individual, and at times more than a competence, in order to remove the fear of destitution. On the other side it forbids that unbridled luxury in possessions and desires, which produces social divisions and classes. It prescribes the claims of the poor upon the wealth of the rich, according to their needs, and according to the best interests of society, so that social life may be full, just, productive.

This, it is not unmindful of any one of the various aspects of life, material, intellectual religious and worldly; but it organized them all, that they may be related together and thus furnish an all-embracing unity in which it will be difficult to neglect any one of their various integral parts. So, these departments of life become an organized unity, similar to the greater oneness of the Universe, and to that of life, of the nation, and of all mankind.

Spiritual Nature

Islam operates on the inner, spiritual side of human nature, rather than on the external; it is from the depths of the conscience rather than on the surface that it seeks to improve man. But at the same time, it is never unmindful of the practical situation in the realm of wordly life; it does not forget the true nature of the human spirit, nor the things which influence if for good or evil, for better or worse: it has a care both for the aspirations which soar aloft and for the material necessities which are chained to Earth, for human strength which is ever limited and for the perfection which is always absolute. Thus because it has a profound knowledge of the depths of the human spirit. Islam makes use both of laws and of exhortations, it formulates commandments and prohibitions, it lays down limitations and enforces them. But it also encourages the human spirit to rise above such legalistic responsibilities as far as it can.

Life becomes possible and profitable only as we observe the lowest limit of the legal responsibilities of this faith; but even then it still lacks the perfection at which Islam aims, so long as it is not inspired by the promoting of conscience towards self-control, loftiness, and nobility. So, in Islam this prompting of the conscience is complementary to all legal duties; conscience must reinforce these duties, making their performance a pleasure, and thus imparting to human life a value and a nobility which are above the range of compulsion.

When Islam seeks to establish complete social justice, it sets it on a higher level than mere economic justice, and on a more elevated plane than can be attained merely by legislative measures; thus, it establishes a comprehensive human justice, established on two strong foundations: first, the human conscience, working within the spirit of man; and second, a system of religious law, working in the social sphere. These two powers it unites by an appeal to the depths of feeling in the human consciousness. " Verily in that there is a reminder for everyone who has a heart, or who will lend an ear; he is a witness of it Islam does not overlook the weakness of man, or his need for external compulsion, "Allah guides by his power more than by the Quran."

Anyone who bestows even a passing and casual glance on this religion must perceive the immense effort which it devotes to the reformation of the human spirit in all its aspects and from every side. And it is not without our subject to take a brief and summary look at this effort. It is designed for the good of society only to the point at which there can be a permanent control by human conscience; it works to guarantee all human society only until the individual becomes aware of his own practical obligations. " Do not play the spy, and do not backbite one another. Would one of you care to eat his dead brother's flesh? You would abhor it Spying is the worst crime against personal freedom and against the sanctities of the individual, just as backbiting is the worst characteristic which can find a lodgment in the weakness of personality; not only does it render a character incapable of praise, but it robs it eventually of all vital and practical courage.

"O! you who believe, do not go into houses other than your own, until you are received as friends and have greeted the inmates."

Individual sanctities must be respected, because individual honour is the first requisite of social justice. "O! you who have believed, let not one people mock another who are possibly better than themselves. And let not women mock other women who are possibly better than themselves. Do not scoff at one another, nor shame one another with nicknames; it is bad to get the name of evil conduct when you are a believer; and those who do not repent are evil-doers."

Mocking one another and scoffing at one another and calling one another by unpleasant nicknames are things which are forbidden alike by the essential values of personality, by human equality, and by social justice. "And do not walk the Earth in pride; verily you cannot split the Earth, nor can you reach the mountains in height."

Vanity and arrogance are characteristics which are unpopular in personality; similarly they are in opposition to the instinct for equality and justice and brotherhood. In a word Islam has the highest regard for the saying of its Prophet that " Verily you are of a great character." Character is the most essential foundation for the building of a firmly based society, for the joining of Earth to Heaven, the temporal to the eternal in the human consciousness with all its finitude and its frailty.

Islam places a great deal of reliance on the human conscience when it is educated; it sets it up as the guardian of the legal processes, to see that they are observed and maintained, and for the observance of the major part of the laws conscience alone is accountable. The giving of evidence, for example a fundamental matter which must be governed by laws, yet which, at the same time, must ensure the rights of men; and the giving of evidence is a question which runs back to the individual conscience and to the dependence of society on the conscience.

As for those who cast imputations upon innocent women, and then do not bring four witnesses in corroboration, flog them with eighty lashes and never again accept evidence from them; they are those who deal corruptly. And as for those who cast imputations upon their wives, and who have no witness but themselves—let the evidence of one of them be a four-fold testimony in the name of Allah that he is those who speak the truth. And let the fifth testimony be to invoke curse of Allah upon himself if he is of those who lie.

And punishment may be averted from the woman if she testifies four times in the name of Allah that the man is of those who lie; and the fifth testimony shall be to invoke the curse of Allah upon herself if he is of those who speak the truth. So too even, where a written agreement is demanded, it must necessarily be witnessed. "O! you who believe, when one of you contracts a debt to another for a stated time, write it down; let a scribe write it down between you justly; let not the scribe refuse to write as Allah has taught him, but let him write, and let the debtor dissect."

"Let him fear Allah his Lord, and let him not lessen the amount in any way. If the debtor is a fool, or if he is in weak health, or if he is unable to dictate, then let his kinsman dictate for him, justly. Then have the writing witnessed by two of your men; or if there are not two men, then by one man and two women out of those on whom you agree as euthanasias; so, if one the women should err, the other may remind her." The duty of witnessing is statutory and a matter of principle: "Let not witnesses refuse when they are called." Similarly, the giving of evidence is a statutory responsibility in cases of legal dispute:

> "And do not conceal evidence; for whoever does so,
> his heart is guilty."

Thus, Islam places reliance on the human conscience in matters which go as far as flogging, or stoning, and in matters touching the rights of property. Such a reliance must necessarily ennoble human nature and raise it towards the equality for which it longs and searches.

Islam does not leave the human conscience to its own resources; it allots to it these noble duties, making it the guardian of the observance of the law and of the carrying out of human responsibilities, and at the same time challenging it to rise above what law and responsibility prescribe for it. It has set the fear of Allah as a sanction on the conscience, and has placed over it the thought of Allah's omniscience, with the aim of ensuring and inspiring its activity. "There is no private talk between three, but, He makes a fourth, nor between five, but He makes a sixth; and whether there be less than that or more, he is always with them wherever they are.

On the Day of Resurrection, he will tell them what they have done. "Verily Allah is aware of all things." "We have created man, and We know that his soul whispers within him; We are nearer to him than his jugular vein. When the two meet and sit, one, on the right hand and one on the left, he cannot utter a word without a watcher being beside him, ready." "Verily he knows what is secret and what is hidden."

Islam preached to men in warning, taking into account not only in this world but also in the next every single human action, for which there is no escaping punishment and no avoiding recompense. "We shall set up the balances of justice on the Day of Resurrection, and no soul will be wronged in the slightest degree; even if it is only the weight of a grain of mustard seed. We shall produce it; for We are sufficient as a reckoner." "When the Earth—quakes with a great quaking; when the Earth brings forth what has been buried in it; when man says, 'What is the matter with it?; on that day the Earth shall tell her tidings, because your Lord has inspired her. On that day men shall come forward separately to see their works—whoever has done the weight of an atom of good shall see it; and whoever has done the weight of an atom of evil shall see it.

Thus, runs the constant teaching of Islam, making reverence and piety a sanction upon the conscience and thus it makes the human conscience the means of advancement by making it responsible for the observance of all that the faith lays down in the way of laws and duties.

The Poor Tax

In the two-fold way, Islam proceeded to set the foundations of social justice, and by this means it succeeded in producing a balanced and interrelated human justice. We shall examine some aspects of this justice in another chapter; for the moment it will be sufficient to consider one example of this system of law and custom. I shall choose the subject of the poor – tax and the alms, because it has an intimate connection with the subject of this title.

Islam makes the poor-tax an obligatory claim on the property of the wealthy in favour of the poor. It is a due which the government can exact by the authority of the law and by the power of its administration; but the public conscience has progressively taken .over the enforcement of the payment of this due, until such payment has become a natural part of the will of the wealthy.

The poor-tax is one of the pillars of Islam, one of the essentials of the faith. "Prosperous are the believers who are humble in their prayers, who turn away from idle talk, and who are active in paying the poor-tax." "These are the signs of the Quran, which is a book which makes clear, a guidance and a gospel for the believers, who observe the prayers, who pay the poor-tax and who are certain of the world to come."

On the other hand, the act of withholding the poor-tax is a form of heresy and of unbelief in the world to come. "And woe to the heretics who do not pay the poor-tax and do not believe in the world to come." But payment of the poor-tax is a method of gaining the mercy of Allah:

> "Observe the prayers, pay the poor-tax, and obey the Messenger; it may be that you will receive mercy."

Help from Allah comes to those who pay this due and who discharge their obligations to society, this meriting their place in the Earth.

"Allah will surely help the man who helps Him; verily, Allah is Powerful, Mighty. Such, if We establish them in the Earth, will observe the prayers, will pay the poor-tax, will urge to do good and will restrain from evil."

The poor-tax is a human institution of long standing, advocated by the commands of the prophets before Islam; thus, there is no religion devoid of this important social responsibility, "And make mention in the Book of Ismail, he was true to this promise, and was a messenger, a prophet; he bade his people pray and pay the poor-tax, and he was acceptable in the eyes of his Lord." So the Quran says of Ibrahim:

> "We gave to him Isaac and Jacob as extra gift; We made them upright men and We made them patterns to guide men by Our bidding. We inspired them to good work, to observe the prayers, and to pay the poor-tax; so, they served Us."

And woe to him who does not discharge this legal obligation. Said the Messenger of Allah:

> "The man to whom Allah has given wealth, and who yet will not pay his poor-tax shall be thus recompensed on the Day of Resurrection; a huge snake with glowing eyes will encircle his neck on the Day of Resurrection, will grasp him by the maxillaries—that is to say, be the jaws—and will say, I am your wealth; I am your treasure. Which is a fearful, terrible and awesome picture."

This poor-tax is a due imposed by the force of the law, an amount of money in a specified proportion. But in addition to this, there is the institution of alms-giving which is imposed on the individual conscience without any fixed rate, it is at the discretion of the will and the conscience.

It is the outward sign of charity and brotherly feeling, to both of which Islam attaches supreme importance; it is an attempt to establish the mutual ties of mankind and the responsibilities of society along the lines of an individual perception of what is necessary, and along the lines of a personal conception of charity. It serves two purposes: first, to establish an inner control of the conscience; and second, to foster a belief in the inherent solidarity of mankind.

Islam makes this charity a pure and humane thing, not limited by the bounds of a religious fellowship, so the Quran says:

> "Allah does not forbid you to act righteously and justly towards those who have not fought against you in the matter of religion, and who have not expelled you from your homes." And the Messenger says: "You will never be Believers until you show charity." They said to him, "O! Messenger of Allah, all of us are charitable." He replied: "It is not a question of your charity to your neighbour, but of your charity to men in general." And thus he sets a lofty pattern of charity which is pure and universal, to the point of making it a feature of the faith.

He even takes the final step and includes in the scope of charity all living things. Thus, the noble Prophet of Islam said: "Once while a man was travelling, he became violently thirsty, so, finding a well, went down to the water, and drank. When he came up again he noticed a dog panting and licking the dust in an agony of thirst. He said to himself," This dog has the same violent thirst which I had, whereupon he went down again to the water and filled his boot with liquid. Grasping it in his mouth, he climbed out of the well and gave the dog to drink.

And Allah the Exalted, gave him praise and pardon." His hearers asked him: "O Messenger of Allah, is there such a reward for us in the case of animals?" He replied: "There is such a reward in the case of every living creature." And again he said: "There was a woman who went to Hell only on account of a cat; she had tied it up, and had not fed it, nor had she even given it to eat the herbage of the earth."

Such charity is a fundamental part of Islam, as it is one of its characteristic signs; it indicates the religious sincerity and depth of the conscience, and it testifies to the existence of that humane spirit without which, in the Islamic view, there can be no religion.

It is on this basis that Islam establishes the custom of alms-giving and charity; it makes one fond of spending voluntarily and freely, in anticipation of the approval of Allah, of a return from Him in this world, and of a reward for Him in the world to come. Thus too one may escape His anger, His vengeance, and His punishment.

So, the good news is for the humble, those who are obedient to Allah, and who spend of their wealth according to His will. "And give good news to the humble whose hearts are afraid when Allah is mentioned, who are patient in their afflictions, who observe the prayers, and who expend freely of what We have given them." This is a picture to inspire the heart of man, and the same idea appears in another connection, where it is written:

> "Only those believe in our signs who, when they are reminded of them, fall down in adoration and celebrate the praises of their Lord, and are not puffed up. As they leave their beds they call upon their Lord in fear and in hope, and of what We have given them they expend in alms. No one knows what pleasure is reserved for such, as a reward for what they have been doing."

And the same inspiration is to be found in the beautiful and touching picture of the character of the people of Medina when they received the emigrants and gave them shelter, sharing with them their property and their houses in cheerfulness and gladness of spirit. "As for those who occupied the houses and the faith before them, they loved those who emigrated to them and they found no desire in their hearts for the share which had fallen to the others; they preferred them before themselves, though, there was poverty among them. Those who are preserved from niggardliness of soul shall be prosperous."

This is a picture of human nature in its highest and best aspects; and here is another description which is not inferior to the first, of the kindness, the compassion, and the sympathy of a community of Allah's servants; some authorities hold that the people in question here are Ali and his wife, Fatima, the daughter of the Messenger, and their household. They fulfil their vows, and they fear a Day the evil of which will fly broadcast. For love of God they give food to the poor, the orphan, and the prisoner, saying, "It is only for the sake of Allah that we give you food; we want from you neither reward nor gratitude. We fear from our Lord a day which will be grim and forbidding."

So, Allah has preserved them from the evil of that Day, and has given them cheerfulness and joy; He has rewarded them for their endurance with Paradise and silk clothing. There, they recline on courage, and there, they see neither not bitter cold nor extreme hot; near over them is the shade of the garden of Paradise, and hanging low around them are its clusters of fruit. They shall be served round with vessels of silver and goblets of glass, with glasses of silver whose measure they have themselves determined; in these they shall quaff a drink tempered with ginger, drawn from a spring named Salsabil. There pass round among them boys of eternal youth, whom to see is to imagine that they are unstrung-pearls, and whom to see is to envisage delight and a great kingdom. They are clothed with garments of green satin and brocade, and they are adorned with bracelets of silver; their Lord has given them to drink a pure drought. Verily, this has come to you as a reward, and thus your life's striving has been recompensed."

So, the giving of alms is to make a loan to Allah, a loan which is certain to be repaid: "Who is he who will make a fair loan to Allah, and He will double it for him. For, such a one there is a noble reward." "Verily, men and women who give alms thus make a loan to Allah, He will double it for them. For such, there is a noble reward." Or it may be regarded as a profitable and remunerative business:

> "Verily, those who recite the Book of Allah, who observe the prayers, and who expend in alms of what We have given them, both secretly and openly—such hope for a business that will not fail. So, He may pay them their rewards in full, and may give them increase of His bounty; verily he is forgiving, grateful."

In either case alms-giving is profitable, and does not involve loss or injury:

> "That which you expend in alms of your possession is to your own advantage, even though you expend it only for the love of Allah; what you expend in alms of your possessions will be repaid to you in full measure, and you will suffer no injury."

So, in the next world Paradise is the worthy recompense of those who expend freely in alms:

> "And hasten to f rgiveness from your Lord, and to a Paradise whose width is as that of the Heavens and the Earth, a Paradise prepared for those who are pious; they it is who expend in alms both in prosperity and in adversity, who curb their wrath, and who deal leniently with others. Allah loves those who act well."

Again, alms-giving is a means of purification for one's

character and for one's property; the Messenger of Allah commanded that a portion of their property should be taken from people who have sinned and have acknowledged their sins, and that this should be spent on good causes thus, such people might be purified and cleansed. "Others have acknowledged their sins; they have done both, deeds that are good and deeds that are evil; it may be that Allah will relent towards them, for Allah is forgiving and compassionate. Take of their property an alms which will purify and cleanse them, and pray over them; verily your prayers will mean a repose for them, for Allah hears and knows. Have they not learned that He is Allah who received repentance from His servants, and who accepts the alms? Have they not learned that it is Allah who is relenting and compassionate?"

Thus, expenditure on alms is encouraged by repayment according to the compact of Allah, by reverence for Him, and by fear of an evil record; to give alms indicates wisdom and understanding. But to refrain from alms-giving is to nullify what Allah has commanded to be accomplished; it is a form of violating the compact and of dealing corruptly on the Earth. Only those who have insight are reminded, those who fulfil the compact of Allah and who do not violate the agreement. They accomplish what Allah has commanded to be accomplished, they revere their Lord, and they fear an evil record. They endure with patience out of regard for the love of Allah, they observe the prayers, and they expend in alms out of what We have given them, both secretly and openly; they drive away the evil by means of the good.

Such shall have the recompense of the Abode, gardens of pleasure into which they shall enter, they and those of their fathers and their wives and their descendants who have been upright; angels shall come in to them by every gate, saying, "Peace be upon you for your patient endurance; good is the recompense of the Abode". But as for those who violate the compact of Allah after coming to an agreement with Him, who nullify what Allah has commanded to be accomplished, and who deal corruptly on the Earth—for them is the curse, and for them there is an evil abode."

To refrain from expenditure in the way of Allah is destruction:

> "Expend freely in the way of Allah, and do not hand yourselves over to destruction."

The 'destruction' of the individual is to lay oneself open to the punishment of Allah in the world to come, and to the vengeance of others in this world. The 'destruction' of society is the discrimination and the oppression which come in the train of the absence of free expenditure in alms, together with the accompanying discords and hatreds, debility and weakness.

To hinder good works is a form of hostility: "Cast into hell every obstinate unbeliever who hinders good work, who is hostile and contentious." "And do not obey any contemptible swearer, any slanderer who goes about maligning, who hinders good works, who is hostile and guilty." He is hostile to the claims of Allah, to the claims of his own soul as a member of that society.

Charity leads to Paradise, and the charitable man will pass over the hard path which leads thither; the path consists in the setting free of slaves, and in the provision of food in a case of hunger and destitution. "And what has taught you the nature of the 'hard path'? It is to set free slaves, to give food in a day of famine to an orphan who is of your kin, or to a poor man in destitution." But to refrain from charity leads to the Fire, and he who merits it will go thither alongwith the unbelievers. "What made you go into Hell-fire?" They replied: "We were not among those who prayed, nor were we among those who fed the poor; we plunged into discussion with others, and we scoffed at the Day of Judgment. Until the final account came upon us." "As for those who have been niggardly with what Allah has given them of His bounty, let them not think that it will be well with them; nay it will go ill with them, for on the Day of Resurrection that which they have stingily withheld will be hung about their necks." "As for those who have heaped up for themselves treasures of gold and silver, and who do not expend them in the way of Allah, announce for them a painful punishment. On that day their treasures will be heated in the fire of Hell, and they will be branded with them on their foreheads, their sides, and their backs. These are the treasures which you heaped up for yourselves. So taste now of what you have heaped up."

The treasures which are referred to in this verse are explained in a tradition; "Whoever collects dinars or dirhams, gold in the nugget or silver, and does not pay it over to a creator or expend it freely in the way of Allah — a treasure, and he will be branded with it on the Day of Resurrection." Treasure, properly understood, is not merely money on which no poor-tax is paid, as some have maintained; all money which is hoarded and which is not paid out for these specified purposes is treasures, even if poor-tax has been paid on it. And the other tradition which indicates that money on which poor-tax has been paid is not treasure, is not in opposition to this tradition; for the latter tradition merely makes the former specific.

Indeed, in the case of men who hoard, punishment sometimes overtakes them in this world as a reward for their niggardliness, and for their hindering of good works. The noble Quran tells a parable of such in a short story concerning a community which had a walled garden, from the produce of which they used to feed the poor. Then, it occurred to them to be niggardly and to keen the fruit for themselves; but a change of fortune fell upon their garden, and Allah took away their produce, so that the next morning they were regretful. "We have tested them as We tested the owners of the garden when they resolved that they would reap it in the morning, and made no qualification of their resolve. So, while they slept a disaster from your Lord encircled it, and in the morning it lay like a garden already reaped. That morning they called to one another, 'Come early to your field, if you intend to reap', and they went their way, whispering to one another. 'Let no poor man come upon you in the garden today. ' So, they went out early with this settled purpose, but when they saw it they said, 'Verily we have erred, and we are cheated of our fruits.'

The most fair-minded of them said, 'Did I not say to you, Will you not give praise to Allah?' They said, 'Praise to our Lord. Verily, we have been evil doers.' So they turned upon one another, blaming one another, and saying, 'Alas for us. Indeed, we have been presumptuous; it may be that our Lord will give us something better than this in exchange. Verily, our desire is towards our Lord.' Such was the punishment; and the punishment of the world to come is yet greater, if only they knew."

The Quran summons men to be generous before the opportunity is lost to them. "Say to My servants who have believed that they must observe the prayer and expend freely of what We have given them, both secretly and openly, before there comes a Day on which there will be neither bargain nor friendship." "And expend freely of what We have given you, before death comes upon one of you, and he says, 'O! my Lord, Would that my death might be deferred for a short space, so that I might give alms and thus become one of the righteous,' But Allah will not defer the death of any soul when its time is come." Similarly, the Quran cautions men against avarice, that they may guard themselves from it, and that they may not be betrayed into it by their desire for wealth and children; for these things are only a trial and temptation for men. "Your wealth and your children are only a temptation, but Allah has a great reward. So be pious towards Allah as far as you are able, attend and obey. Expend freely in alms; that is better for yourselves. It is those who are protected from avarice of soul who prosper."

The Prophet makes alms-giving a duty for every Muslim,

even though he may have nothing. The explanation of that is this saying of his: "The giving of alms is a duty for every Muslim. They asked him; 'O Prophet of Allah, what of him who has nothing?' He replied: 'Let him turn his hand to labour, and thus profit himself, and then let him give his alms.' They said, 'And what if he can find nothing to do?' He answered: 'Let him find some unfortunate soul who is in need'; They said: 'Suppose he cannot find such a one?' He replied: 'Then let him do some one a service, or let him restrain someone from evil, and that shall be his alms. "Thus, all men have an equal opportunity for generosity, each according to his means, and each according to his ability."

Universal Charity

The recipients of charitable expenditure must vary according to varying needs and circumstances; relatives have the prior claim on a man's benefactions, but there are others also who are joined with them, and who are mentioned side by side with relatives in the passages of the Quran which urge to charity. For charity is a universal emotion, and must take precedence over family consciousness; and indeed the mention of charity in the Quran is generally linked with that of faith. More than that— it is an indication of faith, as we have shown. " Serve Allah, and do not associate any other with Him. Show kindness to parents and relatives, to orphans and to the poor, to the stranger under your protection, whether or not he be a relative, to the companion at your side and to the wayfarer, and to those who are your possession (i.e, such as slaves). Verily Allah does not love any crafty boaster. Those who are niggardly and who urge others to niggardliness, who conceal what Allah has given them of His bounty — for such unbelievers We have prepared a shameful punishment." "They will ask you how they should expend money in alms. Say, what you expend is for benefit of parents, relatives, orphans, the poor and the wayfarer. Whatever good you do, Allah is aware of it

Thus, the stranger under a man's protection and the

companion are placed alongside the parents and relatives, just as the poor and the wayfarer are grouped with all of them. All have an equal right to alms. And this is so, even in the case of those who have committed some evil deed, as in the occurrence connected with Mistah, a relative of Abu Bakr, who shared in the slanderous story about Aishah, the daughter of Abu Bakr and wife of the Prophet.

Islam ordains that such persons be forgiven, and it forbids that they be punished in this way. Abu Bakr swore that he would cut off the charity which he had been extending to Mistah, for he was exceedingly angry at the calumnies which the latter had been spreading about the character of Aishah. But this verse was revealed to Muhammad: "As for those of you who have abundance and ample means. Let them not abstain from giving to relatives and the poor and to those who have emigrated in the way of Allah; rather let them pardon and forgive. Do you not wish that Allah should pardon you?" Thus, Islam seeks to raise human instincts to a high and noble level which does honour to human nature in all ages, which makes human nature a proud thing in the past, the present, and the future, as long as Allah wills.

Islam also elevates the conception of charity itself by making it charity for the sake of Allah the Glorious. It depicts charity in this striking picture which has come down through the traditions. "On the Day of Resurrection Allah will say: "O! man, I was ill, and you did not visit Me. "Then man will reply: "O! my Lord, how could I visit You, since You are Lord of the Worlds. "Then, Allah will say: "Did you not know that such and such a servant of Mine was ill, and you did not visit him? If you had visited him, you would have found Me there. "O man, I gave you your food, but you have given Me no food." He will answer: "O my Lord, how could I give You food, seeing that You are Lord of the Worlds?' And Allah will say: "Did you not know that such and such a servant of Mine gave you food, yet you gave him none? Surely if you had given him food, you would have found it with Me." 'O! man, I gave you to drink, but you did not give to Me." Man will say, "O my Lord, how could I give You to drink, seeing that You are the Lord of the Worlds? And Allah will reply: "Such and such a servant of Mine gave you to drink, yet you did not give to him. Had you given him to drink, you would have found it with Me."

Islam also makes alms-giving a matter of the public conscience, thus raising it above the stage where it is merely a mark of the superiority and pre-eminence of the rich over the poor, and thus raising it also above the stage where it may be only a form of hypocrisy arising from ignoble instincts. For if the impulses leading to alms-giving are allowed to deteriorate, or if charity is followed by a sense of obligation on the part of those who receive it, then it becomes an ungracious business which can only injure the soul, the nature, and the conscience, and which can only injure society also by injuring its individual members. There is nothing like attaching a sense of obligation to an act of benevolence for paining people, for humbling them, and rendering them unwilling to accept benevolence. Similarly, there is nothing like hypocrisy in alms-giving for corrupting the conscience and sapping the moral fibre.

Accordingly, Islam labours to elevate the nature both of those who give and of those who receive, and it is this result which it seeks most strenuously to achieve. "Those who expend their wealth freely in the way of Allah are like a grain which produced seven ears with a hundred grains in each ear; so Allah will give a double return to whom He wills, and verily Allah is powerful and aware. Such as expend their wealth in alms in the way of Allah and do not follow this expenditure with obligations or annoyances shall have their reward with their Lord; no fear shall oppress them, nor any sadness rest upon them. Favourable speech and forgiveness are better than alms followed by annoyance; Allah is rich and clement. O! you who have believed, do not make your alms in vain by putting obligation or annoyance upon the recipients, as he does who gives alms for the sake of appearance before the people.

He has no belief in Allah or in the Last Day, and he is like a smooth rock with earth in it; if a heavy rain falls upon it, it is left bare. Such men have no power over what they have stashed, and Allah does not give guidance to people who are unbelievers. But those who expend their wealth in alms out of a desire for the approval of Allah and as a support from themselves are like a garden on a hill; if a heavy rain falls upon it, brings forth its fruit in double measure; and even if no heavy rain falls upon it, yet still there is the dew. Allah is aware of what you do. Would anyone of you like this to happen? Suppose he has a garden of palm trees and vines with perpetual water flowing through it, so that he has all kinds of fruits in it; old age comes upon him, and he has only a weak family; then a fiery whirlwind strikes his garden, so that it is burnt up. In such a way does Allah make the signs clear to you; it may be that you will consider."

For this reason it is desirable that alms be given in secret and privately to the needy. Thus on the one hand the self-esteem of the recipients is safeguarded, and on the other hand a check is put upon conceit and pride. "If you give alms in public, that is good; but if you do it secretly and give to the poor, that is better for you. "And there is a tradition of the Prophet in praise of the man who "Gives his alms, but conceals the fact to the point where his left hand does not know what his right hand is giving."86 This is an outstandingly fine picture of the way charity should be kept secret, and should not be accounted as a matter for pride or publicity.

Sway of Materialism

Islam is aware of the power of the love of material gain, and the power of the love of money. It is convinced that avarice is always threatening the soul and is never far away. "Souls are ever liable to avarice." So, it treats all of these as a personal matter, using the methods which we have seen; it stimulates the will, it warns, it exhorts, it depicts; in this way, its aims may be achieved, and thus, it can beseech this naturally niggardly disposition of man to attain a standard of nobility in dealing with that which he loved dearly and which has a powerful hold upon him. "You will not attain charity until you expend in alms of that which you love."

In this way, man reaches the height of generosity, the limit of liberality, and the noblest form of beneficence which can possibly arise from the human spirit. Thus, man is raised above his natural state, and thus the higher side of his nature overcomes the lower, his spiritual nature conquers his animal nature. By its very nature this is by itself a lofty and universal aim which must command all support. How much more so, then, seeing that it is also an objective for society. The purpose is to create a balance of wealth, to oppose destitution, to establish the responsibilities which exist between the rich and the poor, and thus to shape a society which has a sense of mutual relationship and mutual help, and which is therefore a healthy society.

Islam follows this method, with one example of which we have now dealt in detail. Islam is concerned with persuasion of the conscience in the case of every duty which it prescribes. It imposes no more duties than are demanded for the safety of society, and no more than can be accepted by the limited ability of the general mass of mankind.

Beyond that stage it appeals to the conscience, persuading it of its responsibility and seeking to raise it above its normal scope; thus it attempts to elevate human life, and to draw it ever onward and upward. It recognizes the wide gap which lies between the lower level of duty which is prescribed by the law and the higher level of conscience which is so desirable, and towards which individuals and nations have striven in every age and century.

Thus, as an example, Islam prescribes a principle of vengeance, awarding it as a legal right to the next kin, and permitting him to exact it in full; yet at the same time it exhorts as strongly as possible that men should forgive, forbear, and pardon. "If any man is unjustly killed. We have given authority to his next of kin; but let him not be immoderate in killing; verily, he has been helped."

Again, it prescribes holy war in the way of Allah as a responsibility incumbent on everyone who is able for it. But over and above that it kindles a love for holy wars by inciting the conscience to accept it, by depicting it in glowing terms, and by emphasizing its justice and the glories which it brings to a society. "Allah has purchased from the Believers their persons and their wealth that the Prince of Paradise reserved for them; so they fight in the way of Allah, so they kill and are killed" "And, if not Allah set some men against others, the cloisters had been destroyed, and the churches and synagogues and mosques in which the name of Allah is often repeated." What is the matter with you that you do not fight in the way of Allah, and in defence of the oppressed, men, women and children."

It forbids usury, and goes on to attack its evil character and the evil character of its results. It seeks to arouse the conscience to condemn usury and to reject it. Those who eat up the fruit of usury will not arise on the Day of Resurrection, except in the same way as he whom Satan has sent mad by a touch. That is because they have said: 'A bargain is just the same as usury.' But, Allah has allowed bargaining, though He has forbidden usury. If anyone receives a warning from his Lord and desists, he shall keep what he has already gained, and his destiny shall be in the hand of Allah. But if anyone continues to practise usury, then he is one of those destined to Hell, there to abide; Allah will blot our usury, but He will multiply money. Allah does not love any guilty unbeliever," "O! you who have believed, act piously towards Allah and abandon the usury which is still unpaid, if you are really Believers. And if you do not do this, then know that there will be war from Allah and from his Messenger."

Islam forbids the drinking of wine and gambling, and it links up these things with the custom of divining the future by the casting of lost or sacred arrows; this occurs in one verse which places all these things together as being outside the bounds of commonsense and logic. Then it goes on to persuade the conscience of the reasons for this prohibition. "O! you, who have believed wine and gambling, scared lost and arrows are only an abomination, a work of Satan. Turn away from them, then, and it may be that you will prosper. Satan desires only to raise enmity and hatred among you by means of wine and gambling, to keep you from the remembrance of Allah, and from the prayers; so will you refrain?"

Islam, thus, continues through all its commands and prohibitions; the same course is followed. It is the wisest and the most profitable course for human nature, and its results have already been proved in the early history of Islam and throughout the long period of the past fourteen centuries. This method can be repeated for the present and the future, so long as its essential nature is understood, so long as this direction is followed, and so long as men will follow this straight path.

Society's Role

Generally, the judicial tribunal in Islam is composed of a single judge – the Qadi. The ruler cannot, says Kharshi, appoint two Qadis to pass judgement concurrently on the same matter. It is possible to appoint two qadis for the same town, with each Qadi having his separate jurisdiction, within a certain district, but both of them could not be appointed to pass judgement at the same time. Ibn al-Jawzi reports of an earlier precedent where in Ubayed Allah bin al-Anbari and Umar ibn Amir were appointed joint judges in Basara, they sat together as a bench and combined in hearing and deciding.

The basis of the institution of the Qadi consilium shura is contributed to the system of committee of jurists established by Caliph Umar at Medina. The advice of the consilium was, however, not binding and the decision always remained in the hands of the Qadi. The system of the appointment of reliable witnesses Shuhud Udud was also recorded in the history of Islamic judiciary. The Shuhud Udud played the role of assessors and protected the validity of legal acts and assisted the Qadi in serving as witnesses. They were personally appointed by the Qadi and were relieved in the Qadi's removal or dismissal from the office.

Apart from shuhud udud other officials connected with the court were court clerk-interpreters and assistants entrusted with the maintenance of order during the court's session. The officials entrusted with supplementary judicial functions were termed a 'wan or legal assistants. The katib recorded the full written statements of the parties in the suits along with defence statements, and connected matters. The muzzak investigated the character of the shuhud and also that of the ordinary witnesses. The qasam or qasim supervised the division and apportioning of goods, and the amir al-hukm took into custody the assets of legally incompetent persons, orphans and absentees while khazin diwan al-khan was entrusted with the safekeeping of the court archives. Wakils were the lawyers or attorneys who appeared or prepared for appearance on behalf of the parties in the courts. Wilaya literally means to be the incharge of something; to have power, authority or command over something.

In Islam, the Caliph is a substitute law-giver and all powers necessary for its rule are centered in him. The exercise of Qadi was to have been the personal task of the Caliphs, but they entrusted others with it because they were busy with general politics and pre-occupied with Jihad. The delegation of power precisely meant representation. The idea of delegation/ representation is an important principle in Muslim law. Yet, it has been misunderstood by some scholars. For instance, Tyan remarks that the Qadi is the delegate/ representative of the ruler and by virtue of the fact he lacks autonomy.

The Qadi appointed by the Caliph could further delegate powers to a third person who in turn could sub-delegate his powers to another and this process could proceed in a chain. In other words, Tyan uses the hierarchical organisation of the judicial personages to support his thesis that the Qadi lacks autonomy and that he is a subordinate of central authority. The distribution and redistribution of power was expedient to make the judiciary effective and easily accessible to all.

The survey of source material brought for the existence of two definite stands of thought: one asserting the independence of judiciary in Islam, and the other contending that judiciary in Islam is not free from political interference. The first group comprises the majority of Muslims and can be said to represent the standard Muslim point of view.

Muhammad Hamidullah, a representative of the first group, writes that what the Prophet enunciated for the administration of justice was equality of persons before law. Law is the same for the rich as well as poor. Even the Caliph could be sued before the Qadi. To make the point clear, he cites the instance wherein the Prophet towards the end of his life publicly announced that anyone having a claim against him should come forward. A man claimed few dirhams which were paid him then and there. Caliphs 'Umar and 'AH' writes Hamidullah, presented themselves and gave their accounts before the Qadi during their respective caliphates.

It follows, therefore, that the judiciary was absolutely free from outside control or interference, that the ruler could not prevent the decision of the Qadi from coming into force, as long as the decision of the Qadi was not openly in conflict with the tenets of Islam.

Rahman, writing on the same issue says that no person in an Islamic state, not even the elected head, can be above the law and he is as much subject to the hudud as anyone else. Rahman cites the incident that Abd al-Rahman bin Tariq, a

Qadi of Spain, during the reign of Abd al-Rahman al-Muawiya, gave a ruling against one Habib, a personal friend of the Caliph. Habib complained to the Caliph, who ordered the Qadi to reconsider the case. Ibn Tariq replied, writes Rahman, that his office, just as that of the Caliph derived its authority from the Prophet, hence his duty, therefore, was to follow the example of the Prophet and administer justice impartially to both the strong and the weak, and had his decree established.

The latter view is largely held and supported by the orientalists. N.J. Coulson states that Islamic legal theory and practice lacks powerful and independent judiciary. Coulson quoting Tyan writes that a Qadi was merely the legal secretary of the political authority. While investigating the cause of reluctance of many a personage to accept judicial office, Coulson concluded that their reluctance was essentially due to the dependence of the Qadi's upon political authority.

The doctrine of wilaya which defined the scope and nature of the Qadi's jurisdiction affected the decisions given and actions taken by the Qadi. He cites the incident wherein the governor of Egypt Abd ul-Aziz bin Marwan, who got the decision of his Qadi Abbas bin Said reversed. According to Coulson, the whole spirit of the religious law is fundamentally opposed to the notion of an independent judiciary fearlessly defining the limits of the power of the state over the individual and powerful enough to give effect to its decisions.

The doctrine of separation of power was first formulated by John Adams who set forth in Article XXX of the Massachusetts Constitution of 1780 that "in the government of this commonwealth, the legislative department shall never exercise the executive and judicial powers, or either of them, the executive shall never exercise the legislative and judicial power or either of them, the judiciary shall never exercise the legislative and executive power or either of them."

Adam's proposition meant that the executive, legislative

and judical institutions should have autonomous constituencies. The doctrine of separation of powers as it is understood from its definition is inapplicable in an Islamic state. For, an Islamic state is an ideological state-sovereignty of Allah is its starting point. Allah alone is the real law-giver and the authority of absolute legislation is vested on Him. He alone is the source of judicial, legislative and executive authority.

Islamic political system is based on the foundation of the vice-regency of man, under which the Muslims have been given limited popular sovereignty. The Muslims through *baya* delegate their authority to the Caliph. The Caliph thus possesses the overall authority in a limited sense. Through the doctrine of wilaya, he can further delegate his authority to other persons.

In a secular state, the doctrine of separation of power is implemented for checking absolute power, that is to create checks and counterchecks on the people at the helm of affairs. In the Islamic state, in ideal circumstances, the question of absolute authority does not arise at all. Right at the apex, the authority is a restrained one.

In addition to this, the Muslims in Islamic state are endowed with a right to political action. The underlying principle of Islamic state is religion. Hence any violation of law is not a violation of a state regulation but an act against the divine commandment, thus a sin. It is on account of the religious and ideological basis that the Islamic state does not require a disconnection of the judicial process from the political system. The fact that contextual reality is far from ideal reality hardly requires emphasis here.

The Organisation

Justice is neither only the very foundation of the true Muslim society such as it was, and such as it ought to be, nor is it only one of the five pillars of Islam as symbolized by the Zakat, that part of income due to the State annually—nor all the related legal provisions. It is not solely one of the attributes of Allah revealed in the Quran: "He who holds the scales in balance (on the last day)" (5:18), nor is it simply that element present in hundreds of Islamic laws concerning ibadat or acts of devotion, even though these acts are a valid criteria. Justice in Islam is much more than the sum of all these things. It is the foundation upon which dogma (aqida) is built, and it is directly bound to the sphere of faith (iman) itself. In the Quran, we read:

> "Hast thou observed him who belieth religion ? That is he who repelleth the orphan, and urgeth not the feeding of the needy."

And in a Hadith of the Prophet:

> 'No, he does not believe in Allah, nor in Last Judgement, he who eats his full at night whilst his neighbour is raked with hunger.'

It appears from this that adi or social justice, is brought to full completion by social solidarity, and that both are firmly attached to iman, the basis of aqida itself.

But where the bond which ties adi to the foundation of dogma-that is, faith seems most apparent, is in the examination of belief in the Last Judgement. What, in fact, would this Judgement Day mean without faith in the Resurrection, in the accounting of deeds hisab in retribution and in punishment: without faith in Allah, in His scriptures and in His Prophets?

To believe in this Day of Judgement, therefore, is to believe in the finality revealed to us by the scriptures and the chosen prophets, in other words, the Resurrection, the Last Judgement or the accounting of deeds whereby each one shall be punished or rewarded according to his deeds, in conformity with the rules of divine justice, or even of human justice, in so far as it requires and aspires to fulfil the human justice, in so far as it requires and aspires to fulfil the divine justice.

For this reason that the Islamic doctrine held by distinguished scholars such as *Zamakhshari* and *Qadi Abdal*

Dabbar given the concept of free will—without which neither retribution nor the punishment of Allah would make any sense but would be seen rather as injustice—the name theory of justice, on the understanding that in this case it is a matter of divine justice.

Since the man who repels the orphan and does not readily encourage feeding of the poor is really the negator of religion, and since the man satiated, forgetting his starving neighbour, is really denying food and the Last Judgement which itself constitutes divine justices, we can affirm that all societies calling themselves Islamic, yet which do not realise this justice, have nothing to do with Islam, and even less to do with faith, other than in name.

Having adduced this philosophical or ideological evidence by way of introduction—which in these days of ideological confrontation may not seem entirely inappropriate—let us now try to give some examples of this social justice in Islam. We shall look at it from two aspects:

> "Formal and spiritual, and also on the plane of behaviour— suluk and of goals— maqasid— which are sought by the legislator, bearing in mind that the social justice which was the mark of Islamic civilization during its days of splendour remains as much in the letter as in the spirit, a far off work, offering to those who wish to realise it, a vast field of theoretical moral codes and objectives yet to be attained."

Let us first recall that Islam regards the son of Adam, honoured by the Creator as his vice-regent on earth, as a being endowed not only with a body, but also with a spirit, limited certainly by certain physical constraints in the manner of other living creatures, but possessing dignity and spiritual, moral and social dimensions. For this reason, man cannot survive on a purely material and economic plane of life.

As far as it is possible to define it from the law, Islamic

society constitutes a balanced, humane community, where each individual must feel that he forms with the others a compact and solid unity, based on fraternity, social solidarity and equality of rights and duties. This society must work towards a common objective. Its activity must be organised under the aegis of a just arbitration which can assure work to everyone according to his capability and merit, and an equal chance to all. The wealth of the Ummah – the Islamic community – must be evenly distributed to all the members according to need, taking into account the solidarity which binds them.

Islam has fully defined matters relating to income and expenditure under various heads. It has instigated rights and duties, but it has also exhorted man to generosity in the highest sense badhl, to financial sacrifice (tadhya) to the purification of wealth by the zakat-tazkia, all directed to the achievement of social justice. In all, it maintains a double objective to educate souls and preserve the interests of the community (jamaa). When educative methods prove ineffectual, Islam exercises coercive redress-zair.

Further, where methods of religious persuasion no longer work on the conscience, when neither the exhortations of the preacher (wadh) nor the counselling of the murchid – director of conscience – bear fruit, it brings forth the whip of the Qadi (judge) or the sword of the supreme authority of the State.

Social justice, thus, based on economic justice in Islam has been able to guarantee certain standards to all members of the Ummdh, be they capable or incapable of performing any work, be they poor, weak, widowed or children. It includes among the weak, both Muslims and Dhimmis – those, who live in an Islamic country but do not profess Islam. Animals, too, are included among the weak. However, the social justice of Islam has neither approved nor encouraged poverty engendered by laziness or inertia.

Islam absolutely forbids begging. The muhtasib – commissioner in charge of economic affairs – has the authority to command a beggar physically capable of work, to do so. If the beggar refuses, the responsible commissioner should employ coercive means until the beggar ceases to hold out his hand. Islam neither encourages parasites, malingering under the protection of zaouias or hospices, nor living on charity, regardless of who may be dispensing it.

Justice for Livelihood : The Islamic principle is that man must earn his living by work. Approximately five hundred verses of the Quranextol the expense of energy in useful work. The Prophet has glorified labour in several of the Hadith. It is necessary to understand by amal as much the work of a man in his personal enterprise, agricultural, industrial, or commercial and other forms of profit and production, as the work carried out by salaried workers such as civil servants, industrial workers and other employees.

There are a number of Hadith devoted to the protection of wages for workers, dealing with taxes, remuneration itself and the need for rapid payment. The Prophet adds to this subject:

> "He who willingly works and does not have shelter, must be given shelter. If he is single, then he must be given a wife. If he does not have a camel let him claim one."

Sheikh Abu Zahra commenting on this subject further states:

> "All this evidently is to be accounted for by the beit-ul-mal of the Muslim state, that is to say, the public treasury."

These benefits to the worker are productive of many advantages which will in the last analysis benefit the whole of the Muslim community. They imply free housing, transport and also marriage, with the costs to be borne where necessary by the State. Family allowances in the time of the Prophet and Abu Bakr were paid in favour of the husband, wife and children. Under the Caliph Umar, the amount of the allowance was augmented according to the age of the children and continued until they were of age. They were not only granted to the so-called legitimate progeny but equally to illegitimate children. This provision was perpetuated under the Caliphs Othman and Ali and well into the succeeding period.

The spirit of Islam guarantees the well-being of workers. It guarantees the same tranquillity even to animals. The Imam Ahmad said that it is incumbent upon the muhtasib to forbid persons possessing animals to use them in work which they cannot accomplish. The French author Peltier, in his translation of Bukhari, was led to examine these various aspects of solidarity and of social justice in Islam, as well as the guarantees offered to workers by our religion. He is not alone in expressing his admiration of the system. Little of this exists in the Muslim world today. Even so as a model or ideate the Islamic concept of social justice has a degree of perfection still to be attained even in the most highly developed non-Muslim states.

Islam has given emphasis in favour of employees and workers since the time of the Prophet. It has promised with equal guarantees to families without sufficient resources at their disposal. The Prophet said, "He who leaves after his death dependents deprived of support or very young children, his affair is my concern. I become a guardian." In other words, the State assumes responsibility.

Justice and Social Solidarity : The domain of social justice or social solidarity is extended to the protection of several categories of the weak (ajaza) and needy. The aged, the *Dhimmis* – non-Muslims – are amongst those allowed the advantages of social benefits. A celebrated instance from the time of the Caliph Umar illustrates this. Addressing an old Jew, he said:

> "We have not been fair in our treatment of you, since we have exhausted your youth and abandoned you when you aged."

Umar immediately invited him to his home, and there gave

him his own food and had the treasury bestow a pension on him to the end of his days. The same measures were passed in favour of the poor, the needy, the sick, the blind, the crippled, displaced persons and prisoners, as well as orphans, the weak and illegitimate children as already mentioned.

The concept of social justice was expressed further in quite unique ways. An example may be found in the waqf or zabadi, instituted to cover the damages caused by the children of slaves, so that they might avoid the pecuniary sanctions or corporal punishment that their parents or masters could otherwise inflict upon them. Provision was also made whereby the public treasury would intervene to help the insolvent debtor pay his debts, and aid was given to poor travellers who found themselves far from home.

Other implementations were devoted to psychiatric hospitals where the sick were given therapy with music and popular comedy, a field where modern psychotherapy has proved the value of methods being used to great effect so many centuries ago. Justice and social solidarity however are not confined to the material side of life.

Social justice goes one step nearer to attaining solidarity by stipulating the need for love, a necessary part of the Islamic community which must present itself as a single body, a compact edifice, It is this which embodies the idea of humanitarian justice. Though the spirit of class and race still prevails in our own days, Islam established equality between all men. This equality is proclaimed in the Quran:

> "The noblest among you in the sight of Allah are the most Allah-fearing." And in the Hadith of the Prophet: "Muslims are all equal, just as the teeth of a comb."

This principle is repeated in several other hadith or deeds of the Prophet and his companions. A brief reference to some of these will illustrate the point. On the equality of race and ethnic origin, there is the example of the Prophet's rebuke to his companion Abu Dharr Al-Ghifari. Abu Dharr had mocked Bilal I'Abyssin, evoking, "the colour of his mother." The Prophet said to him:

> "O Abu Dharr, you are still a man belonging to pagan (jahilyya) times. Lift your head and look. Then know that you are hardly superior to a man of colour, be it black or red unless you surpass him in deeds."

In the legal domain, it is established that the Prophet submitted himself truly voluntarily when it came to the execution of corporal punishment, as the occasion in the mosque when the Prophet was in the process of joining the ranks of the faithful for prayer. Someone claimed that the Prophet had hurt him by knocking him over. Muhammad immediately offered him the right to avenge himself upon his person if he so wished.

A somewhat similar instance was the intervention of Usama Ibn Zaid in a case concerning a theft by a woman of the Banu Maktum. The chiefs of this large and powerful tribe asked Usama Ibn Zaid to intervene with the Prophet, who held him in great esteem, since the honour of the tribe would be at stake if the woman were to be subjected to corporal punishment. The Prophet came in, angrily admonishing:

> "Would you intervene in the punishments set forth by Allah?"

Then, he turned to the Muslims declaring:

> "What has been the downfall of nations before you is that when a thief of noble origin was caught, he was allowed to go free without punishment, whereas the thief of humble origin was submitted to punishment. I swear by all the oaths of Allah that if Fatima, daughter of Muhammad, committed a theft, I would have her hand cut off."

It was thus that the Prophet applied the rites of justice and equality even to himself, and to his family where necessary, demonstrating the truth of the concept that there is no distinction of class or caste in Islam.

The Caliph Umar behaved in like manner with regard to his son Abdar Rahman when he applied the famous principle, "From where do your possessions come?" (min ayna laka hadha?). He made even the greatest of the Prophet's companions submit to this law-men like Khalid Ibn-Walied, 'Amr Ibn al' As, Sayad Ibn Abi Waqqas, Abu Hurayrah and many others.

This form of Justice is not limited to the conduct of Muslims only among themselves. Islam makes it an obligation for Muslims in their dealings with the faithful of other religions, and there are many instances of its practical implementation in the early history of Islam, as for example in Umar's resolution of the dispute between a Copt and the son of Amr Ibn al'As, Governor of Egypt, and his own appearance before the Qadi Shoreih with a Jew.

It would scarcely by possible to find a more perfect model of the just ruler than Umar II, Ibn' Abdul' Aziz, whether democratic or revolutionary, at any time in history.

Means of Attaining Social Justice : What are the sources of revenue sufficient to cover all the expenditure demanded by these and many other measures of social justice? To answer this we must formulate some idea of economic justice which is the pre-requisite and complement of social justice; the two cannot be separated.

Alongside charitable institutions like the awqaf—holy foundations—which often went as far as protecting animals, many individual contributions imposed by the religious law for the good of the community, such as maintenance for close relatives, expiation of kaffarat, funds left by will and testament, or wasiyya and other measures designed to reinforce social solidarity, there existed the Beit-ul-mal or public treasury. This was the chief means of financing social welfare and drew revenues from a number of sources, the most important of which was the Zakat purification dues.

Zakat constitutes the principal base upon which the social structure of Islam is built. It is neither alms nor charity, but an obligatory due. He who consciously refuses to pay this tithe is considered a renegade and runs the risk of mortal punishment. The war of the ridda-apostasy—when the Caliph Abu Bakr declared war on the recalcitrants who wanted the Muslims to return to the days of paganism and destroy the Islamic community, evidences the extremity of the punishment.

There is an element of piety in the Zakat, since, it is act of devotion—ibadat at which brings the human being closer to his Creator. It is an act of solidarity with society and educates the soul, teaching it to conquer selfishness and to practise self-sacrifice and generosity. For the spirit it constitutes a source of joy and of peace, and for the conscience procures the satisfaction of having fulfilled its duty to Allah. For all these reasons, the Zakat is different from anything which may appear to have a superficial resemblance to it in the modern world. It is not simply a tax which may be avoided by cheating the government fiscal system in one way or another.

Another source of revenue which feeds the Beit-ul-mal is derived from what Ibn Hazm describes as expenditure due besides the Zakat. In this connection, Ibn Hazm has commented upon a hadith stressed by Ali which states:

> "Allah makes it an obligation for the rich of a country to provide for the needs of their poor. Authority must compel them when the resources of the Zakat is insufficient."

Ibn Hazm and other jurists have proclaimed that when a man dies of starvation, the people in whose house he has died—should consider themselves collectively responsible for his death and should, in consequence, pay the diya or price of blood. Scholars learned in the Hadith have indicated how the

Prophet enumerated the superfluous possessions that a Muslim should give to one who has only the bare minimum.

After this enumeration, the companions of the Prophet began to perceive that fundamentally, no person has the right to possess anything superfluous to his needs. Caliph Umar in a public address also said:

> "If I was to live longer, I would take the possessions that the rich have in excess and give them to the poor. No man is more worthy than another to be in possession of wealth. And following this, I would raise those who are last to the ranks of the first."

It emerges from this, that the just man in authority must intervene to stop arbitrariness and iniquity. He must ensure justice and equity. When he finds that there are enormous disparities in the heart of the community, and that luxury and wealth exist alongside poverty and misery, he must guarantee economic justice and therefore social justice.

Further way of realising social justice in the Islamic point of view is that of public ownership, that is ownership by the Ummah or community. It consists in suppressing large-scale ownership in general, when it exists, by returning property to the State. This is the situation most frequently encountered.

The objective of Islamic law, though in principle it respects and protects individual ownership, is to establish justice, by preventing wealth from accumulating in the hands of an oligarchic plutocracy who live in opulence and luxury, circulating money solely among its members, whilst the majority of people exist in hunger, destitution and contempt. The poor will not be slow, in these circumstances, to form an army of malcontents capable of threatening the stability of the community, of weakening and undermining it. Allah has prescribed that our community be strong and flourishing.

Islam abominates the fact of poor in its bosom. The Prophet said:

"I am in the hands of Allah with regard to poverty and infidelity—for poverty is tantamount to infidelity."

The Prophet sequestered hama—a piece of land at Medina called Naqui—to serve as pasture land for horses belonging to the Muslims, which was to be shared by all Muslims. For the same purpose Umar put aside a piece of land at Rabdha. The proprietors of this land came to him complaining, "O, Prince of Believers! This land belongs to us! We have fought for it during the Jahiliyah. It belonged to us even when we entered the Islamic religion. Why then have you sequestered it?" 'Umar, after reflecting for a moment, replied, "All goods belong to Allah! People are the creatures of Allah! If I were not obliged to do certain things to remain in the path of Allah, I would not have sequestered a single span of the land." The word huma, to sequester, denotes the act of taking a certain area of land which was private property and making it over as a possession of the community, for the benefit of those members of the community in need.

This objective seems clear and incontestable when we read the instructions given by Umar to the agent in charge of land sequestered at Rabdha. He specified that the pasture be " for those who were in need"—muhtadyin. And we can read in several histories, that he had no wish to hear about the beasts of Ibn Affan or Ibn Auf who were wealthy, since if they were to lose their livestock they would still have the time to go to their watering places and gather grain, whilst the wretched poor man, having lost his herd, had no recourse but to come to him with his children crying, "O Prince of Believers."

To the argument that such a man in distress had the right to ask help from the State, since he had a right to part of the Beit-ul-mal. Caliph Umar enjoined, "Should I abandon them to their sad fate: could you anymore lose your own father? To supply them with grazing is easier for me than to give them gold or money. Yes, I know that this land belongs to its owners, that they fought for it in the Jahiliyah and that they owned it when they came into Islam. I know they think I am unjust in this matter, but it is to try to walk in the way of the Lord that I have done all this. "Umar's action put into practice the Hadith of the Prophet:

> "Men are united by three things: water, pasture and fire.".

His conduct is consistent with the principle:

> "One should suffer a small ill to avoid a major harm."

There is a further example of the same kind also stemming from the Caliphate of Umar. It was suggested to Umar that he distribute the regions conquered in Iraq and Syria and give them to the people. He refused, and made these regions the property of the State justifying his action in the following words:

> "If we were to divide these lands, nothing would remain for those who come after you. What would they say, these Muslims, when they saw the land already distributed, inherited and possessed?"

The idea is unthinkable. "What then would be left of these Syrian and Iraqi lands for the orphans and widows of these countries?" The story further relates that Ibn jabel, who with Imam Ali was among those who agreed with Umar, suggested to the latter, "If you distribute these lands, their harvests will be in the hands of these particular people, but after their death all will be concentrated in the hands of a single man or a single woman." Instead of dividing these immense areas between a limited group of the Prophet's companions and forming a new caste of big property owners. Umar and certain others preferred to establish, as Al-Awzal says, a greater number of *small fellahs* and villagers in village groups, allowing them to run their own affairs, and act on their own initiative.

In this way they would be enabled to till the earth profitably, and pay the taxes which would be due to the State. They were fully aware that no Muslim would be able to buy the land whether by agreement or coercion, since all agreed that the possessions thus acquired could neither become an object of sale, nor of inheritance. The greatly mourned Sheikh Abu Zuhra writing on this subject deduced that Umar had made his judgements on three grounds, all of them concerned to promote the general good. His intention was to prevent the creation of large landed estates, since the lands of Iraq and Syria together accounted for many thousand feddans, and if divided between ten thousand people they would inevitably create a class of large landowners. To benefit the State and the progress of Jihad by the land tax— kheraii— these lands would bring in, both of which would be pleasing to Allah, to supply further State revenue for the benefit of the needy.

It is beyond question that Caliph Umar based his judgement on the interests of the Ummah, when he might very easily have taken advantage of certain other precedents of the time of the Prophet. Since, in the first two instances quoted, Islam put large-scale individual ownership at the disposal of common interest, and in the third prevented the development of large scale ownership after the property had actually fallen into the hands of the State, it is established beyond doubt that Islam prohibits the development of private ownership wherever the acquisition or monopoly of wealth threatens to create properties on a large scale. Commenting on these Sheikh Abu Zuhra wrote:

> "The utterances of the Prophet (Hadith) proving that ihtihar is unlawful (haram) are numerous. No matter what form this acquisitive aggrandisement assumes, it is unlawful since it constitutes a *habs* by stopping the circulation of goods, whether food, clothing or other things. Ihtihar, therefore, prevents the weak from gaining access to agricultural property and from working the land. In fact, where there are great landed proprietors, it is they who buy all the land which might be put for sale. The small farmers cannot fight

> against them to acquire this land. It is then the duty of authority to intervene."

The uncompromising attitude of Sheikh Abu Zahra is well known. He stood by his beliefs and was never obsequious to those in power. He was not the kind of man who changed his opinion with each change in government. The lines above were not written out of opportunism or fear since he always resisted all pressures. His firm stand often caused him problems yet, he did not change, and such was his position to the end of his days.

We have touched briefly on the concept of social justice in Islam, examining its literary tradition, its spirit, its finality and the way in which it was realised during the golden age of Islam. We have even examined the content of economic justice upon which it is built. Indeed, the first is conditioned by the second, since it supplies the means by which social justice is translated into concrete form. This idea of complementarity may be compared to that of Kant, who wrote:

> "Understanding is composed of two complementary elements: concept and sensations. The concepts without the sensations are empty. Sensations without concepts are blind: they have neither goal nor significance."

In the context of our subject, social justice is the concept and economic justice its terms, its substance, the condition without which it cannot be applied. How otherwise can Islam go forward and proclaim that the right of the individual is tied to the right of the community, that general interest takes precedence over particular interest and that the good of the Ummah comes before the good of each person?

Our religion has realised all this without leaving the individual suffocated, harmed or crushed by the mass of society. How, otherwise, can it go forward and claim that Islam is at the same time a religion, a State and a perfect social order? Sayyid Qutb wrote on this subject:

> "According to modern terminology, Islam means a system of organisation *nidham* fulfilled by the idea of dogma *aqida* at the level of conscience, by ethics at the level of behaviour-suluq-atid finally by that of divine law—Shariah the social level."

The complementary roles of social and economic justice were protected by the State, which watched over their application. They were enriched and furthered by a network of beneficent popular institutions, like an immense carpet worked by open and outstretched hands working side by side, capable of protecting each man who might be a victim of adversity or in danger of perishing. And all this was the work of a law-giver who persisted in efforts for its application. Has there ever existed, does there exist even today, anything to rival the conceptual order of Islam such as it was applied in times past? At that time of Umar Ibn Abdul Aziz, not only were there no beggars, poor or needy, but no evidence could be found of people liable to receive the benefit of the zakat even thought the legal definition of the masakin—needy—is, "those who do not have the means to feed themselves for one year." An African Governor under the same Caliph said one day:

> "We have to go from door to door to find someone who will accept the zakat."

Can social justice, in its essence, attain a higher degree of development? Call it what you will, the essential is that it should have suppressed tyranny, exploitation and slavery; that it be general; that it guarantee dignity and freedom of man; that it protects spiritual values and that the religion of Allah should predominate. Call it what you will, 'social justice' with Sayyid Qutb, or 'social solidarity' which Abu Zahra, or ishtirakyya - 'socialism'—with Dr. Muhammad Al-Mubarak who wrote:

> "To say that there is no socialism in Islam is to be ignorant of the nature of socialism, and to demonstrate in addition an inability to understand the teachings

and objectives of Islam; to prove that one has no acquaintance with Islamic laws pertaining to the subject. Call it, if you like, the socialism of Islam, as does Mustafa Sibai, or 'Islamic socialism' as does Hassan Al-Banna; give it any other name you can think of, provided that the word chosen contains real substance; for without this, it would be nothing more than a slogan."

The essential is not to be found in names, or in forms, or in slogans. The essential is the content, the substance. The essential is that it should actually exist, this social justice, just as it did during the golden age of Islam, and enriched now by the addition of new substance, which must, above all else, conform to the general interest, that is to the interest of the Ummah, without stifling the individual. It should also take into account the experiences, good or bad, of other nations making use of the criterion of rational effort—ijtihad and its rules for amelioration and perfection. And then let this social justice be designated by whatever name one cares to choose, even that of 'socialism', since, it is this name that the young prefer in our days, provided that it had conferred upon it the original meaning, and that it is anything but shirk- infidelity, shirac-stumbling blocks, or ishraq-idolatry. It will signify, quite simply, el ishtiraq—a community of effort and of fruits. In the major capitals of the developed world, there are beggars and poor wretches who can be described as beggars.

In the European and American press, we read that men have died on the streets from cold or hunger, or even worse evils. What makes one stop and think is not the high number of such cases—and according to the paper they are relatively high, but the very fact of their existence at all. Does this mean to say that the situation in this respect is better in the Islamic world than in Europe or America? Sadly, we are forced to admit that our situation is much worse; we cannot even establish any comparison.

Even in the richest of the Muslim countries (and perhaps more so in these than elsewhere), we see the existence of the most atrocious poverty alongside the most scandalous opulence together with all the tragedy inevitable in such stimulation. In our community it is no longer just a matter of the kind of cases which surprise journalists, as in Europe and America; there is a gulf, a bottomless chasm, between the social justice defined by Islam and the situation of Muslims today. "Where justice reigns there also reigns the law of Allah." Such was the opinion of Ibn Al-Qayyim Al-Jauzyya. In the same vein Sayyid Qutb wrote:

> "In this world which is called 'the Islamic world', you look and then you see a social reality which is not pleasing. Then you open your eyes and ascertain that there are social institutions which do not guarantee justice."

This is the same point of view as that expressed by Dr. Muhammad Faruooq al-Nabhan, Professor at the Kuwaiti University of Law and Islamic Teachings, at the IXth Seminar on Islamic Thought which took place at Tiemcen, where he condensed all these reflections in a few words:

> "To begin with, we have to recognize that reality for the Islamic peoples is gloomy, dismal and a long way from the justice and even the spirit of Islam. We have to recognize that social injustice imposes itself on us in a form which contradicts all religious and human values."

4

Lawful Sanction

The securities provided for the practical enforcement and to guarantee the fulfilment of the fundamental rights, have been discussed by reference in the foregoing chapters. But it will be in the fitness of things that they should not only be briefly repeated here, but putting together all other factors in this connection it should be examined how fundamental human rights were kept safely out of the reach of and constant meddling by the rulers in the Islamic State.

The important problem of humanity today is not the determination of these rights, preparation of their beautiful lists, their inclusion in the constitution of the country, issue of international charter and declarations of rights, and celebration of human rights day. The real problem, instead, is how to save the rights, that are being enumerated, displayed and recognized as human rights, from the usurpation and transplanting by the rulers of the day;

Islam has attached special importance to this practical aspect in its system of governance, and has provided such effective and firm safeguards to the fundamental rights, which on the one hand strike at the root of the possibilities of the development of the germs of dictatorship and Fascism in the rulers and the causes and motives that take them on to the path of oppression and tyranny and compulsion and violence ; and on the other, ridding the common citizens of the fear and awe of human authority and their negative feelings of their own helplessness, arousing in them the spirit of self-reliance, magnanimity and fortitude and doubtlessness, create such a tremendous power of resistance in them that there is no room left for any body to thrust his sovereignty (absolute authority) over them.

The Quran in a short verse has revealed to us the truth about dictatorship, its causes and how it succeeds in getting sway over people. God has presented Pharaoh as the worst pattern of dictatorship before us, and out of the evil traits of his character that have been pointed out, one that was at the root of all of them was this:

> He took his people as facile and worthless.
>
> Al Quran XLII: 54

The Quran conveys to us in this verse that Pharaoh regarded his people as lowly, despised and weak as compared with himself, and it was this estimate of them that was at the root of declaring himself as their god and his dictatorship and Fascism. Immediately following this God says:

> And they obeyed him: truely were they a people rebellions (against God). Al Quran XLII: 54.

This was the reason on which Pharaoh's dictatorship was based and flourishing. His own crime was that he took his people as facile and weak and ruled over them as a tyrant of the worst type. His egoism fed on their misery and suffering in debasement:

> Despressing a small group among them.
>
> Al Quran XXVIII 4

But in the sight of God the people were no less blameworthy and contemptible since they were obeying him in abject subservience and were resigned to their fate of lowness and debasement. The Quran has declared them as a nation of transgressors—transgressing the limits set by God. The first and foremost limit set by God is that none save Him should be taken as their deity and Sovereign. The people guilty of such a heinous crime shall be meted out the fate of the people of Pharaoh, to save His servant from the torment of humiliation and debasement. God on the one hand made ample provision for putting checks on dictatorship in His code of conduct for human life and on the other made people extremely resistant to dictatorship and Fascism. The protections provided in the Islamic system of governance can be divided under four heads.

A. Purge of the concept of Sovereignty.

B. Purge of the leadership.

C. Limitation of powers.

D. Accountability of the emirate.

Let us now briefly examine each of them:

The Authority

Islam has started its scheme of reform with a drastic change in the concept of sovereignty. The declaration of the Quran that God is not only your Creator, Master, Sustainer and Lord and Cherisher but your Sovereign and Ruler also, has struck at the root of the sovereignty of man. Taking God as the Sovereign means that the distinction of the ruler and the ruled between man and man has come to an end. From the common citizen to the highest, office bearer of the state stand at the same level, and man became free of the bondage of another man like himself. And those entrusted with the affairs of their slate, fearing the accountability before the Judge of judges and the punishment in the life Hereafter instead of compelling people to their own obedience, strictly stuck to the path (of righteousness) pointed out by the Quran and the Sunnahs. Under this concept of Sovereignty neither there is any possibility of taking to the dictatorship for any person, nor the necks of the citizens can be made so weak and pliable that they may bow down to any dictator in abject subservience. Neither an amir or Imam can imagine usurping the rights of the people, conferred on them by the Supreme Sovereign, nor can the people themselves be so docile as to permit them doing so.

This concept of Sovereignty drastically changes the attitude and behaviour of the government relating to the human rights. It was this concept of Sovereignty that manifested itself in the harangue of the first Caliph of the Prophet, Abu Bakr, the man of truth:

> To me your weakest individual is mighty, so long as I do not get him his dues (from the usurper) and your mighty ones are weak to me so long as I do not force them to yield what they have usurped from others.

This related to the human rights. And how much the responsibility of enforcing and respecting them, allowed him "to enjoy" the "pleasures and comforts" of authority during the two years and a quarter of his term of office of caliphate, he said a little before his death in a sad tone:

> If only I had transferred the burden of caliphate, that fell to me on the day of Saqifah Bani Saridah, to Umar or Abu Ubaidah; one of them would have been the Amir and I would have been his vizier. (advisor2).

Of the last instructions and advice that he gave before his death this was also one:

> Whatever I have taken from the Bait-al-mal, paid to me as subsistence allowance, be returned to it. And for this purpose such and such of my landed property be disposed off and the sale proceeds be deposited in the Bait-al-mal (public treasury).

So 'Umar, his successor, in compliance with his wishes sold the land in question and deposited the amount in the Bait-al-mal. Abu Bakr had left instructions in connection with his shroud and burial that he should be burried in the same two pieces of clothes that he usually put on during his life, since "a living person was more deserving of new cloth." (usually in vogue in enshrouding the dead bodies Tr).

Where such firm resolve and sense of responsibility exist and such (exemplary) spirit of sacrifice is at work where one'! own rights are concerned, is there the least little bit of possibility of dictatorship gaining front.

The second Caliph 'Umar, after being installed into the seat of the caliphate, said in his harangue:

> If I knew a person who could bear this burden with greater efficiency I would rather have been slain than undertaken this guardianship.

This much about the "aspiration to authority." And now something about his resolve relating to the enforcement of the rights:

> Listen, O people! I have been placed in charge of your (collective) affairs. But you must know that my sternness has given place to gentleness. However, those, who wrong others and usurp their rights, shall find me just as stern as ever. But for others, who are devout believers and God-fearing in their behaviour, I am extremely gentle. I will not allow any one to wrong any one else; I shall rub one of his cheek on the ground with my foot pressed against the other, until he bows down to justice. In spite of this sternness I rub my own cheek on the ground for the pious and the righteous soul.

And now the details of the benefits derived from the Highest Office of Authority. Before breathing his last as a result of the fatal wounds (inflicted by an assassin while he was leading congregational prayers Tr.), he had asked his son:

> O Abdullah bin-e-Umar! How much I owe to my creditors?

On calculation it was found that it amounted to about eighty six thousand dirhams.

(dirham was a small silver coin Tr.).

On learning that Umar said:

> If the family of Umar can pay it off with its assets, let them do so. If not, ask Bann 'Adi to extend their hand for help. And If even then you tail to meet the debt, ask the Qureshites to contribute their mite, but ask no other people for help.Abd-al-Rehman bin-e-Auf said:

> Why not take a loan from the Bait-al-mal to repay your debts? Umar replied, "I seek refuge in God from such an approach. I don't want that you and your friends should say after my death that you relinquished your shares for the sake of Umar. In this way you shall put me under an obligation and in a hard fix from which God alone can deliver me.

What was the spirit behind this character? It was the same creed of the life Hereafter and accountability before the Sovereign; During the last moments of his life, he was in a state of great uneasiness and was trembling with fear. When Ibn-e-Abbas tried to console and calm him, he said:

> By God, If I had gold, the weight of the earth, I would have given it away in the way of God before being confronted with the torments provided by God (for the transgressors).

When Ibn-e-Abbas praised his period of caliphate, he said:

> Do you praise me and my purity of performance in the matter of caliphate and emirate? While I was with the Prophet of God, he was pleased with me. And as an associate of Abu Bakr I remained loyal, obedient to him till the end of his days. But for myself I am mighty afraid of these affairs of your emirate and

caliphate endangering my own safety in the accounability of the Hereafter."

This is that character which emerges on the basis of belief in the Sovereignty of God and making the rulers a blessing for humanity instead of being a scourge, a torment, completely closes the doors upon dictatorship.

The Concept of Trust : In the Islamic state the second powerful safeguard against usurpation of Human Rights is the concept that it is a Trust (from God) and its head is in the position of a trustee. After the covenant between God and His servant:

> Say: Truely my prayer and my service of sacrifice, my life and my death, are (all) for God, the cherisher of the world. Al Quran VI :162.

> And God has purchased of the Believers their persons and their goods; for theirs, (in return) is the garden (of paradise) Al Quran IX: 111

Every thing that a Muslim has, becomes a sacred trust from God, and he is bound (by this covenant) not to use his right of exercise of his own free will and wish his unrestrained powers but strictly in accordance with the will of the real owner of the trust and His instructions. It is the result of this concept of Trust that when a person wrongs another, God accuses him of "Breach of Trust with his own inner self." So when Tamah bin-e-Ubairaq of the Bani Zafar tribe brought accusation of the theft of the steel armour against a Jew, God said to the Prophet in His revelation:

> Contend not on behalf of such as betray their own soul. Al Quran IV 107

Meaning thereby that the servant of God who has sold his innerself to his Lord and cherishing he makes misuse of it, he is guilty of a breach of trust. Honouring the trust by him demands that the servant of God should take to the course of truth and honesty. Falsehood and treachery does more harm to their perpetrator than any one else, since as a betrayer of trust he degrades himself in the estimate of the real owner of the trust and makes himself liable to serve punishment at His court. Pointing to this fact about wrongfulness, it is said:

> And any who transgresses the limits of God does verily wrong his (own) soul). Al Quran LXV·I

Which means the first target of the wronger's misdeed is his own self. His wrong may or may not do any harm to any one else but his own ruination and prediction are assured.

According to this concept of trust every body is burdened with accountability and responsibility according to the nature of the trust. Every one is accountable to his Lord for his deeds of omission and commission proportionate to the resources at his command and the powers, and authority with which he has been entrusted. The rightly guided Caliphs and other companions of the Prophet, in general, were fully conscious of this concept of trust. And that is why they tried to avoid being burdened with any post of responsibility. And once, under pressure from the people or under orders of the Amir, they were charged with any such post and accepted it, they did their utmost to do full justice to it. The fear of accountability pervaded their whole being to such an extent that there was not another man in the society more God-fearing than they.

Abu Bakr, the man of truth, says:

> Whoever is charged with the responsibility of governance, will have to render a heavy account, and will find himself liable to the severest penalty for his lapses. And he who escaped that burden reckoning with him will be easy, and he is not exposed to the danger of minute scrutiny. The rulers are most likely to oppress the Muslims. And one who wrongs and oppresses the Muslims betrays his trust with God.

Umar's fear of accountability before God is evidenced by the following statement of his on one occasion:

> If a kid gets lost somewhere along the river Euphrates, (Several thousand miles, from his seat of authority, the capital town of Medina!) I am mighty afraid of being called to account for it before God.

Whenever 'Umar was overwhelmed with the sense of responsibility of the burden of trust on his shoulder, he would pick up a handful of earth from the ground and clutching at it he used to say:

> If only I were dust, rather a non-entity! If only my mother bad not borne me!

Abu Bakr, Uthman and Ali were no less worried on this issue of accountability of the Hereafter. Umar bin-e-Abd-al-Aziz spent one whole night, after the late evening prayer, weeping. In the morning when asked by his wife, he gave the following reasons for his night-long wait:

> I (suddenly) found myself wholly responsible for the affairs of the entire Muslim Ummah. I came to think of the people away from their homes in strange lands, mendicants in miserable condition, indigents, the helpless oppressed prisoners and such other people. I realized that I will have to answer for all of them to God, and Muhammad (Sal' am) will stand against me in support of them. And 1 was mighty afraid that I would not be able to plead my case before God, and can never satisfy Muhammad (Sal' am) with any argument that I can offer. The idea made me shudder and I was mighty afraid about my own precarious position.

Strictly speaking, to a Muslim, his life and property and every thing over which he has power of utilization, is a trust from God. But where caliphate and emirate are concerned the word "trust" has been used as a technical term. Abu Zar Ghifari once expressed a wish that he too should be appointed the Amir of some territory to which the Prophet said:

> You are weak and emirate is a trust and it will become a source of regrets and repentance to all save one who deserves it and taking charge of it squarely meets all the responsibilities of his post.

Similarly, he said on another occasion:

> Whoever appointed a person as a controller and ruler over something belonging to Muslims, when a better person and capable among Muslims was available, he would be guilty of breach of trust with God and His Apostle.

In another tradition he said:

> When you witness betrayal of trust, wait for the Dooms day. On being asked what is betrayal of trust, he said in reply that when rule governance and leadership are entrusted to an incapable person, they should wait for the Hour (Doomsday).
>
> Bukhari, reported by Abu Hurayrah

This concept of trust is an important means of safeguarding human rights and respect for them, and a great deterrent, in the way of usurpation of rights.

Priority of Duty : Islam in its system of thought and action has laid greater stress on the fulfillment of obligations than demanding and acquiring one's rights. The issue of demanding right is of secondary importance in comparison to the fulfillment of obligations. If the obligations are fulfilled faithfully and consciously the problem of rights simply does not arise. But as soon as the obligations are neglected or suspended, the question of rights raises its head. Whoever is under an obligation is in the position of a giver, and one to whom it is due is in the position of the recepient. Now in case the obligations are being fulfilled regularly in all sincerity, the recepient simply need not put forth his claim for them.

Since state is the Sovereign in the western secular political system, it enjoys the position of absolute authority. All the powers have become associated with it. In some countries, they have come to be concentrated in one place in the form of a communist state, and elsewhere under the theory of Division of Powers. In countries like the United States of America they have become divided into legislature, judiciary and the executive. But the final authority lies in the hands of the State. The logical result of this state of affairs has been that the position of the citizens has become defensive. The anxiety for their safeguards has given the rights greater importance. And the obligations have not been stressed because there is no way of getting them fulfilled. Which is that superior (Irresistible. Tr.) power that can compel the state to fulfil its obligations? If the state usurps any rights, the affected individual with the greatest effort on his part, may get it recovered through the judiciary. But it is not certain that the judiciary can always extend that help to the aggrieved individual in the matter of restoration of the usurped rights. The state through curtailment of the powers of this institution, the judiciary, can deprive the individual of this facility.

Since rights in Islam are eternal and unchangeable, the state is shorn of the power of curtailing or limiting the powers of the judiciary, and is bound to exercise all its powers strictly in accordance with the injunctions of the Sovereign and the limits prescribed by Him. So all the stress here is on the fulfillment of the obligations.

The Quran, wherever it has addressed mankind, various Ummahs, the prophets individuals, the unbelievers and the polytheists, and the believers, has reminded them of their obligations, promising them honour and dignity in this world and in the next also, only on the basis of fulfilling their obligations. The Quran in its entirety, from the beginning to the end, has no where addressed the deserving ones, prompting them to unite, form groups, organise themselves and snatch their due from the usurpers by force. This persuasion is not needed since the Sovereign has taken upon Himself to remove the defaulters in the fulfillment of obligations from the seat of authority, meting out to them chastisement in the form of ruination and perdition, bringing them to degradation and disgrace in the life of this world and effacing them totally and consigning them to the roaring flames of Hell-Fire.

Again, such persuasion is not needed also for the reason that the government of God through delegated authority (the Islamic State) is in fact a government for the guardianship of the recipients of rights its real mission is to ensure the fulfillment of the obligations through the powers of its (delegated) authority, and let the deserving ones have their dues in the smoothest possible manner. The declaration of war against those withholding Zakah by Abu Bakr is a manifestation of this temperament and character of the Islamic State. He had neither been pressed by the recipients of Zakah for their rights, nor any individual or collective complaint in this behalf had been lodged with his government. He was actually appointed by God and His Apostle for this purpose of preventing the usurpation of the rights of people by foroze, if necessary.

Even today none of the eight groups deserving Zakah (under the Quranic injunction), enjoy the legal right of filing a suit in a court of law against any one who owes Zakah to the Bait-al-Mal, to realize his share. The deserving ones can only put up their claim for consideration of the government. Now it is the responsibility of the government to see if it can pay off their dues from the Zakah head of Bait-al-Mal or realize the requisite amount of Zakah due from the moneyed people to meet their needs. In other words, the government is legally the supporter and guardian, and advocate and agent of the deserving lot. It is the factual plaintiff on behalf of the recipients of the right, and all the powers at its disposal are exercised for the fulfillment of the obligations or realization of the rights from those at the paying end. Imam ibn-e-Taimiyah explaining the obligations of the government, says:

> The real objective of the governments and the emirates is to serve the servants of God and looking to their reform and moral rectitude. And when people shall abandon the faith they shall find themselves in great loss. And the bounties of the world conferred on them by God, shall not avail them in the least. And the spiritual gain from the temporal is of two kinds. One of them is to distribute the goods of this world among the deserving ones; and the other is to mete out due punishment to those indulging in excesses and oppression and also those trying to take what is not due to them or more than their due.

Just imagine what are the chances of the problem of human rights cropping up in a society in which devotional acts, teaching and preaching, education and training, the media of propagation and the various agencies and institutions of the government and all its power, put together and all the means at its command are together exerting pressure internally and externally on the, fulfillment of obligations.

Concordance of the Objective : The Quran points out the aim and objective of the existence of the Islamic State in the following verse:

> (They are) those who, if we establish them in the Land, establish regular prayer, and give zakat regularly, enjoin the right and forbid wrong:
>
> Al Quran XXII: 41

And identically, the same is the goal of the Muslim Ummah:

> Ye are the best of people evolved for mankind, enjoining what is right, forbidding what is wrong, and believing in God. Al Quran 111:110

In other words the objective of the individual and the collective life of the Muslims and that of their government and the state is identical – living a life of righteousness and rectitude and enjoining, what is right, on others, and abstaining from the path of evil themselves and forbidding 'others what is wrong. The unity of the objective in the individual and collective life is that be it a common Muslim citizen or the person in their highest seat of authority, they are the trodders of the same path and bound for the same goal. The direction of their journey is the same.

All of them are engaged in the same activity, each one according to his position and capacity and in accordance with the resources and powers at his disposal. One entrusted with power and authority is exercising them to achieve that goal (in his privileged position of greater responsibility. Tr.), and the one with no other assets is striving towards that goal with his body, and soul only.

Where no such harmony exists, there is no longer any issue at stake, for contention between the individual and the state. Under the Islamic order the position of the amir of the state is not that of a ruler but that of a guardian and supervisor, and the relationship between the amir and the people instead of that of the usual ruler and the subjects is that of helpers of each other. God says:

> The Believers, men and women, are protectors, one of another: they enjoin what is just, and forbid what is evil: they observe regular prayers, practise regular charity (pay Zakat regularly Tr.) and obey God and His Apostle. A1 Quran IX:71

Now, even if the unlimited aspiration for power and authority of a ruler creates a situation of contention and confrontation, the citizens can always have recourse to the path illumined by the Quran for them:

> Help ye one another in righteousness and piety, but help ye not one another in sin and transgression:
> Al Quran V:2

The amir, as soon as he digresses towards the path of sin and transgression furnishes the Ummah sufficient ground for withdrawing their cooperation, and he forfeits his right to their obedience.

This concord in the matter of the objective converts the concept of rulership into the concept of brotherhood, and the punishment of turning away from it resulting in loss of the right to loyalty and obedience, becomes a very effective means of the protection of the fundamental rights.

Status of Individual

The problem of the fundamental rights of man is in fact the problem of the dignity of humanity. Those coming to occupy seats so often lose mental balance, and by the spectacle of the wonders worked by their authority and the vast resources at their disposal create an illusion that they come to think of themselves as super human entities, and that they possess such high qualities which necessarily entitle them to sovereignty and rule, and the rest of the humanity (creatures of a much lower order than themselves) were only created to abjectly bow down to them.

This trend of thought has actually taken the form of theories and philosophical thought. It was this pattern of thought which gave birth to such a fabrication as the "Theory of Divine Origin", and the term "Divine Rights of Kings" was coined for the (unlimited) powers of the kings. Again, it was this misleading trend of thought which helped in coining such titles for kings as the "Protector of the World" and "Shadow of God" and presenting them as the ones specially sent by God to rule and thus degraded and put in disgrace the common people. These "Divine Rights and Divine Shadowness" became the cause of great distress for mankind and to save itself from the misery of it, the movement for the protection of fundamental rights had to be launched.

Islam has laid great emphasis on the dignity of man, and he is regarded as the most honoured and respectable entity, next only to God in the universe. In relating the incident of the creation of Adam, it has been said that God breathed into this Divine mould of clay of his own spirit and bowed down the angels to him. The Quran says:

> When I have fashioned him (in due proportion) and breathed into him of My spirit, fall ye down in obeisance unto him. Al Quran XV: 29

This verse also reveals that man, quite different from the rest of the creation that came into existence with the command of the Lord and Cherisher, "He", is a separate and special creation, and as compared with other creatures, he has been fashioned in the best possible mould. The Quran says:

> We have indeed created man in the best of moulds.
> Al Quran XCV 4

Not only this but he was honoured and made superior to other creatures and all his bounties and forces at work in this universe were subdued for him to serve him. The Quran says:

> We have honoured the sons of Adam, provided them with transport on land and sea; given them for sustenance things good and pure; and conferred on them special favours above a great part of our creation.
> Al Quran XVII: 70

> Do ye not see that God has subjected to your (use) all things in the heavens and on earth.
> Al Quran XXXI: 20

This honour, superiority and greatness man came to have as a member of mankind, and there was no distinction of black and white, Arab and non-Arab, oriental and occidental and high and low, since they were born out of a single soul. The Prophet pointing to this greatness once said addressing the sanctum of Kaaba:

> How chaste art thou; and how wholesome thy atmosphere! How great art thou and how venerable thy status But by God, in whose Hands lies the life

> of Muhammad, the honour and dignity of a Muslim's life and property and his blood in the sight of God is more important than thy sanctity.
>
> Ibn-e-Majah, Tradition No.3932.

This was one aspect of man's status. Now let us see how has Quran, in order to tame the devil of pride and arrogance in man, and particularly to keep one in authority and in possession of resources, on the right track, brought home to him his own true position:

> Now let man but think from what he is created!. He is created from a drop emitted—proceeding from between the backbone and the ribs:
>
> Al Quran LXXXVI:'S-7

> (Consider) that We created you out of dust, then out of sperm, then out of a leech-like clot, then out of a morsel of flesh, partly formed, and partly unformed in order that We may manifest (Our power) to you.
>
> Al Quran XXII: 5

> O man! what has seduced thee from Thy Lord Most Beneficent ...Him who created thee, fashioned thee in due proportion, and gave Thee a just bias; in whatever Form He wills does He put thee together.
>
> Al Quran LXXXII: 6-8

Along with making this fact about his position evident to him, he was also told that:

> Every soul shall have a taste of death: In the end to Us shall ye be brought back. Al Quran XXIX : 57

> Wherever ye are, death will find you out, even if ye are in towers built up strong and high:
>
> Al Quran IV :72

When, with all his greatness and superiority, man has neither control over his life nor over death, where is any room for haughtiness.

In many verses of the Quran and the traditions of the Prophet, these two truths have been brought home to man in such a wise manner that he should be inclined to respect fellow men, fulfil his obligations in relations to them, should shun tyranny and excesses and should never be a victim of self-deceit or misunderstanding about himself.

These were the basic concepts which Islam brought home to man, and through them ridding him of the unhealthy trends of any aspiration to enslave any one or show willingness to be enslaved, showed him the way to pass his life honourably under the blessings of the universal sovereignty of God with the mutual relationship of equality and brotherhood.

Now we shall take stock of the Islamic injunctions regarding the practical problem of formation of the government.

Purge of the Leadership : To check completely dictatorship and fascism, in an Islamic state, the Muslims have been directed to be extremely careful in the very first stage of the formation of the government. And prescribing two regulations in connection with the election of the amir the wrong persons have been barred from finding their way to the (most important) post of emirate. The first of these regulations is that the person aspiring to a job, despite all his high qualifications and capabilities is unfit for it, since his aspiration for it is the greatest proof of the unsoundness of his intentions. God says:

> That Home of the Hereafter We shall give to those who intend not high-handedness or mischief on earth:
> Al Quran XXVIII 83

The Prophet says:

> By God, we never appoint any one to any post to which he aspires or is avaricious. Bukhari, Muslim

> The worst betrayer of trust among you is one who is an aspirant to a post of responsibility. Abu Daud

He once said to Abu Bakr in connection with an inquiry relating to Emirate:

> O Abu Bakr! It is for him who is not at all interested in it, and not for him who is madly after it. It is for one who tries to run away from it, and not one who pounces on it. It is for one to whom it is said, 'This is thy due' and not one who himself asserts, 'This is my right.'

After this fist regulation of disqualification, the other instruction to the people was that they should elect the best person (most suitable) for the post of Amir, and norm for this quality, "best", was also elucidated, so that his character may be objectively scrutinized and tested, and personal like or dislike, kinship, territorial, group, lingual and racial prejudices or the outstanding apparent traits of personality, for example his facial beauty, the style of his dress, his style of hair, the fascination of his written word or speech and such other chorus may not recommend him in the election. It is this norm of election in view of which the Prophet said:

> Listen and obey, even if a Negro slave with a small scalp is appointed as your amir, so long as he rules according to the dictates of the Quran.
>
> 7Bukhari, reported by Anas

The same norm 'Umar had before him when he was looking for his successor. Putting up the problem of the caliphate before the members of the Shura or the advisory body, he said:

> If Abu Huzaifa's slave, Salim, had been alive, I would have nominated him for the Emirate. If my Lord and cherisher questioned me about Salim, I would have said in reply. I had heard the Apostle saying that Salim loves Allah very much.

On this occasion when Mughira ibn-e-Sah'bah suggested to him that Abdullah ibn-e-Umar be nominated the next caliph, he said rather gruffly:

> God settle accounts with you! By God, I never for one moment thought of it. We are not interested in your

affairs. Neither did I find, rulership something likeable that I may command it to my family. If it was something good I have had it. And in case it was bad to have it, it would be enough for one member of the Umar family that he be brought to account for the well-being or otherwise of the Ummah of the Prophet Muhammad (P.B.U.H). I suffered much through self-abnegation, and totally deprived my family. I even with all this I am let off (on the Day of Reckoning) without any reward or punishment. I shall consider myself lucky enough.

The tradition of the Prophet and the saying of Umar make it evident that the best Amir is one who is well equipped with the knowledge, intellect and administrative capabilities to enforce the Quranic injunctions, whose character reflects love of God, and has all the traits liked by Him and His Apostle to the maximum degree.

In the election or nomination of those in command of the affairs of the Muslims, in addition to the general condition of his being a believing male, sane and rational and adult, the following qualifications have been regarded essential:

1. Taqwa or Piety

God says:

> The most honoured of you in the sight of God is (he who is) the most righteous of you.
>
> Al Quran XLIX: 13

> Shall We treat those who guard against evil the same as those who turn aside from the right?
>
> Al Quran XXXVII: 28

2. Capability

The person being elected must be fully capable of efficiently handling the job to be entrusted to his care.

> God doth command you to render back your Trusts to those to whom they are due; Al Quran IV: 58

Under this head, the traditions of the Prophet in which he has forbidden us to render trust to those incapable of holding them, and that to make an incapable person the superior and ruler where a better and most pious among the Muslims is available, is betrayal of trust with God and His Apostle, have already been quoted in the foregoing pages.

3. *Justice and Equity*

The first and foremost qualification of a ruler is justice. The following portion of the verse quoted above (IV: 28) mentions Justice as a requisite of a ruler:

> And when ye judge between man and man, that ye judge with justice. Al Quran IV: 28
>
> O David! We did indeed make thee a vicegerent on earth: so judge thou between men in truth (and justice): nor follow thou the lusts (of thy heart), for they will mislead thee from the Path of God:
>
> Al Quran XXXVIII: 26

The Prophet has said:

> On the Day of Reckoning the dearest and nearest to me will be the just ruler, and the most- detested person and one to be consigned to the worst torments in Hell will be the despot and the tyrant.

Umar, the second rightly guided caliph of the Prophet, when bidding farewell to the governors with fresh assignments used to give them the following instructions:

> I am not sending you out as tyrants but as the leaders and guides of people. Do not debase and disgrace Muslim with flogging. And don't put them in trial by praising them. Do not wrong them by depriving them of their dues. Do everything in your power to provide

all possible facilities to the Muslims and go on working untiringly for their prosperity.

4. Wisdom and Administrative Capacity

Those at the helm of affairs of the Muslims must be the people who have the necessary qualifications of wisdom, administrative capability, and knowledge and understanding. The Quran says:

> Say: are those equal, those who know and those who do not know? Al Quran XXXIX: 9

> To those weak of understanding make not over your property which God hath made a means of support for you. Al Quran IV: 5

What those charged with authority among the Muslims, should be on the whole, is amply borne out by what Abu Bakr and Umar have said about them. Nominating Umar as his successor, Abu Bakr gave him sound advice:

> Umar! The first thing I warn you against is your own inner self. Every one's inner self has some cravings and some aspirations. And if you satiate one, the other must come up for satiation. And listen! Beware of those companions of the Prophet whose bellies have become distended. Their eyes show greed, and every one of them has his own interests foremost on his programme. If one of them stumbles due to a false step, the whole lot will be amazed. Beware! You are not the one that goes tumbling down. Get it well into your head so long as you fear God, they will be afraid of you. And as long as your own behaviour is good, the people will also behave in the right manner with you. This is my advice to you and I pray to God for your peace and well-being.

The will of 'Umar which he left for his successor comprises the following instructions:

(1) Taqwa (Piety) (2) Favouring the righteous and forgiving the evil doers (3) Taxing only the surplus goods of the Zimmis and treating them kindly (4) To realize Zakat from the rich among the Bedouins and returning it to the poor (deserving) among them. (5) Justice for all that need it among the people and meeting their needs (6) Defence of the frontiers. (7) Abstaining from giving priority to the rich over the poor. (8) Strictness in the enforcement of the Commandments and limits prescribed by God and those showing no respect for the Divine injunctions to be disgraced publicly. (9) Keeping yourself at the same level with the people in dealing with them (no priorities, privileges and distinctions. Tr.). In the realization of the (peoples) dues no regard for the personality of the defaulter and heedlessness in the matter of reproach. (11) Equitable distribution of the spoils of war and self abnegation (12) Neither oppressing the Zimmis nor allowing others to oppress them (13) Giving thought to the Hereafter and making provision for it and disregard for the bounties of this world (14) To guard against the cravings of the innerself getting the better of him (15) To stand like a rock before the most violent storm for the sake of the Truth (16) To be compassionate to the Muslim Ummah (17) Respect for the elders giving dignity to the young and reverence for those learned in the religious lore (18) Neither beating any one nor disgracing any one. (19) Not to deprive the believers of free gifts and grants. (20) Not to station the troops permanently guarding the frontiers lest the propagation of the race should come to an end. (21) Not to let the national wealth and resources keep confined to the rich people (22) Not to close your door on the poor and the needy lest the mighty should devour the weak.

When Umar took over as the caliph. Ali gave him the following advice:

> If you want to follow your companion (Abu Bakr) and keep up to his level patch up your shirt, keep your trousers above your ankles, mend your shoes yourself, patch your leather socks, curtail your aspirations and never fill your stomach fully.

And Umar did live up to these counsels during the entire period of his caliphate. For the rest of his life since he died in harness a martyr's death.

This is the norm of the election and the essential qualifications of those charged with authority in Islam. If the Ummah elects its rulers according to this norm, and they too come up to it, there will be an atmosphere of mutual well-wishing and cooperation instead of confrontation between the individual and the state, and there will be no hindrance in the protection of the fundamental rights.

Limitation of Powers : After imposing stern conditions for the elections of those charged with authority, as soon as the Amir is installed into the seat of authority, Islam binds him with the limitations of powers in such a way that he can neither give himself the airs of the rulers nor can he put together the means of display of pomp and glory. These are some of the restrictions placed on the powers of the Amir:

1. Delegated Authority

The head of the Islamic state by virtue of, his office, discharges the duties of a two fold representation. He is on the one hand the vicegerent of the Sovereign on the basis of the responsibility of enforcing His commandments and instructions practically And on the other hand he is the deputy of the true vicegerents of the Sovereign being their elected representative. Since the vicegerency has been conferred on every Muslim individually and they all delegate it to an individual of their choice, through manifestation of their free will in an election, thus devoting the responsibility of a duty to be discharged on the behalf. So he is the deputy (or representative) of them all. This dual deputation signifies that the head of the state is on the one hand accountable to God and on the other responsible to the people. This peculiar position of his, limits his own will and power to a very small sphere. This is the first and the greatest restriction placed by Islam on the powers of those charged with authority.

2. *Eternal Constitution*

The greatest safeguard of the fundamental rights in the Islamic State is that eternal constitution which is with us in the form of the Quran and the Sunnah and which has determined a code of conduct for man's life that can neither be amended nor cancelled. The Sovereign, determining the checks on the legislative powers of those charged with authority and the conditions of loyalty and obedience for the common people, has commanded:

> Follow (O man!) the revelation given unto you from your Lord, and follow not as friends and protectors, other than Him. Al Quran VII: 3

And those guilty of the slightest digression from this commandment have been given the divine verdict in very clear terms:

> If any do fail to judge by (the light of) what God hath revealed, they are (no better than) unbelievers...... they are (no better than) wrongdoers, they are (no better than) those who rebel. Al Quran V: 44.47

This law the following of which is being enjoined on the believers, since it does not change with the change of the government, is passed on to every new comer in authority, and so the rights conferred by it are never curtailed, suspended or cancelled. They are immutable and totally immune from the interference of the state.

3. Eternal Pattern of Sovereignty

This constitution has not only been preserved in the form of written word and the book comprising them, but also presents before us a permanent pattern to follow in its interpretation, elucidation and practical enforcement; and being embodied in the person, of the Prophet, makes such a solid and lucid manifestation of its sense that there is no chance of playing with words, to give them meaning suiting the lusts of the rulers and through desired interpretation, and even distortion and perversion, to chalk out new paths of digression (from the straight path). The Sovereign who has strictly forbidden following other than His own commandments, says about His Prophet:

> We sent not an Apostle, but to be obeyed, in accordance with the will of God. Al Quran IV: 64

And this obedience, too, should not be with any feeling of compulsion and revulsion but with perfect readiness of mind and willingness of the heart. The Quran continues in the same context:

> But no, by thy Lord, they can have no (real) Faith, until they make thee judge in all disputes between them, and find in their souls no resistance against thy decision, but accept them with the fullest conviction.
> Al Quran IV: 65

In the light of this commandment, from a common citizen to the head of the Islamic State, the real fountain-head of leadership, guidance, giving instructions and governance is the sacred person of the Prophet of God. In every thing pertaining to man's life their attitude shall be a demonstration of the following instruction of the Quran:

> So take what the Apostle assigns to you, and deny yourselves that which he withholds from you. And fear God; for God is strict in Punishment.
> Al Quran L1X: 7

And,

> Ye have indeed in the Apostle of God a beautiful pattern (of conduct). Al Quran XXXIII: 21

With the practical pattern of Sovereignty of the Prophet, no Islamic state any where in the world, can afford to overlook the word or deed of the Apostle of God in any matter pertaining to human life, and his interpretation and elucidation of any Quranic injunction. This eternal pattern of Sovereignty compels every head of the Islamic state to follow the Prophet. And this check on him putting an obstacle in the way of transgression or overstepping the limits of his powers puts an end to any oppression and excess.

4. *Supremacy of the Judiciary*

The eternal position of the Quran and the Sunnah means that the judiciary has supremacy over both the executive and the legislature. The executive cannot do any thing against the Quran and the Sunnah, and the legislature cannot legislate against the spirit of the Quran and the Sunnah. The judiciary is the protector of the citizen's rights. It can declare any laws violating these rights as null and void and can stop their enforcement, and making the orders issued by the executive ineffective, can provide strong protection to the citizens.

5. *Limits of Obedience*

Obedience of the Amir is conditional in Islam. And in this connection the Sovereign has Himself laid down a general rule:

> O ye who believe! Obey God and obey the Apostle, and those charged with authority among you. If ye differ anything, refer it to God and His Apostle.
> Al Quran IV: 59

The limits of obedience in an Islamic State determined by this Quranic verse are the following:

(1) Obedience is, in fact, due to Allah alone, and is binding upon the Muslims including the Apostle.

(2) Obedience in the second place is due to the Prophet of God, and is not different from that in the first item, but the only practical form of the obedience to God. Obedience to God for us (mortals) is nothing else but our obedience to the Prophet. That is why at another place it has been said in the Quran:

He who obeys the Apostle, obeys God:

Al Quran IV: 80

Like the first, this obedience too is binding upon the Muslims, ordinary citizens and the rulers alike.

(3) Thirdly, obedience is due to one in authority. But like the first two, this is not unconditional. It is associated with the basic condition that the person in authority must be bowing with the rest in the first two items of obedience.

(4) If there is a contention between the person in authority and the believers on any issue, it will be decided on the authority of the Book of God and the Sunnah of the Prophet.

Along with this fundamental article of the constitution of the Islamic state, the Muslims have been given clear instruction that they should never obey any person who is a slave of his own innerself, mischief maker, tyrant and one violating the obligation of enjoining what is right and forbidding what is wrong. Certain Quranic verses in this context are noteworthy:

Nor obey any whose heart We have permitted to neglect the remembrance of us, one who follows his own desires, whose case has gone beyond all bounds.

Al Quran XCII: 28

And follow not the bidding of those who are extragent,......who make mischief in the land and mend not (their ways). Al Quran XXVI: 151-152

And hearten not to the sinner or the ingrate among them. Al Quran LXXVI: 24

> Heed not the despicable man,—ready with oaths, a slanderer going about with calumnies, (habitually), hindering (all) good, transgressing beyond bounds, deep in sin, violent, and cruel),...with all that, base-born.......because he possesses wealth and (numerous) sons, when to him are rehearsed our signs. "Tales of the Ancient," He cries! Al Quran LXIIt: 10.15

In this connection, the Traditions of the Holy Prophet further stating in detail the principle of obedience, have so much elucidated all its various aspects that there is no confusion left. He says:

> Listening and obedience is binding on Muslims whether it is pleasing or repugnant to him, so long as he is not ordered to do something sinful.' And when he is ordered to commit a sin, there is neither listening nor obedience. (Bukhari and Muslim)

That is to say, as soon as the Amir has made himself independent of the two items of obedience (God and His Prophet), he forfeits his rights to the obedience of the people, and the Muslims in that situation are bound to openly refuse to obey him. The Prophet has said very plainly:

> There is no obedience in transgression and sin. Obedience is only in what is right.
>
> (Bukhari and Muslim)

> There is no obedience for one .who is a transgressor.
>
> (Bukhari and Muslim; Abu Daud and Nasai)

> No obedience for His creatures at the cost of disobedience to God. (Bukhari and Muslim)

His forfeiture of the right to the obedience of the people means in plain words that he is no more their Amir. He has been divested of his powers. No orders from him have any legal position, and the Muslims have now been entitled to have another Amir for themselves through fresh elections. If he goes so far in his transgression that the system of prayer is in disarray due to him, he has given a handle to the believers to take up arms against him.

There will come such people to rule over you whose programme in life manifests good and evil both mixed up. So those who showed disgust for their evil deeds, discharge their duty. And those who disapproved of them were also safe. But he who approved of their evil deeds and followed them, would be brought to back. The companions asked the Prophet, "Shall we not take up arms against such rulers?" The Prophet replied, "Not so long as they establish regular prayers." (Muslim)

When Abu Bakr took upon himself the responsibilities of the caliphate, recalling these limits of obedience, said:

> Obey me as long as I obey God and His Apostle, but if I am found guilty of something involving disobedience to God and His Apostle, you are no more under any obligation to obey me.

Umar, the second caliph, addressing a gathering, said:

> The greatest and most important duty of the ruler is to see whether the people are fulfilling the obligations enjoined on them by God. We shall enjoin upon you only that has been enjoined on you by God, and forbid you what God has forbidden you. All that we want is that the Divine injunctions be enforced far and wide.

And it was during the period of the caliphate of 'Umar that after the conquest of Iraq, many people had taken Christian women for wives in view of the permission granted for it in the Quran. 'Umar wrote to Huzaifah bin-al-Yamn that he did not approve of it. He wrote back to enquire whether it was his personal opinion or under an injunction of the Islamic Shariah, to which Umar replied that that was his personal dislike of it. Huzaifah wrote to him that they were under no obligation to follow his personal opinion.

Ali, the fourth caliph, said in one of his harangues:

> You are under obligation to obey me in what I order you, while I am myself obeying God, whether you like it or not. And what I enjoin on you, while transgressing the Divine Injunctions, there is no obedience" in transgression. Obedience is only in Maroof. Maroof:. Literally well known (to human nature) and having an affinity for it. As a technical term of the Islamic Shariah, it comprises the acts, attitudes, and the behaviour, that the normal people with an unsullied nature have approved in every age. Truth, keeping of one's plighted word, justice, equity and kindness, to name a few, have always been regarded as desirable and laudable. Obedience is only in Maroof. This conditional obedience of those in authority left no room for their high handedness in the matter of people's rights conferred on them by God. They are entitled to people's obedience only so long as they respect these rights and do not take any step detrimental to them. If they contravene this principle the people need not obey them. And as a reaction against this they will be justified in their striving to depose him from the emirate. These limits and conditions of obedience provide the citizens, a guarantee for the protection of their fundamental rights against the onslaughts on them by the rulers.

6. The Obligation of Consultation

There is yet another obligation, for the person those in authority, that cannot take any step without first consulting those persons of the Ummah who can give sober advice. The way he is elected by the mutual consultation and concurrence of the opinions of the Muslims, he is also under obligation to manage the affairs of the state by consultation under the following injunction of the Quran:

> Who (conduct) their affairs by mutual consultation;
> Al Quran XLII: 38

Even the Prophet of God was no exception to it. He is being instructed:

> And consult them in affairs (of moment) :
> Al Quran III : 159

The Prophet of God was himself in authority (by virtue of being commissioned by God). He was directly guided by God. So he was not so much in need of consultation. But since he had to leave a pattern after him for those succeeding in the office of authority to manage the affairs of the Islamic state, he was made to establish a tradition of mutual consultation. He often consulted his companions on various major and minor issues. This tradition (of consultation) was so much liked by God that in some matters before giving him instructions be waited for the companions of the Prophet to opine on those issues, and when one of such opinions was approved by Him, by authorization and approval of it through revelation, the person offering the opinion was encouraged. So we find that the revelation approved the opinion of 'Umar on the issue of the prisoners of war of Badr, the death service of the hypocrites. Burdah, prohibition of alcohol, taking the station of Ibrahim as the place of prayer, and entering the house unannounced during the time people usually rest in bed. The Prophet once addressed Abu Bakr and 'Umar, the most eminent among his companions, saying that if they come to a consensus on any issue he would not oppose them (Musnad Ahmad).

Ali is reported to have said:

> Once I asked the Prophet if a certain problem confronted them after his passing away which was neither mentioned in the Quran nor he (the Prophet) himself had opined on it, what should be our course of action. The Prophet said in reply that they should bring together the most devout among the believers

> of his Ummah and put the puzzling issue for their mutual consultation, but never take a decision on a solitary opinion.

About its importance and real spirit the Prophet had said:

> Whoever suggested to his brother something about which he was certain was not the right course, betrayed the trust reposed in him by his brother.
>
> (Abu Daud)

After the definite Quranic injunction and the Sunnah of the Prophet, no Amir of the believers can take any action (in important matters) without consultation. This obligation of consultation impedes the course of dictatorship and inspires the political life with spirit of democracy. It is worthwhile to note here the basic point that the principle of consultation in Islam depends not on the majority of opinions but their soundness. In other words, only the opinion that is nearest to the spirit of the Quran and the Sunnah will be acceptable, and it will be put into practice after Ijma. The consensus of the Mujtahids of the Ummah on a certain issue during a certain period. The consensus of the learned ones raises the status of Ijma for above the personal opinions of individuals however great in learning and piety, when the majority of the erudite in the religious love has conceded to it. Without the support of the Quran and the Sunnah the majority of opinion carries no weight and is to be given no importance.

Abu Bakr consulted the eminent companions on the issue of those withholding Zakat. The majority of the companions were not in favour of declaring war against them. But he did not concede to their opinion, since according to his understanding of the Quran Jihad was the right course to take in their case. Later on all the dissentients agreed that Abu Bakr's decision was based on sound reasoning and participated in the Jihad. Similarly, 'Umar dissented from the majority of consultants on the issue of distributing the arable lands of the conquered Iraq and Syria. Companions of the stature of Bilal and Abdur-Rahman bin-e-Auf were insisting that the lands be distributed among the conquering armies. A general meeting of the advisory body was called and after long deliberations extending over several days, 'Umar succeeded in convincing them of the soundness of his own opinion. He had come upon a verse of the Quran (LIX:7) which he brought powered in support of his stand on this controversial issue and they came to a consensus.

These precedents also make it evident that the Amir, with all his, superiors in sight, cannot take any decisive action on the basis of his own personal information and satisfaction on any issue, unless and until he has had a consensus on the satisfaction of the majority on the soundness of his own opinion.

The relationship of the Amir and the advisory body had been brought out by 'Umar in the meeting called by him on the issue of the distribution of lands in these words:

> Gentlemen, I have given you the trouble to come here because I wanted that you should take off some of the heavy load of your affairs on my shoulders, since I am also a weak mortal like you. Today you are called upon to determine the right. Some of you have differed from me, and some have concurred. It is not my desire that you should come to my way of looking at the problem. You have the Book of God with you that tells you only the truth. By God! I have said a·y thing on which I want to act, I had no other intention but following the truth.

It was also Umar who had said:

> No (office of the) caliphate without consultation.

Emphasizing the importance of consultation he goes so far as to say:

> The person who invites you to the emirate for himself

> or any body else without seeking the opinion of Muslims it does not become you not to kill him.

After Uthman died a martyr's death, and people wanted to install Ali in the seat of authority-thus vacated he said:

> You people are not authorized to do it. It is the business of the Shura or the advisory body and the companions of (the battle of) Badr. The person whom they elect for this purpose shall be the caliph So we shall get together and deliberate over it.

Abu Musa Ashari regarded this consultation as the difference between caliphate and monarchy:

> Emirate (caliphate) is that instruction which comes into existence as a result of consultations (sort of referendum Tr.). And monarchy is that established with the might of the sword.

This principle of consultation has fully guaranteed the expression of opinion to all those whose rights are under consideration. This consultation is not limited to the members of the Shura. A common citizen can change the opinion of the entire Shura and the Amir if he can bring the authority of the Quran and the Sunnah in support of his contention. An old lady was exercising this right on others when she made 'Umar, the second caliph, realize the error of his decision of living the quantum of women's dower, and he took back his order immediately.

7. *The Obligation of the Objectives and the Priorities*

Yet another restriction on the person in authority is that he cannot make any amendments in the objectives and the priorities of the state, since such alterations will go against the concept of the Trust. He can utilize the monetary resources of the state (Bait-al-Mal) only under those heads that have been determined by the Islamic Shariah, or by the decision of the Shura. And how much he (the Amir) is himself entitled to from the Bait-al-Mal (as subsistence allowance) is also for the Shura to determine. After the election of the first caliph (Abu Bakr) when the question of his subsistence arose, 'Umar took him to Abu 'Ubaidah, the Nazim of the Bait-al-Mal (Treasury Officer), from the market place where he (Abu Bakr) was standing with cloth for sale. The Nazim, elucidated the principle of determining the allowance to him saying:

> We are fixing an allowance for you equivalent to the income of an average person among the migrants (from Maklesh), which is neither equal to that of the richest, nor that of the poorest among them.

This subsistence allowance was fixed at four thousand dirhams: an old oriental weight and silver coin, originally two thirds of an Attic drachma. It is about 3.071 gms annually. But through a testament of his before his death he had got returned to the Bait-al-Mal, all that he had received (during the twenty seven months of his term as caliph. Tr.).

'Umar, elucidating the principle of the share of the caliph from the Bait-al-Mal, had said:

> For me nothing more from the bounties of Allah is allowance than a pair of clothes for the summer season and another for the winter, and subsistence for my family equivalent to that of an average person among the Quraish, for, I am a common man among the believers.

He determines the following basic principles regarding the responsibility of the Bait-al-Mal:

> With regard to this goods (the resources of the Bait-al-Mal) I do not consider right save these three things— taking justly, giving away justly and withholding it from (serving the cause of) falsehood. My relationship with you is that of the guardian of the orphan with his (the orphan's) goods. If 1 am not in need, I shall

> not take any thing from it. And, if in want, I shall take according to the barest minimum of my needs.

Ali, the fourth caliph, also kept his subsistence allowance at the level of Shaiklain (Abu Bakr and Umar), and passed a life of great austerity.

We have already thrown ample light on the aims and objectives of the Islamic state. Its only objective is to proclaim the religion of God over all others:

> Establish the Faith Or the way of life and make no divisions therein. Al Quran XLII: 13

The goal of the collective power of the Islamic state and each and every one of its citizens is this:

> And religion is all for Allah. Al Quran VIII: 39

The person in authority cannot afford to keep any other objective in vein. The Prophet has severely warned his successor and all the believers:

> The person who introduces something into our faith which is to be rejected. (Mishkat, chapter on Adherence to the Book of God and the Sunnah)
>
> Whoever honoured an innovator, helped in the demolition of the Faith. (Mishkat, chapter of Adherence to the Book of God and the Sunnah)

These are the restrictions placed on the powers of the person in authority. The ruler, tightly bound by the delegated authority and along with that fully observing the limits prescribed by the Quran and the Sunnah, obligation of consultation, conditional obedience, and obligation of the objectives and priorities of the Islamic state, can hardly dream of usurping the fundamental rights.

Along with the concept of the government, purge of the leadership and limitation of the powers, Islam has made extraordinary arrangements for keeping an eye over the activities of the Amir and calling him to account. In the foregoing pages we have discussed the way and means of vigilance. In this connection it would be better to recall the sequence of the means of vigilance to have an idea how Islam has established the superiority of the people over the government, making it a democracy in the true sense of the world.

1. Reckoning of the Hereafter

The first and foremost agent of vigilance is the fear of the (reckoning of the) Hereafter, which has always a tight grip over his mind and nerve. The omniscient and well-acquainted and omnipresent Entity, (God), Who is going to call him to account for each and every deed of his, and here in this life, is closer to him than his own jugular vein, has forewarded him, that:

> Whosover follows My guidance, on them shall be no fear, nor shall they grieve. But those who reject Faith and believe Our Signs, they shall be companions of the Fire; they shall abide therein. Quran II: 38-39.
>
> Not one of the beings in the heavens and the earth but must come to (God), Most Gracious, as a servant. Al Quran XIX 93.

The Prophet has said:

> Every one of you is an overseer and protector, and will be asked to account with regard to those entrusted to his charge. So the Amir (of the believers) will be called to account in connection with the people. And the house wife is an overseer over her husband's household and his offspring, and she will be asked to render account on that score. Bukhari and Muslim, reported by Abdullah bin-e-Umar
>
> One who has been entrusted with the collective affairs of the Muslims and he betrays that trust, Allah shall bar his entry to heaven. Unanimous
>
> When somebody has accepted the responsibility of

> the collective affairs of the believers, and he did not strive for their well-being and did not tire himself as he would in the management of his own affairs, Allah would throw him into Hell-Fire face-down.
>
> Tabrani, Kitab-al-Khiraj.

Accountability of the Hereafter is an internal vigilance that never leaves man alone, in company or in solitude, and continues the process of self-reckoning all the time. In the presence of this internal system of watch and ward, even if there is no external vigilance, there is hardly any likelihood of his going astray and taking to the path of oppression and evil. It was the result of this acute sense of accountability that during the caliphate of Abu Bakr, 'Umar as the Qadi of the Islamic state for two years had not a single case brought to his court. That was because every individual of the Society, including their Amir, were discharging their duties so efficiently that no question of (usurpation of) any rights ever cropped up.

2. *Accountability Through the Courts*

The head of the Islamic state enjoys no immunity against the citizens. And any citizen can bring a suit against him.

The caliph of the believers, 'Umar had a contention with Ubai bin-e-Kab on some matter. The latter filed a suit against him in the court of Zaid bin Thabit, the then Qadi of Medina. The Qadi issued someone to 'Umar to present himself in his court. He came to attend the court but neither he nor the plaintiff had any witness to testify in their case. According to rules, 'Umar had to make his statement on oath. When Ubai discerned that 'Umar was ready to take an oath, he withdrew his case.

'Ali, the fourth caliph, saw a Christian selling his (Ali's) armour in the market, and claimed it as his. On his refusal to oblige, the case was brought to the court of Qadi Shariah, who asked 'Ali to produce a witness which he failed to do. So the case was decided in favour of the Christian, and 'Ali accepting that decision of the court said, "Shariah, you have pronounced the right judgment in this case." The Christian was amazed at this decision and said, "Such justice could come only from the Prophets of God, that the Amir of the believers is dragged to the court and has to put up with the decision against himself. To tell the truth the armour belongs to the Amir of the believers. It had dropped down from his camel's back and I had picked it up."

This status of the judiciary was maintained even during the period of the Umayyid caliphate. Utaiba says:

> "I was sitting with bin e-Imran, the Qadi of Medina, when the head of the bodyguard of the caliph Hisham bin Abdul Malik came to him with Ibrahim, bin-e-Muhammad, and said, 'In a contention between the Amir and Ibrahim, the former has sent me as his agent or attorney to your court.' The Qadi asked him to produce his credentials. He said in reply, "Do you mean to say I have told a lie?" The Qadi said to him mildly, 'Not that 1 doubt your statement, but it involves a point of law, and until you produce evidence to this effect no decision on your case can be pronounced.' He went back and acquainted the caliph Hisham with the situation. Hisham personally attended the court and after hearing the case the Qadi pronounced judgement against the caliph."

And it was from the court of this same Qadi Muhammad bin-e-Imran in another case that caliph Mansoor was summoned. The complaint was lodged by some owners of camels in connection with certain rights of their's. The Qadi wrote to him "Give them their due or present yourself at the court." The caliph presented him at the open air court in the Prophet's mosque, and the Qadi decided the case against him and in favour of the camel drivers.

These precedents make it evident that in an Islamic state

a common citizen can file a case against the highest office bearer and bring him to the dock and can get his right restored. The power of the state that it can summon the greatest man to the court, makes its grip on the executive so firm that fear of facing the court alone becomes an effective vigilance and people's rights' are not jeopardized.

3. *Accountability Through Shura*

The importance and function of Shura has come for mention earlier. Here we shall take up only its aspect of calling the ruler to account. The function of the members of the Shura is not just .o express their opinion when the Amir calls them to opine on a certain issue. Their real job is to keep an eye on the activities of the government. They are the brain of the Ummah as well as its eyes. Their vigilant eye keeps back the person in authority from overstepping the limits of their powers and mis-appropriation of the public lands or the Bait-al-Mal. As a matter of fact every citizen of Islamic state Muslims in particular, have a right rather it is an injunction to them from God, that they speak the truth, enjoy what is good and spread it as far as they can, and put checks upon evils and do every thing in their power to keep their society on the path of justice and equity. But this duty devotes on the members of Shura most, who are elected only for this function in an Islamic state. In connection with management of the collective affairs of the believers they are the select addressees of the following instructions of God and His Prophet:

> Help ye one another in righteousness and peity, but help ye not one another in sin and transgression.
>
> Al Quran V 2.

> O ye who believe! fear God and always say a word directed to the Right. Al Quran XXXIII 70

> The Believers, men and women, are protectors of one another: they enjoin what is just, and forbid what is evil. Al Quran IX 71

The Prophet says:

> Whoever of you witnesses on evil should change it with the might of his arm. If he cannot do that, he should try to stop it by word of his mouth. And if even that is not possible, he should have a disgust for it and an urge to remove it. And this is the lowest degree of belief. Muslim, Tirmidi, and Abu Daud The most superior type of Jihad (striving in the way of Allah) is to say what is right before a despotic ruler. Abu Daud, Tirmidi, Nasai

There will be rulers coming after me. Whoever supports them in their falsehood and helps them in their tyranny is not from me and I am not from him (such a man has nothing to do with Islam and its teachings).

Shura in a way has ascendancy over the ruler. The latter is under obligation to consult the Shura, but the members of the Shura are not bound to express their opinion only when they are called by him for consultation. They can opine on the activities of the person in authority, give him useful suggestions and can call him to account publicity whenever they feel it is necessary to do so. Under these conditions it is not possible for the person in authority to do as he is pleased, to usurp somebody's right, or take coercive measures against the deserving.

4. *Accountability Through the People*

Islam does not allow the Ummah, after they have elected the Amir and the members of the Shura, to leave all the business of the state to them for their appointed term and remain unconcerned themselves and leaving them alone to do what they like until the next elections. Since the government is the most important and most effective and the riches in resources to achieve the objective for with each and every individual of the Ummah is striving with his life and resources, they can never afford to shirk the responsibility of vigilance, and from time to time taking stock of their performance with regard to achieving that objective. For them it is not just the problem of bread and butter, clothing and shelter. Much above that is the establishing of the Religion of God. Neither any individual of the Muslim Society can afford to squander the limited resources at his disposal and be guilty of betrayal of trust, nor allow others to go on recklessly washing the collective resources of the believers, entrusted to their charge.

It was the demonstration of this sense of responsibility that prompted Salman Farsi to object to 'Umar having two sheets of garments instead of one that everybody had received as his share, and publicly interrupting him and refusing to listen to his harangue, even knowing well enough how much 'Umar was given to sacrifice, public service and austere piety, and agreed to listen to him only when 'Umar had explained his possession of an additional sheet as a gift from his son, who also testified to it on the spot.

Similarly, the old woman had publicly opposed 'Umar in his declared intention of delimiting the power of women, asking him to remain within the limits of his powers and not to meddle with a right conferred on women by Allah.

The rightly guided caliph never tried to crush this sense of calling their rulers to account. Rather, they encouraged it. Abu Bakr in his inaugural public address, on taking, over as the first caliph of the Prophet, had said, "If I keep on to the right path in my conduct (of managing your affairs) cooperate with me. But if I fail in that, do correct me (with .force)." Similarly, 'Umar, his immediate successor, just to test the sense and the power of the people of holding to account their rulers, once said to a gathering: "What will you do if I slacken in my vigilance, and adopt a policy of drift in the management of your affairs?" Bishr bin-e-Sad stood up and drawing his sword from its scabbord said:

> "We shall behead you?" 'Umar feigned to get angry and said to him rebukingly. "Does thou say that about

me regardless of my high position?" He said with emphasis," "Yes you, you and none else." Umar was very much pleased with this bold reply and said, "Thank God, there are men among my people who will drag me to the right path were I ever to digress from it.

The same was the course adopted by. 'Uthman and 'Ali. Uthman was the target of criticism but he never tried to stop the wagging tongues through bribe or coercion. The Khazrites went to the extent of virtuperation in case of 'Ali, and even threatened to kill him but he took no notice of it and said, "Verbal demonstration of antagonism was not enough to justify any action against them."

Along with all these means of the accountability of those in authority, it should also be borne in mind that Islam has not limited its sphere of vigilance to Public Affairs alone, but the Private Affairs too are encompassed by it. In the matter of Maroof and Munkar: Literally means alien to human nature. In the Islamic terminology it includes acts, attitudes and behaviours for which men of wholesome nature in every age and under any order, true or false and corrupt, have, had abhorrance. Barring the few perverts, nobody ever approved and acclaimed falsehood, breach of trust, tyranny and injustice and other evils.

The fundamental rule of Islam is that whatever is determined for the collection is equally bad for the individual. A crime committed secretly is no less an evil than one committed openly. If drinking and gambling in public are cognizable offences, they are just as much cognizable in the privacy of a hotel, a club or one's own home. Since the law of the Islamic Shariah does not divide life into two compartments of individual and collective (public and private. Tr) associating itself with only one of them but encompasses the whole of it, and does not allow the private life of an individual to be ruined through pursuit of lusts by excluding it from its sphere of vigilance. It was in keeping with this principle that the lives of the Prophet, the rightly guided caliphs and other companions were exposed to public view.

After this review of the fundamental concepts of the status of the person in authority, the conditions of his election, the limitation of his powers, the limits of obedience to him and all the measures of holding him to account one can have an idea how powerful and effective are the safeguards against usurpation of the fundamental rights in the Islamic society. And the great wealth of peace and security, prosperity and satisfaction of those groups of people and the territory to which these protections are afforded, can only be imagined. Did the Islamic order last only thirty years?

While studying the safeguards provided for the fundamental rights in Islam a pertinent question can arise in the mind of the reader that with all these powerful and all-pervading protective measures, how Islam came by this tragedy that its unparalleled order of Justice and Equality could not survive the brief span of thirty years' of the rule of the rightly guided caliphate. The spirit of democracy came to an end during this short period. Monarchy came to have full sway over the democratic order. The Ummah had no say in the election of the caliph. Inherited monarchy usurped the place of elected caliphate. Bait-al-Mal was no more a public trust controlled by the believers, but became the personal property of the rulers.

The order of the Shura, freedom of self expression, and the freedom of the judiciary also ended with the other institutions. The tribal and territorial prejudices raised their heads and murders, plunder, bloodshed and tyranny and oppression made their appearance here in the Islamic order in all those forms in which it would have existed in any other un-Islamic system of government. During the dynasties of Banu Umayyah and Banu Abbas and the following period such incidents came to be of common occurrence which could not be called by any other name but tyranny. What explanation can be offered for this remarkable change? And does this change not prove that the Islamic order could survive only thirty years after the Prophet's death, and failed after that period?

This question appears very pertinent and weighty enough in the light of the historical facts. But in fact it is based on a misunderstanding. Such questions come to the minds of those who regard Islam and the behaviour of the Muslims as one and the same thing, when it is a fact that Islam has an entity of its own quite independent of its votaries. Its principles and rules and regulation are themselves arguments in its favour. The behaviour of the Muslims is not a criterion to judge Islam. Rather, the opposite is the case. The behaviour of the Muslims shall be judged on the criteria provided by Islam to see to which category of the votaries of Islam they belong, and how far they are sincere in their assertions of devotion to Islam. It would not be proper to take Muslims for other peoples and nations of the world. If their true position is properly understood there would be no justification for posting their misdeeds to the ledge of the Islamic order.

The other states of the world are themselves sovereigns in their states. So the royal farmans issued by their kings, the laws framed by their parliaments and other legislatures, the orders promulgated by their rulers and the decisions pronounced by their courts have the position of an authority and arguments in their favour. And as we have already explained under the discussion of constitution in these states law is another name for the will of the rulers. The law has no independent entity of its own beyond the state and its manipulations. Rather, it is bound by their wishes. If the law in vogue obstructs their path in taking any step, they clear it through amending that law or replacing it by another serving their purpose. And then this amended or new law becomes an authority. The former law becomes cancelled since it is no more effective, and has no legal position in the courts. Now reference is made to the new or the amended law, and it remains in force so long as afresh one does not come to take its place. This process of legislation only keeps the entire legal system involved in regular amendments, cancellation, limitations and suspensions, but also serves as an authority to make any law effective or ineffective. And in this entire process at no stage the legislator is considered law-breakers. The courts go on discarding the laws cancelled by the legislators and decide the legal cases on the basis of the latest legislation.

As against this, in Islam, neither any rulers of the Muslims nor the Ummah as a whole enjoys the position of legislator. Their power of legislation is conditioned by due regard for the spirit of the Quran and the Sunnah. Those of their rulers who turned away from the Quran and the Sunnah, promulgated laws contrary to Islam or adopted an attitude in direct conflict with the injunctions of God on His Prophet, their position is that of rebels, traitors and law-breakers. They have been much more despicable to the Muslims themselves than to others, and the Muslims have in fact adopted this very attitude towards them. The orders and laws promulgated by them could never become a part of the Islamic legal code. They could never attain the position of authority and argument.

Their authority could not bring about the slightest change in the law of the Shariah, which has a separate entity of its own independent of and beyond the powers of the state. The Muslims recognized and accepted the decisions of only those Muslim rulers as precedents who strictly followed the law of the Shariah. They recognized as authority the orders and decisions of only 'Umar bin-e-Abdul-Aziz among the rulers of Banu Umayyah. Among the Banu Abbas no ruler was considered worthly of consideration in this respect. And only the collection of edicts that Aurangazeb among the Mughal emperors of India got compiled under his own supervision found its way into the books on Muslim jurisprudence. But his grandfather, Akbar's Din-e-Elahi was despised and rejected in his own period. In the Islamic history extending every fourteen centuries, the laws framed by the monarchs and dictators were never considered worthy of notice even. And as against this the laws framed by the lowly and ascetic legists like Imam Abu Hanifa, Imam Malik, Imam Hanbal and Imam Shafii which had been derived from the Quran and Sunnah attained the position of Law, and today Muslims all over the world follows these four schools of the Islamic jurisprudence. In the subcontinent upto the middle of the nineteenth century this Fiqh (jurisprudence) was the law in the courts, and even during the British period justice was dispensed in the courts according to this law where the personal matters of the Muslims were concerned.

In short, the law of the Islamic Shariah has never been cancelled or suspended during any period of history. Even the kings abided by its laws. Their person could not become the fountain-head of law. Few of them like Akbar tried to invent Din-e-Elahi in opposition to the law of the Shariah, and tried to thrust it on people but could not succeed in his attempt. The law framed by him also got buried with him. The Muslim millat (community) never allowed that it should be absorbed in the law of the Shariah.

Undoubtedly, there were remarkable changes in the system of governance. The concept of vicegerancy and trust that was the guiding spirit of the Islamic state disappeared. The delegated authority got converted into personal authority, and then commenced that long drawn series of tyranny and mischief with which every student of history is well acquainted. But how can any one infer from the historical facts that Islam failed them? The historical record is the record of the failure of the Muslims and not that of Islam. How can the objectionable or disgraceful behaviour of any Muslim ruler or a Muslim group be regarded as the failure of Islam? And how does it prove that the measures provided by Islam for the protection of the fundamental rights became ineffective after thirty years?

Every creed, ideology, school of thought, principle or tradition really depends for its efficacy or inefficacy on the firmness of the belief and faith and living upto it. This is the first and foremost condition to bring into play the effects and fruits of any system or ideology. Without fulfilling this basic condition of the firmness of creed and obligation of living upto it, no system or ideological way of life can bear fruit.

Truth is admittedly the best principle of life. But can we be benefited by its blessings without taking to truth of speech in practical life. If it is not so, would it be proper to decide in face of the abundance of falsehood and the majority turning away from the truth, that the principle of truth has become ineffective, since it has failed to make itself binding on a large number of people. And would we be justified in advising people to give up truth on the plea that the majority of people do not practise it? Or will those banishing it from their lives be deemed despicable and guilty, and every sensible and conscious person will advise this defaulting majority to give up the apparently very effective falsehood and talking to truth, make it effective?

In fact, it is man's own belief and conscious resolve and effort which give their effectiveness to principles and ideologies. Without this spirit of belief and exercise, every principle and every ideology is no more than a collection of words. The British unwritten constitution is considered as the ideally democratic constitution. But do mere abstract words of the constitution have all the effectiveness and force to make them as practicable, useful if enforced in any Asian or African country as they have proved in Britain? If not, who will be held responsible for failure of the constitution or the nation that made it a failure through its own behaviour.

The failure of a way of life and the failure in giving effect to it are two different things, which should not be mixed up. We can declare any system a failure only when the answer to any one of the following questions is in the affirmative.

1. Has experience proved it defective and useless?

2. Has the advanced knowledge and discernment of man proved wrong the principles presented by it, in the light of intellect and reasoning?
3. Has man discovered better and more practicable principles than these?
4. Has the long journey of history made them outdated and impracticable?
5. Has it become so much deformed and perverted that it is no more possible to sort out the right from the wrong elements?

None of these questions can be answered in the positive where Islam is concerned. Islam in practice has proved itself superior to all other systems of life in the world. Which is that ideological way of life, ancient or modern which has, in comparison to Islam, during the thirty years of its enforcement might have brought about such a magnificent revolution of justice and equality and prosperity and goodness? Islam alone has the distinction of not only remaining in force for thirty years with its true spirit and teachings but attained its ideal form. No other system could be enforced in its ideal form on this earth even for a second.

Thirty years is not a brief period for the practical experiment with any ideology. Which of the Islamic principles or regulations were proved wrong during this period of trial? Which are those defects, if at all any, have been discovered? Again, has man really discovered any system superior to it? We have earlier in this book, taking stock of Islam and other systems of life, seen that the utmost that human intellect has been able to present does stand no where in comparison with Islam. There are no valid reasons to declare Islam outdated and impracticable. Historical facts provide ample evidence that whenever Islam was into practice strictly in accordance with the conditions imposed by it, the Muslim society came to enjoy all the blessings of the rightly guided caliphate, and Islam once again appeared in its true form and full glory. The evils that had crept into the political system of Islam after the rightly guided caliphate, have been mentioned earlier. But with all the corruption and perversion about sixty years after the rightly guided caliphate, when 'Umar Abd-ul-Aziz was installed into the seat of authority, and removing all the traces of monarchy, resolved to enforce once again the Islamic order with its original spirit, the entire society was revolutionised.

The Islamic revolution was brought about anew in all its full former glory, and it appeared that the period of the rightly guided caliphate had returned. This proves that Islam had not failed them, but the Muslims, and particularly their rulers had become victims of inaction and negligence in the matter of living upto it. When after sixty years, he made a firm resolve to reform the practice of Islam, and tried it all over again, he found the system just as true, dynamic and fruitful as regards the results, as it had proved during its first trial by the rightly guided caliphate. And after thirteen centuries, when Syed Ahmad Shaheed wanted to enforce it in his short-lived Islamic state in Peshawar it came into action with all its comprehensiveness and perfection, and not one of its principles proved—impracticable.

It is neither the case with Islam that its teachings have become so much perverted that sorting out the sound from the unsound is no more possible. The Quran has been preserved for us without the change of an iota in it. Each and every incident of the life of the Prophet, every deed and word of his have been so carefully preserved of which there is no other example in the world. The period of the rightly guided caliphate history has preserved in its pages like the true image in a mirror. The work done in the field of the Islamic Fiqh (jurisprudence) by the (most capable men of the) Ummah is there in its original form. Moreover, detailed literature for guidance exists concerning every walk of life and on all the problems of the modern age. Any person wanting to know what are the Islamic teachings on a particular issue, would find difficulty in access to them? The fundamental teachings of Islam and its principles and laws are before us in a very clear and definite form. No part of them has been perverted and none became ambiguous. In other words, the thing known as Islam, has been with us on the highway of history continually for the last fourteen hundred years without any defects. During this long journey Muslims at times remained very close to Islam and at others too far from it. But it was never their sad experience that the Muslims intended to come close to Islam but finding it non-existent or buried in the pages of history. They had failed to do so.

Under these circumstances the objection levelled at Islam that it lasted only thirty years aims at creating misunderstanding and nothing more. The fact is only this much that the Muslims lived up to the dictates of Islam with their heart and soul in it, for thirty years only. Later on their political system got corrupted and corruptions formed in the society. But the question may be asked how did it effect the soundness of Islam. On what basis was it regarded impracticable? Does the presence of certain kings and dictators in the Islamic history prevent us from putting true Islam into practice? Shall we be justified in putting up the excuse that since people like Hajjaji b. Yusuf and Hassan b. Sabab have stood between us and the rightly guided caliphate, it will not be possible to rehearse the order of that period once again? After all, what is the relevance of the activities of the rulers and monarchs in the context of the mutual relations between Islam and the Muslims? The Muslims never established any relation with them for guidance.

The common man among the Muslims does not remember their names even. Their orders and edicts were never considered worth mentioning even or making reference to them in any matter. As against this, even the Muslim children are acquainted with the names of the rightly guided caliphs, the eminent companions, and the four Imams of the most popular schools of jurisprudence, Abu Hanifah, Malik, Shafii, and Ahmad b. Hanbal, as also Imam Bukhari, Ibn-e-Taimiyah, Ghazzali, Shah Wali-Ullah and such other Muslim elite in the religious sphere, since these personages, right from the time of the Prophet, have relevance in the matter of transferring to the Muslims their religious legacy and in maintaining continuity of their attachment to Islam. It was due to them that the Muslims never lost contact with the contemporary world and Islam never evaded contemporary problems. It has been advancing in every age with the times and offering guidance to the Muslims in every age.

Now let us take stock of the objection that the Islamic order lasted only thirty years, from another angle. This objection is applicable to the political system of Islam and that too only partially. But the individual and collective life of the Muslims in general has always been subservient to Islam. The Islamic law has been at work in their moral, social, educational, private, cultural and judicial aspects of life. Their political life, too has not been altogether cut off from Islam. Under the Islamic order the religion and politics never parted ways as they did in the Christian Church and the state in Europe, When the ascendancy of the Church ended in Europe, the state totally banished religion from the collective life and limited it to the individual life. The legislative powers of the state were no more governed by the religious injunctions and rules and regulations. The philosophy of secularism freed it from the hold of religion on it. As against this, in the entire history of the Muslims before the period of colonialism, there is not one example where a Muslim monarch or any ruler completely suspending the law of the Shariah might have enforced the law framed by himself. The Muslim monarch did violate the law of the Shariah, but consigning it to the care of the mosque and the *Madrasa* (religious bodies and institutions), they never became totally unconcerned with the law of the Shariah. The law of their states was the law of the Shariah, and all the affairs of the life of the people were decided by the courts according to the law. All the Muslim monarchs were not tyrant, oppressor, and given to a life of ease and luxury, voluptuousness and de bauchery. There have been among them many who are famous for their piety, righteousness and austerity. There have been kings like Nasiruddin Mahmood and Aurangzeb who had imposed upon themselves austere piety and never touched the public treasury where their own upkeep was concerned.

They prepared caps and made copies of the holy Quran for their own and their families, subsistence. A majority of them we find just Godfearing and mindful of their people.. Their characters bore a deep imprint of Islam. Undoubtedly they were far superior to the contemporary monarchs of the non-Muslim world. Since we judge them on the norm of the rightly guided caliphate, they appear low in our estimate, but compared with the contemporary rulers and their systems of governance with the contemporary systems of governance in the world, their position becomes entirely changed.

These facts amply reveal the truth that the objection levelled at Islam that it lasted only thirty years, is incorrect. It would, however, be correct to say that the Muslim Ummah could not maintain it at the level of the rightly guided caliphate in the sphere of practice. But we would like to repeat our question to these fault-finding people that if a firm resolve is made today to enforce Islam in it pristine purity what is there that stands in our way. Is it the fault of Islam or the evil intentions of those drunk with the lust for power and intoxication of ruling over fellowmen as their god?

Another objection raised in connection with the "failure" of Islam by the orientalists and their camp followers among the Muslims, is this that in the Islamic society of the early period after the Prophet, political, economic, judicial and social institutions could not come into existence or at least could take no definite mould on whose basis a definite structure of the Islamic system of governance could emerge. The Islamic society according to its structure was a rather advanced type of the tribal society in which the central position of the tribal chief had been taken by the caliph. In this type of personal rule, the reigns of the state were in the hands of an individual who managed all the affairs of the state from his seat of authority in the mosque.

He distributed the spoils of war, issued orders and instructions to the governors and the military commanders, received their reports of their performance, dictated replies to their queries, supplied them with the necessary resources, gave a hearing to their complaints, helped the common people in distress, settled their disputes and furnished guidance in matters relating to jurisprudence. Since every body had access to the caliph, they approached him directly with their major and even minor problems. In this way, the caliph came to have a central position and centralization of powers instead of decentralization obstructed the path of the autonomous and semi-autonomous institutions coming into existence. Since the rightly guided caliphs were extremely pious, righteous and selfless and with God-fearing heads of the state, every thing was in its proper place and the affairs of the state ran smoothly.

But, when the rulers who were shorn of that selflessness excellence and the magnanimity and purity of character of their predecessors, came into power, this system which had not been based on firmly established institutions rapidly deteriorated and so many evils found their way into it.

This objection is based more on prejudice than on ignorance of facts. And the real motive behind it is this aspiration of the west that all the credit of the concept of human rights, the movement launched for their attainment, and like the philosophy of democracy credit for the political, economic and social institutions should be added to this account alone. Otherwise the fact is that during the period of the rightly guided caliphate, particularly during the period of Umar, the foundations of the Islamic state had been firmly established on well-founded institutions, and during the period of Banu Umayyah and Banu Abbas these institutions became much more expanded and much better organized.

Protection by Law

After taking stock of the rights in the democratic and socialist countries we shall now see how far have the protections provided for the practical enforcement of the fundamental rights by these countries been effective and have succeeded in protecting the individual against the oppression and tyranny of the State.

In the western system of law and politics, constitution is regarded as the greatest protector of these rights, and the effective form of their practical enforcement suggested is the inclusion of these rights in the constitution and making them enforceable through the judiciary. On the surface it appears very effective and in some Western countries, particularly Britain, America and France, it is in fact so in a big way. Nearly all the countries of the world act on the constitutional method of rule, and the people regard the most sacred legal document of the constitution as their great source of strength. But when we analyse the constitutions of various countries and study the course of events in these countries, the fact is revealed that the constitution which is considered the greatest protector of the fundamental rights is itself not immune from the usurpatory and plundering action of the government.

Barring America and Britain, whose written and unwritten constitutions we shall discuss later on a look at the constitution of any country of the world, will show that there is a whole chapter of "Constitutional amendments", through which the ruling party with the requisite majority and the appropriate modus operandi gets a free hand in amending the constitution and moulding it according to its own wishes and requirements. In this way these constitutions, which usually get framed by the majority party or under its aegis arm this party with unbridled and unlimited powers to rule in a dictatorial fashion. And usually they see to it that in the early stages of constitution making the firmness and definiteness of the constitution are badly damaged so that what remains is a rickety business. Dorothy Pickles analysing this state of affairs writes:

> Constitutions are made by politicians who are bound by their loyalty to their own party doctrines and attitudes, and sometimes in addition by the requirements of coalition governments.

The basic philosophy of a constitutional government is that the sphere of the powers of the rulers may be delimited and they must be made to abide by it. And if they overstep their well-defined powers, the judiciary should prevent them from doing it. But we find that the practical shape of things is just the opposite. The judiciary which is entrusted with the responsibility of keeping over-bearing rulers in their place, itself comes to work under the constitution framed by these same rulers and politicians and the powers conferred by them. What is, after all, the fountain-head of the powers of the judiciary? That same constitution in framing which it has had no say, and which is constantly tampered with by the rulers in the form of amendments, and abrogations, pruning and suspension; which serves no other purpose except to nationally limit the powers, which after all they manipulate to suit to their wishes and motives.

More so by amending some clauses or by including some others and deleting yet another or by declaring a state of emergency and exercising the powers acquired under it, they suspend the concerned sections and then in case of the enforcement of new laws, effective with retrospective effect, they find a way for every desired move at their own sweet will. The judiciary, whose powers are constantly changing due to frequent amendments and deletions in the constitution, can never stand in the way of the rulers, since the legislature has ascendency over it, and this legislature is overridden by the ruling party by virtue of its brute majority. The Supreme Court of Pakistan, in the case State versus Zia-ur Rahman, elucidating the sphere of the power of the judiciary has remarked in its judgement:

> While it is true that judicial power cannot be taken away, the jurisdiction of the functionaries entrusted with the administration of justice can legitimately be defined by the Constitution. Thus it is for the Constitution to say what jurisdiction the High Court will exercise and what the Supreme Court. Similarly, the Constitution itself may even prescribe that certain categories of classes of cases shall be decided by Tribunals other than the High Court or the Supreme Court. No objection can be taken to this kind of demarcation of functions. Indeed, if such demarcation is not done, there would be chaos, for, no one would know what are the precise limits of their own respective jurisdictions.

Now, it is evident that the determination of these powers is in the hands of the legislators, or in other words, the rulers. Therefore the courts are bound to conduct their business of dispensation of justice with these limited powers, which the rulers are pleased to confer on them. It is the result of this bitter truth that even such measures of the rulers which totally pervert the spirit of the constitution, are regarded as perfectly in keeping with the constitution since they can always find legal justification for amending it, and in this way a step that was prohibited and illegal till yesterday, would become justifiable and legal the next day only because of an amendment in the constitution. No moral principle or any well known code of justice and equity comes in the way of effecting such changes. The court is simply bound by the codified law and not by any moral code. So we find that the Supreme Court while pronouncing its verdict in the case of Brigadier (retd.) F.B.Ali and Colonel (retd.) Abdul Aleem Afridi, has written:

> It is first sought to be contended that the Ordinances were not law at all, because, they purported to unreasonably deprive a citizen of even the norms of a judicial trial. But this generalization cannot be accepted. Law has not been defined in the Constitution of 1962 and, therefore, in its generally accepted connotation, it means positive law, that is to say, a formal pronouncement of the will of a competent law-giver. There is no such condition that a law must, in order to qualify as a law, also be based on reason or morality. The Courts cannot strike down a law on any such higher ethical notion nor can Courts act on the basis of philosophical concept of law as pointed by me in the case of Asma Jilani.

In the circumstances, I too find myself unable to say that the impugned Ordinances are not law, and, therefore, violative of Fundamental Right No. I.

Now, where the codified law enjoys such supremacy, and the law itself is the formal declaration of the Law-givers, will and 'pleasure, the courts can provide the citizen with only that much of protection as has been permitted to them by the limits of the powers approved by the constitution in force for the time being and the ordinance issued by the rulers. How shall these laws be deemed legal or illegal? Expounding this point, the Chief Justice of the Supreme Court, Justice Hamid-ur-Rahman says in the case of Asma Jilani.

So far as a Judge is concerned, a definition is necessary, all that he has to see is that the law which he is called upon to administer is made by a person or authority legally competent to make laws and the law is capable of being enforced by the legal machinery. This, in my view, brings in the notion both of legitimacy and efficacy.

The supremacy of the rulers in the matter of framing the constitution or in sphere of the legislation, and the determination of the powers and jurisdiction of the judiciary also being in their hands, makes it clear how helpless in fact the judiciary is before the framers of the constitution and law. The raw deal received by the provisions of the constitution relating to the fundamental rights in Bangaldesh, India and Pakistan in the later half of 1975 is clear proof of the helplessness of the judiciary in the matter of protecting these rights.

In Bangaldesh, Mujib established the dictatorship of a single party, put a ban on other opposition parties and incarcerated their leaders, gagged the press, made the legislative assembly a non-entity and by depriving the judiciary of the powers of enforcing the fundamental rights, made it wholly ineffective, but all this was held as perfectly constitutional. In India, when Mrs. Indira Gandhi, in order to save herself from the penalty of winning the election through malpractices, tried to render ineffective the decision of the court against her, the majority of the ruling party in the parliament amended the constitution and thus provided her protection.

The powers of the judiciary were curtailed, the opposition parties were banned, Indira's opponent in the elections Raj Narain, who had won the case against her in the High Court and his supporters in the political field were all put behind the bars, declaring a state of emergency all the fundamental rights were held suspended and the newspapers raising voice against all this were throttled to death. When all this was over, Indira's advocate, Mr.A.K. Sen stood in the highest court of the country, but shorn of powers, and said:

> "The concept of free and fair elections is notional and it cannot be treated as a basic feature of the constitution. The courts are not competent to sit in judgement whether the elections were conducted fairly and in a free atmosphere or not.

And this entire game, too, was played under the constitution and the powers conferred by it. Therefore the supreme court, which was bound by the amended constitution for its decisions had to exhonerate Mrs. Gandhi of all the malpractices the High Court had held her guilty of and penalised under the unamended constitution.

In our own country, Pakistan, where the fourth constitution is now in force, simultaneously with its enforcement, the fundamental rights were suspended under a state of emergency. Later on, through an ordinance and by means of the fourth and fifth amendments they were curtailed. As the declaration of the state of emergency, issue promulgation of ordinance and the series of amendments in the constitution were also under the powers conferred by the constitution, all this was regarded as constitutional. And by virtue of this constitutionality the rulers cannot be charged with the commission of any offence by the law court.

The same state of affairs exists in other countries of Asia, Africa and South America where the constitution, instead of acting as the protector of fundamental rights, has become the protector of the dictatorial authority of the rulers, supporter of their tyrannical measures and a means of unlimited powers for them. Commenting on this state of affairs CD. Kernig says:

> In the 20th century, however, the representatives of the people have themselves often proved to be unreliable where the safeguarding of fundamental rights was concerned. Not infrequently majorities have modified the fundamental rights laid down in the constitutions, and with them often the entire constitution itself.

Every constitution in the world along with giving a free hand to the rulers to amend the constitution, under a "state of emergency" confers such powers on them in a state of emergency which enables them to do away with what little remains of the fundamental rights. And then for a state of emergency the existence of objective conditions is not necessary. The rulers can declare it at their discretion whenever they feel like doing so. And immediately after such declaration, the constitution frees them of all the limits imposed by it under normal condition. They can impose martial law under the constitution, can deprive the judiciary of all its powers and the people of all their fundamental rights. Neither the constitution nor the law of the land can stop them from doing such things.

In addition to these shortcomings of the constitution and its helplessness before the rulers, there is the problem of its very existence and survival which is a much more complicated one. It is a commonplace phenomenon, and we have a very bitter experience of it here in Pakistan, that the change of government, internal revolutions, rebellion of the army, external aggression, and the irreconciliable differences between the political parties, all give the constitution the sack.

With every outgoing ruling party or person the constitution enforced by it also departs, and every newcomer appears on the stage of power with the draft of a new constitution, and the powers of political authority which he wields, confer the same legal position on this new constitution, which in its predecessor's time was occupied by the earlier constitution In the Asma Jilani case, referring to the international law the learned Chief Justice of the Supreme Court observed:

> According to the international law a victorious revolution or a successful coup detat is an internationally recognised legal method of changing a Constitution.

Factual evidence and this elucidation of international Law can give us an idea how frail, uncertain and unstable the legal document called the constitution is, notwithstanding it distinguished position of supremacy. When its own existence is not guaranteed, how much trust can be reposed in it for the protection of the fundamental rights, which are part and parcel of it? How can the constitution, which is itself constantly mutatory, become a protector of immutable and inalienable human rights?

This also makes it evident that the claim of the inalienability of the fundamental rights is not correct. The only means of determining and enforcing these rights is the constitution. Without constitution these rights have no legal basis left for their existence. And the constitution is a puppet whose strings are in the hands of the government. At times it is amended at others something is added to it, at yet other times some portions of it are curtailed or suspended and so often it departs alongwith the outgoing rulers. Under these changing conditions, the fundamental rights at times find a place in the constitution, at others they get abridged, at yet other times they are suspended and now and then alongwith the abrogated constitution they themselves get eliminated. If the inhabitants of a country are lucky in having them intact, the traps of the varying interpretations given to them make them ineffective. In principle they are much above that common law, but their enforcement is always "in keeping with the law", and within the limits of the constitution the are made lawful with the addition of prefixes and suffixes like 'if, but', 'provided', 'unless' etc. And this law is put into practice according to the will of the rulers, C. D. Kernig writes in this context:

> That fundamental rights are rooted in the texts of modern constitutions and yet have always been subject to interpretation "according to law" (although in essence they are considered to be inviolable).

It is the result of this accord with the law that the fundamental rights regarded as inalienable and inviolable can be suspended merely by enforcing section 144 of the criminal procedure code by a Deputy Commissioner (or Collector) of a district and the constitution is unable to come to the rescue of the affected citizens.

This helplessness and inconsistency of the constitution

clearly indicates that it is not a reliable protector of the fundamental rights. Nor is there any ground to regard these fundamental rights as inviolable on the basis of guarantees provided in the constitution.

After this general survey of the position regarding the enforcement of the constitution in the world, let us now have a look at the British and American constitutions also, which are deemed the best model of democracy, and at the first sight the form of their enforcement also appears fairly satisfactory.

In Britain no written constitution exists at all. Therefore these fundamental rights there are not guaranteed constitutionally. The British parliament is a sovereign body. Its legislative powers suffer no limitations whatsoever. No court in England can strike down the laws enacted by the British parliament, nor can it stop their enforcement. There, the fundamental rights are protected by the common law of the land, and for their enforcement one has to go only to the common law courts. But in spite of having no written constitution, in the matter of fundamental rights, the British citizens are much better placed than the citizens of other countries of the world. That is why Jennings says with great pride:

> In Britain we have no Bill of Rights; we merely have liberty according to law: and we think—truly, I believe—that we do the job better than any country which has a Bill of Rights or a Declaration of the Rights of Man.

But this satisfaction is gradually declining, and the legal experts in Britain are stressing the need of a written constitution for the protection of fundamental rights. Thomas Paine was the first person to realize this need, who had written in a very sarcastic manner, in 1971, in his book *Human Rights*:

> The boasted English constitution is a fraud: it does not really exist at all:

> One member says this is constitution, and another says that is constitution, it is one thing, tomorrow it is something else while maintaining the debate proves there is none.

A prestigious British journal *The Economist* in its issue of November 8, 1975 had written in its latest survey report on fundamental rights:

> Twenty years earlier, the assertion that "Britain had the best position in regard to the fundamental rights", appeared very strong. The supporters of this claim can bring in their support to the argument that during the passage of the reformative bills on abortion, divorce and racial discrimination, the parliament has established a commendable record in the matter of its regard for the civic rights. But now the conservatives will put forth the examples of delimiting the rights of property and restrictions on membership of the unions. And the supporters of the labour party in the same vein shall out forth the law of the migrants passed by the conservatives with retrospective effect and the restrictions imposed by their Industrial Relations Act on the right to strike work.

"Moreover, there are some other aspects in which the law of land is opposed to the general principles of the international law rather the European convention for the Human Rights. One such example is the power of preventive detention of the suspected people under the law of Prevention of Terrorism. This law has been passed by the parliament in November 1947.

According to this report the liberal member of the parliament Alien Beith introduced a bill in the parliament to invite attention to the distressing fact that the document of European Convention for Human Rights which Britain had signed twenty years ago, had not till then been brought on Britain's statute book.

A protracted struggle between the parliament and the king in Britain has resulted in the king getting divested of all powers and being replaced by the parliament as a dictatorial body since there are no limits of any sort on its powers of legislation, whereas the constitution's only purpose is to keep the rulers's powers within proper limits. And today this aspect is the cause of greatest anxiety. *The Economist*, analysing the problem of the fundamental rights in Britain writes: "A law relating to rights can be passed and for its protection a constitutional Court can also be established with powers to declare certain law against the fundamental rights, but the real difficulty is that if in spite of these powers of the court, the parliament enacts a law that is unconstitutional, what can the helpless court do to remedy the ill. Can it enforce its verdict against the parliament? At the most it can declare a certain law unconstitutional. But to kill the powerful giant of the strong tradition of the parliament's supremacy is not so easy." The analyst arrives finally at the following conclusion: (p. 25)

A satisfactory Bill of Rights depends on the change in the political system and particularly the system of holding elections, the effects of the rival partisanship arising from this system and the effects on the mutual relations between the government and the Parliament. In other words before any Bill of Rights a constitutional document will be needed. (p. 25)

Throwing light on the general trend of the public opinion, this report tells us that in the decade beginning from 1970, the campaign for the demand of the Fundamental Rights has been gathering momentum and from 1974 onward, it has become intensive. The Ministry of Interior is now having consultations with other government departments whether such a law is going to be practicable and will receive general appreciation.

Since Britain is regarded as the cradle of democracy, and most countries of the world including Pakistan, where parliamentary system of government is in vogue, follow the British pattern. Therefore, it will be in the fitness of things that we have a look at the opinions of those demanding the Bill of Rights, so that we may have an idea of what the Britishers themselves think of their Constitution.

The well-known legal expert, D.W. Hanson commenting on the supremacy of the Parliament with reference to the greatest charter of human rights, the "Magna Carta", says:

> From a legal point of view, the most important event is this that the Barons did not allow their antagonistic political role to follow the path of the principle of the common law. As against this they adopted a course, as a result of which, a political compromise was arrived at between the Lords and the common members of the Parliament. That is why to solve the problem of Double Majesty, which had arisen powerfully in the seventeenth century, instead of the supremacy of the law, the idea of the supremacy of the Parliament was adopted. This supremacy of the parliament has deprived the fundamental rights of the protection of the constitution and has left them entirely at the mercy of conventions.

The well known legal expert, a former judge and dean of the Faculty of Law in Birmingham University, Professor Hood Phillips, writes:

> "The British constitution contains 'Fundamental' rights in the strict sense. The principles relating to individual's liberty can be altered by ordinary act of Parliament, and there is no legal limit to the extent to which Parliament can abridge or abolish rights which in many constitutions are regarded as fundamental."

In this connection, citing the examples of the performances of the parliament, he tells us that the parliament passing the Defence of the Realm Act, during the first world war and during the second world war the Emergency powers Defence Act, conferred on the government such extensive powers encompassing all aspects of the national defence and economy which are unparalleled in the history of parliaments. Later, in

1940, another act was passed which passed through all the stages of discussions and readings in the Houses and the royal sanction in just one day. Through this act the citizens were bound to surrender their lives, properties and services to His Majesty. In 1920 under conditions of peace, to arm the government with the emergency powers, an Act was brought into existence under which civic liberties could be suspended by declaring a state of emergency during internal turmoil and chaotic conditions. This law has been pressed into service several times in cases of strikes by the labour at the ports and the employees of transport department and power houses.

Professor Phillips explaining the real cause of insistence on the supremacy of parliament and denial of a written constitution to the nation, says:

> It has invited the leaders of both sides in the political 'game' giving inordinate power to the Prime Minister of the day, which will be inherited by the leader of the opposition in due course, while the general public are apathetic or unaware.

After taking stock of the British constitution in detail, he arrives at the following conclusion:

> A written Constitution with judicial review is desirable for this country. We have seen that there are no legal limits to what Parliament can do by ordinary legislation, that the Government virtually controls the activities of Parliament, that the maximum "duration of a Parliament is too long, that the existence of a (reformed) Second Chamber with some power of rejection or delay is essential, that important areas of law and practice are uncertain, that the Parliament Act 1949 is of doubtful force, that too much power is concentrated in the hands of the Prime Minister, that the dissolution of Parliament needs to be regulated, that the law relating to judicial tenure should be

improved, and that there is a call for a new Bill of Rights

A judge of Britain, Sir Leslie Scarman, exposing the respect for the fundamental rights, observes:

> Do you think that the deeply disturbing practices of interrogation to which rest was had in Northern Ireland would have occurred had Birtish law possessed at the time fully developed code of human rights.

Making a demand for the Bill of Rights he says:

> If human rights are to be protected in a manner consistent with our international obligations, some means other than the common law must be found. Legally at the mercy of a legislature, which is itself, save in a minority situation, at the mercy of the executive, is no sure guarantee of human right.

Without a Bill of Right protected from repeals, amendment or suspension by the ordinary process of a bare Parliamentary majority controlled by the government of the day, human rights will be at risk.

J.J.Craik Henderson, exposing the sovereignty of the parliament says:

> Perhaps instead of referring to a supreme Parliament it might be more correct to say that the Cabinet is supreme in the exercise of Executive power and of law making through its control of the majority Party in the House of Commons.

Expressing his dissatisfaction over the present protections in connection with the fundamental rights, he goes on to say:

> If one could be sure that Ministers could be relied on to observe the niceties and conventions of the constitution and always to act wisely, then a strong Executive and a flexible constitution giving all power

> to the Cabinet would be best, but unfortunately nobody can be sure of this and accordingly some safeguards ought to be provided.

The campaign now going on in Britain for the constitutional safeguards to the fundamental rights. Professor Charles' Howard Macllwain of the Harward University, had foretold in 1947. He says:

> As the restraining influence of tradition grows weaker, the danger of a tyranny of the majority comes nearer and the time may arrive when convention must give way to law if the rights of minorities are to be respected and safeguarded as they have been in the past. A popular despotism must result if the omnipotence of parliament ever becomes in practice what it now is in law.

And today the Britons are witnessing emergence of that dictatorship. And it is for this reason that they are carrying on a campaign for a written constitution and a Bill of Rights so that dictatorship may be checked and it may be brought and kept under the judiciary. It is really strange, but a fact, that not only in Britain, but even in its colonies like Canada, New Zealand and Australia no where the fundamental rights have constitutional safeguards. In Canada a Bill of Rights was passed in 1960, but it does not restrict the parliament's power of legislation. It has been made clear in it that even if a law is in contravention of it, the courts cannot stop its enforcement. Justice Borar Laskin of Canada, has elucidated it, in the following words:

> "The Bill of Rights is only meant for the guidance of the Ministry of Law so that it may be before it when it comes to legislation."

Its main importance may lie in the direction to the Minister of Justice to examine all proposed legislations for consistency with the purposes and provisions of the Bill of Rights and to report any inconsistency to the House of Commons.

The Canadian Prime Minister, Lester Pearson tried, to have the Bill of Rights incorporated in the constitution but failed. Prime Minister, Trudeau somehow got it passed in 1969, but its status remained the same as in 1960. In 1963, the Prime Minister of New Zealand, J.R. Hanan tried to get the Bill of Rights passed but the parliament rejected it. More or less the same is the situation in Australia.

The citizens of Britain and its colonies are at the mercy of the parliament in respect of the fundamental rights. Their only support lies in the respect for traditions and customs. Undoubtedly the roots of respect for these traditions are deep enough and no government dare deny them. But due to the ascendency of the parliament and helplessness of the judiciary there is no firm guarantee of constitutional protection of the fundamental rights. According to Justice William O. Douglas of the Supreme Court of America:

> "British constitution is really the tradition of 'self-control' practised by the members of parliament and the British rulers.

But the judges, legal experts and citizens of Britain do not believe in this tradition of self control alone as the reliable protector of the fundamental rights, since this tradition cannot stand in the way of the suspension, abrogation and curtailment of these rights. The parliament can put an end to them whenever it is pleased to do so, and there can be no appeal against its action.

After Britain, let us have a look at the American constitution. It is regarded as the ideal democratic constitution in as much as it entrusts the judiciary with the task of protecting the fundamental rights, and it enjoys supremacy over the legislature. It can strike down the laws framed by the Congress if it finds them contrary to the Constitution and can stop their enforcement. But notwithstanding the supremacy of the judiciary, in the event of internal turmoil, upsurge or external aggression, the executive and the Congress acquire unlimited powers. Under Article I, Section 9 and Clause 2, martial law can be clamped on the country, the fundamental rights can be suspended and the courts shorn of the powers of entertaining writ petitions.

Explaining this clause Willoughby writes:

> In time of war, or of domestic insurrection or disorder when so called martial law has been declared the privilege of the writ of habeas corpus, together with all the other civil guarantees may for the time being, be suspended.

In 1954 the Congress passed the Immunity Act under which under certain conditions any body could be deprived of the right of not being compelled to bear witness against himself, which has been unconditionally recognized in the fifth amendment of the Constitution. In the same year in spite of the freedoms of assembly, and forming organizations, guaranteed by the constitution, the communist party was banned and the supremacy of the judiciary could not help by declaring the step unconstitutional and getting the ban on the party lifted.

Professor MacIlwain commenting on the protection of the fundamental rights in the American constitution says:

> There is a constant threat to all the rights of personality we hold dearest—such rights as freedom of thought and expression and immunity for accused persons from arbitrary detention and from cruel and abusive treatment. These have always been endangered when-reasons of state have been thought to require it. At times it seems to me that just now we are in special danger of forgetting these rights and these dangers.

These facts amply reveal that the fundamental rights are not wholly inviolable even in America and Britain. As for the real reasons behind the somewhat seemingly satisfactory conditions in Britain and America, Dorothy Pickles says:

> The only ultimate safeguard of constitutionality would seem to be the practice of it over a long period of time, and circumstances do not always permit this. Invasion, defeat in war, deep-seated and irreconciliable political division within a country-these can make the normal development of constitutional government very difficult, and even impossible. The United State and Great Britain have both been fortunate in that they have enjoyed long periods of comparative invulnerability from external aggression and have been relatively free from the internal instability.

This would mean that the protection of fundamental rights in America depends much more on the favourable conditions prevalent in these countries than on the strength of their constitutions and traditions. If these conditions change and these counties too are exposed to foreign aggression or internal disturbances, their constitutions and traditions would not be able to help their citizens. The strength of the constitutions of these countries is based on the peculiar conditions prevailing there and the continuity of their history. Therefore the countries that borrowed from their constitutions overlooking their historical background, instead of coming by any advantages or blessings got involved in difficulties. Confessing it Lord Amery says:

> The rise of dictatorships and of one party government has been the almost inevitable consequence of the ineffectiveness of constitutions which reproduced the outward force of the British Constitution without that spirit of strong and stable government which is of its essence.

Burke, in a letter of his to a member of French Assembly, advising him to abstain from imitating the British constitution, writes:

> When I praised the British Constitution and wished it to be well studied, I did not mean that its exterior form and positive arrangement should become a model for you or for any people servilely to copy.

From this discussion we arrive at the conclusion that the British and American constitutions too do not guarantee the irrevocability of the fundamental rights. And even if the people of these countries are being benefited by their constitutions, it is limited to them alone. If any other country tries them, the result will soon be apparent in the form of dictatorship.

About the socialist countries we have already said that barring "economic rights" there are no other rights in existence there. And the other rights that have been mentioned in the constitution are not realizable through the judiciary. That is why there is no problem of the protection of the fundamental rights there in any form. A socialist state itself decides all the rights, and also prescribes the limits of their enforcement. It is, so to say, all in all—(to quote a Persian saying, the cup, the cup maker and the clay of the cup, all rolled into one,)—beyond that (the party) there is neither any right nor any authority to enforce a right.

This examination of the constitution of the democratic and socialist countries reveals the fact that the constitution itself provides no certain guarantee of the protection of the fundamental rights. Our own observation and experience bear testimony to the fact that we cannot rely on just the document of the constitution for the determination and practical enforcement of the fundamental rights. The greatest fault of these constitutions is that there is no sanction power behind them that can compel the rulers to abide by the limitation placed in the exercise of their powers and which may thus provide eternal protection to the fundamental rights.

5

Equal Status

Right of Marriage

'There are three essential elements in every normal marriage,' says Dr. Westermarck in his book, *The Future of Marriage in Western Civilization*, 'the gratification of the sexual impulse, the relation between husband and wife apart from it and procreation of children.' Let us see what is the angle of vision from which Islam looks at marriage and what is the central value in it which it stresses more than any other. Let it not also be forgotten that, unlike Christianity, which looked upon marriage as if it were a necessary evil, Islam regards it as a most sacred institution and makes it incumbent on every Muslim man and woman, unless prevented by valid physical or economic incapacity, to lead a married life. The following traditions of the Holy Prophet stress the importance of marriage:

> It is necessary for you to marry, because marriage is the most powerful shield against the allurements of sight, and the protection of your private parts; if one of you cannot afford it, let him fast because fasting weakens the sexual impulse.
>
> The Prophet declared that marriage was one of his most sacred practices and added: 'Whoever dislikes my way of life is not of me' (Bukhari).

> A tradition reported by Arias says, 'When a man has got married he has made his religion half perfect. Then let him fear Allah for the remaining half.'
> (Baihaqi)

The Quran also exhorts the followers of Islam to enter into marriage with chaste women:

> Then marry such women as seem good to you.
> (iv. 3)

> And lawful for you are all women, besides those mentioned above, provided that you seek them with your property taking them in marriage not committing fornication. (iv. 24)

> You are sprung one from the other; so marry them (slavegirls) with the permission of their masters and give them their dowries justly they being chaste, not fornicating, nor forming secret relations. (iv. 25)

> This day all the good things are allowed to you, and the food of those who have been given the Book is lawful for you and your food is lawful for them; and the chaste from among the believing women and the chaste from among those who have been given the Book before you (are lawful for you), when you have given them their dowries, taking them in marriage, not fornicating, nor taking them for paramours in secret. (v. 5)

The Quran has constantly used the word Mohsin for chaste men and Muhsinat for chaste women both of which come from the Arabic root Him meaning 'fort'. The underlying idea is that marriage safeguards and protects chastity in the same manner as a fort protects the garrison within from a besieging army.

From the above quotations it appears that Islam recommends marriage because, first, it helps men and women to lead a life of chastity, that is, it secures them against promiscuous sexual indulgence; secondly, because it prevents the formation of secret sex relations. These two values are the cornerstone on which the institution of marriage rests and Islam's conception, of woman's rights in marriage flows logically from them.

Let us see what the social importance of chastity and open sex relation is as opposed to secret love. In modern times, the ideal of chastity has lost hold on man and it has been claimed by some, even among men of science and learning, that chastity is by no means a very important social value and that happiness in marriage as well as the proper upbringing of children need not suffer from sexual promiscuity on the part of either partner. Some would go to the length of abolishing the family system in order to secure the release of men and women from the bonds of conjugal fidelity. It is presumed by these people that alternative methods of bringing up children can be organised more efficiently. It is difficult to bringout the importance of chastity as a social value unless we discuss all such proposals and ideas.

Let us first deal with the importance of conjugal fidelity and its healthy effects on the happiness of the family and the health of society. Islam has made no distinction in this respect between man and woman; both are equally punishable under the law of Islam if they are guilty of sexual laxity. But, in practice, public opinion has always, even in Western countries, taken more alarm at unchastity in women than in men, the reason being that the disturbing social and family effects of a woman's misconduct are deeper and more widespread. Discussing this inequality of treatment as regards men and women, Dr. Westermarck says in the *Future of Marriage in Western Civilization*.

But there are also more special reasons for that inequality between the sexes. It was a doctrine of the Roman jurists that adultery is a crime in the wife, and in the wife only, on account of the danger of introducing strange children to the husband.

It has been argued that the danger of confusion of pregnancy has disappeared with the development of methods for preventing conception, but it is anything but certain that the lovers trouble themselves about contraceptives. Von Krafft-Ebing writes [in his book *The Modern Family*): 'The unfaithfulness of a wife, in comparison with that of a husband, is morally much more weighty, and should be more severely punished legally.

The unfaithful wife dishonours not only herself, but also her husband and her family....' 'The man,' says Kisch in [Die Sexuelle Untreue der Frau], 'can make a lapse in this marriage without the consequences of it being necessarily of vital importance; he can at any moment do remorseful penance without the mischief he has caused being irreparable. The infidelity of the wife poisons the soul for ever, shakes the foundations of the harmony between mother and children, makes the legitimacy of the latter uncertain, and leads to an irreparable rupture of the 'domestic life.' Hedwig Wega observes that while the adultery of the husband is in many cases a purely social act, which need not spoil marriage, that of the wife is in no case merely bodily attachment. Stendhal remarks [in his book on Love] that where love is absent, the fidelity of a married woman is something contrary to nature, but that, 'with love there, one has no taste for any mate but that of the beloved fount.' He also writes: 'The difference between infidelity in the two sexes is so real, that a woman of passion may pardon it, while for a man that is impossible!'

These are some of the consequences of female unchastity, but so less grave are the consequences which follow from the sexual irregularities of men. We shall again quote Dr. Westermarck who says:

> However useful sexual intercourse may be to the unmarried, it has also its disadvantages. It may give venereal diseases to him who practises it; and it may be fraught with serious consequences for the female

> partner.... The illegitimacy of birth affects the offspring even more than the mother. The death rate for illegitimate infants is very much higher than for legitimate ones.... Another result of them is the comparatively large number of criminals among the children of unmarried parents, who grow up in so unfavourable circumstances. The way in which they have been treated in the Western world is a disgrace to its civilization... It certainly seems both absurd and unjust that the legal rights of any citizens should be influenced by the judgments which society passes upon their mothers; but however much legislation may improve the condition of illegitimate children, it cannot make them equal to those under which most other children develop. Family allowances may be granted, to their mothers where the father is unknown or indigent, founding institutions may provide them with an education that is the best possible in the circumstances, but nothing can compensate them for the lack of an adequate home.

It may of course be argued that all such evils can be avoided through the use of contraceptives. Dr. Ellis maintains that the much smaller rate of illegitimate children in England, compared with the rate of such children in Germany, is due to the wider adoption of methods for preventing conception, but when we hear that their number is rapidly increasing in Germany, in spite of the fact that contraceptives are used on a large scale in all classes we can by no means feel reassured that extra-matrimonial procreation will some day become an anachronism. Strictly speaking, however, the censure to which the unmarried mother is subject refers to something else than the birth of the child; this event is an impressive and conclusive testimony of an act which itself is considered degrading.

The above quotations should suffice to establish the fact that immodesty and unchastity have a serious disturbing effect on married happiness, family ties and the proper development of children. Apart from these effects, conjugal infidelity breeds jealousy, one of the most destructive human passions, both individually and socially. There are people who try to minimise the effects of jealousy, and regarding it as a relic of primitive barbarity foresee its disappearance with the spread of education and enlightenment. Dr Westermarck himself is one of those who believe that with proper education this primitive feeling would disappear, but even he has been forced to admit that there is one kind of sexual and conjugal jealousy which is not traceable to primitive barbarity.

This kind of jealousy, he says, arises from the uniqueness of the relationship between two persons and the endeavour to stamp this uniqueness on the whole relationship, sexual and moral. If this is true, civilisation and culture may be expected to increase this kind of jealousy rather than refuse its proportion. Let us see what Dr. Westermarck himself has to say on this subject. He writes:

> The jealousy of a man, particularly a civilized man, differs from that of a male animal, apart from any feeling of injured rights ownership or any other right. It is coloured by the nature of his love, It is accompanied with humiliation, because the loss of possession to which jealousy refers or the failure to obtain it, is of such a nature as carries with it a lowering of a man's self valuation. There may also be envy of what the other has obtained by depriving him of it. There may be fear of another man's offspring being born into the family. But there is one characteristic common to sexual jealousy in all its forms, namely, that it is an angry feeling aroused by loss, or fear of the loss, of the exclusive possession of an individual who is the object of one's sexual desire. It is impossible to suppose that the feeling of anger will ever disappear, however ugly and useless it may be. How violent ...

> it sometimes is among ourselves is illustrated by the fact that in analysing 188 murders committed by some persons in England, a prison commissioner recently found that the highest number, 46, were due to jealousy.

But even when the infidelity of a husband or wife does not give rise to the angry feeling of jealousy it causes deep sorrow; and I think it can be demanded of a: spouse to consider whether he or she has a right to inflict such suffering upon the other party. Helene Stocker observes that the refined feeling of love implies instinctively an obligation to avoid, as far as possible, making the beloved person feel pain. It is true, as Bertrand Russell said, that love, is a generous emotion. But it is not generous to the person who has to suffer for his generosity towards another.

Communist-minded persons in our country who really desire to maintain their capitalistic way of living under the garb of communism have spread the false idea that Soviet communism does not attach any importance to the ideal of feminine chastity, because all such ideas and values are really the product of outmoded religious teaching. But a writer of the eminence of Havelock Ellis writes: 'There has been an erroneous idea abroad in the world that the Bolsheviks believe in sexual intemperance and promiscuity in sex relations, an idea no doubt based on the chaos which inevitably resulted at first when the new regime was so suddenly inaugurated. That disorder much distressed Lenin himself, who was entirely opposed to promiscuity and all mere physical indulgence, and held that the highest human elements entered the love relationship. It is Lenin's doctrine which now permeates Soviet society.'

The same writer tells us that unchaste women command little respect in Soviet society. It would almost seem that the polyandric woman whom, in the opinion of some Western persons, Soviet conditions favour, is there unduly depreciated....

Blonsky points out that the depreciation of polyandric women is shared by men, even the men who form temporary relationships with them, for men are inclined to look on such women as a convenient means of satisfying sexual needs, simply as substitutes for prostitution, and feel for them no high regard. That, Blonsky considers, is an influence making for the degradation of polyandric woman whose life courses are not usually, happy. It is unnecessary to add that the monoyandric woman, who is peculiarly adapted for motherhood and family life, will not be easily deprived of that career.

It is sometimes argued by those who wish to lead a life of unlimited sexual indulgence that there is no reason why a man's sexual desires should be tied down to one woman, why he should be put under an unnecessary obligation to bring up a family with all its cares and responsibilities. To such persons Havelock Ellis replies: 'It used sometimes to be asked: What has posterity done for me that I should do anything for posterity? The question was wrongly put. "Posterity" is only another name for mankind, and when we pose the question rightly, there can be no dispute about the answer. If we put aside the part that belongs to nature or God we owe everything to mankind. All that we are, all that we possess in civilization, we owe to the everlasting aspiration and struggle of mankind before us, and to the slow accumulation of knowledge and art on the topmost level on which we now stand. Our immense debt to mankind in the past can only be repaid to mankind in future. It is our privilege, if we do not regard it as our duty, to pass on in even finer shapes the great traditions which have been handed to us.'

Such passages enable us to understand why Islam insists on marriage both for men and women. Without married life involving the care and education of children, human personality can never find its full development and the great traditions of religion, culture and civilisation cannot be passed on to the future generation. It should also be remembered that children contribute as much to our education and personal self-development as we contribute to their proper growth and upbringing, so that it can be safely asserted that a childless man is necessarily a half-developed man. Then there is an additional consideration. If human individuality is a value of some importance, then it is not only necessary for every person to develop his individuality to the fullest extent possible but also to transmit it for the future use of mankind by bringing into the world fresh individuals who will retain at least a part of his individual characteristics.

It is possible, however, to admit the necessity of procreation and the importance of chastity as a cementing and healing bond in family life and yet maintain that by abolishing the family and evolving alternative institutions for the training and upbringing of children, we may allow a large amount of sexual latitude to men and women without any serious social disturbance. Such methods were tried in Soviet Russia for some time and, though the Soviet Republic has widely abandoned them, their echoes are still heard even in our backward country. It is true that if once we can get rid of the family and evolve other means for the preservation of human race and the education of children, modesty, chastity and all other such values lose their necessity. But what is the possibility of success in this attempt? Is it possible to abolish the family or is it rooted in our social nature? Let us deal with the question, as it has a very important bearing on the rights of women versus men.

There are three biological tendencies common to men and animals which form the foundation of family life and which cannot be overthrown now or in any conceivable future. They are the impulse of sexual attraction which leads to mating, the tendency to a close and enduring comradeship with the opposite sex and the instinctive impulse of mates to care for their offspring. Even an authority like Havelock Ellis admits that 'it is vain for even the most conservative of human beings to lament the failure of marriage, it is futile for even the most light-hearted of radicals to hope to get beyond it. The family is at the root of our bisexual constitution, and needs no formal institution. Again the same writer says, 'it has too often been forgotten that the family possesses this manysided flexibility and has in different ages and lands shown endless variation of shape in adjustment to varying social conditions. Those who overlooked this essential fact have frequently cried out in rebellion against the whole conception of the family.

Because they themselves have chanced to come out of an unhappy family life. Though the excellent qualities they have, notwithstanding often displaced, so far show that even an unhappy family life may have happy results they impetuously demand the complete abolition of the family. Havelock Ellis also replies to those who believe that the economic independence of woman achieved by her in modern society, her increasing participation in civil and industrial life and the growing use of contraceptives will in the end lead to the disintegration of the family. He does not believe in any such consummation and says in his essay on the 'Renovation of Family' that these factors, instead of abolishing family, may even strengthen and purify it, if they are well handled.

Institutions like the maternity home, the nursery school and the kindergarten which are increasingly taking over the functions of the home have encouraged a large number of people to believe that as this process goes on to its perfection, the family will soon become unnecessary as a social institution. Those who harbour such notions should not turn a blind eye to evils which are likely to arise from the disappearance of personal and intimately affectionate relations between the parents and children. Mechanical instruments involving depersonalisation of human relations are a source of danger to the growth of human personality.

This aspect of the matter is well brought out by Margaret Mead in her book *Male and Female*. Writing about American mothers, she says: 'Birth in America is ideally, more and more frequently and actually in a hospital. This means that but for a few exceptional cases, the father is absent and the mother has been given over to the care of professionals, doctors and nurses. For months before the birth she has been preparing to leave her home and her husband, not for the home of her parents or her brothers, as in many primitive societies, but for a strange, segregated spot, where she and many other women unknown to her will live together, giving birth among strangers. When the baby is born, it is against the force of gravity, on a delivery table designed not to let the child's own weight assist the birth but rather to facilitate the ministrations of the obstetrician. Its first cry is often induced by a vigorous slap. The mother, deep under an anaesthetic dose, does not hear this cry, although recent research has suggested that the cry has a function in making her uterus contract.

The infant is taken away to a row of cribs; its lips, ready for sucking, are left to press helplessly against each other. The primary bodily capabilities with which the child enters the world are initially unrewarded. It can suck, but no breast is given it; it can cry for help, but no one holds close and feeds it. Its body is wrapped completely in soft cloth, the first lesson in expecting cloth to intervene between one body and the next. The second lesson will come when it is taken to its mother, at the proper hour for its birth weight, neatly laid out on a moving table, and placed against her fully clothed body, with the carefully sterilised breast exposed just a few inches, and persuaded to suck.

This persuasion is often a grim business, the nurse knows how to take the baby, who very often is so exhausted with hunger that it no longer wants to eat, and, holding it by the scruff of the neck, puts it on the mother's breast. Whether it eats or not, it is supposed to be taken away again after the appointed number of minutes. The mother is left sometimes worried and enraged because the baby would not eat, having very doubtfully enjoyed in routinised cloth-developed experience. During the nine or ten days that follow, the mother handles her baby clothed, and only at regular hours. The father does not handle it at all. Breast-feeding is frequently abandoned altogether, and by the time the child goes home, the mother, if not the baby, has learned that contacts between mother and child have a certain form. The failure of milk, the failure of the baby to nurse, the obstetrical and paediatric pressure towards at least supplementary feeding are all natural enough in a setting where the new child is treated as if its health and well-being depended on the machine - like precision with which it is fed and on what it is fed.

The mother learns impatience with her milk, which is too rich or too weak, too much or too little, pouring through nipples that are inverted or sore or otherwise unobliging. She can turn with some relief to the bottle and the formula, the reliable rubber nipple with a hole that can be enlarged with a pin, the graduated bottle into which just the right formula at just the right temperature can be measured. No recalcitrant individual unregulated body here, to endanger her baby's gain in weight, the chief criterion of its healthful existence. At once or in a few weeks, most American mothers reject their own bodies as a source of food for their children, and, in accepting the mechanical perfection of a bottle, reaffirm to themselves, and in the way they handle their babies, that the baby too will be much better the more it learns to use that beautifully mechanical bottle accurately on time, in the right amounts, the more it accepts an external rhythm, and abandons its peculiar rhythms that it brought into the world.

'For primary learning experience, that is, the physical prototype of sex relationship, a complementary relation between the body of the mother and the body of the child is substituted by a relation between the child and an object, an object, that imitates the breast but which is not handled as either part of the mother or part of the body. If the mother holds the baby as she gives it the bottle in most instances it becomes an implement, an extension of her hand so that it holds food, rather than an extension of her breast. At what age the child distinguishes the exact difference between a glass bottle and a rubber nipple, loose in space, and a human breast, we do not know, but the mother experiences the difference from the state, and her experience is available to the child, in her voice, in her hands, in the very tempo of her being. She is not giving the child herself; she is faithfully, efficiently providing the child with a bottle, external to both of them substituting for a direct relationship mediated by an object.'

This ironic description of an ideal delivery in an ideal hospital shows how the substitution of mechanical inventions for direct human contacts retards the growth and mars the personality of the child. Evidence is not lacking to prove that institutional care of children is a poor substitute for home life. A White House Conference on Child Health and Protection held in America in 1930 declared that 'institutional care for the most part has produced uninspired individuals poorly adjusted to the outside world.' Dr. Nimkoff writes: 'We can show that normal family life is indispensable to the proper development of the child's personality.' Fioyd Dell writes: 'Institutional life at its best has been notoriously drab and barren in comparison with ordinary family life.

Institutional life has been found to fail in developing individual powers and in furnishing incentives for growing up. It has characteristically turned out spiritless creatures who do not know how to get along in the outside world. The best modern institutions for children now model themselves upon the parental home and try to give what it should give. Even at their best, however, these institutions, when they replace the private, home entirely, are regarded as makeshifts, as poor substitutes for a real home with real parents. And real home and real parents are known to be so important to the child's development that it is more and more the practice that only as a last resort are homes broken up and children taken from parents.'

After giving an account of the methods tried by Soviet Russia for providing alternate education to children and the results experienced, Dr. Westermarck says in his book, *The Failure of Marriage in Western Civilisation:*

> Many facts thus support the general belief that there is no adequate substitute for the beneficial influence which parents as a rule exercise upon their children, that the love of the parents towards the child is one of the most essential features, if the child's moral and emotional development is to proceed harmoniously.

In these circumstances I can find no reason to suppose that it could be in the interests of the state in the future to break up the family. The Bolsheviks' suspicious attitude towards it is due to the view that private property has always served as a cementing bond in the family; and to demolish private property is the object of the most feverish efforts of the new society. It is considered to be of great importance that the mentality of the Russian youth should be largely moulded by agencies outside the home, away from the family circle; in the kindergartens and schools it is always made to feel that the supreme aim of life is the promotion of the purposes of the new society.

Yet, though the rulers of Russia regard the family as a menace to their ultimate designs, they find it at the present stage of readjustment indispensable to the maintenance of social stability. But they have obviously underrated its vitality. The persistence of the family does not depend upon the preservation of private property. Its safest guarantee is the love of man and woman for each other and for their children, and the Bolsheviks are even said to assure themselves that this bond will gain in firmness when property has passed from private to social control.

In conclusion, Dr. Westermarck says:

> So far as I can see, then, there is every reason to

> believe that the unity of sexual and spiritual elements, in sexual love, leading to a more or less durable community of life in a common home, and the desire for and love of offspring are factors which will remain lasting obstacles to the extinction of marriage and the collapse of the family, because they are too deeply rooted in human nature to fade away, and can find adequate satisfaction only in some form of marriage and the family founded upon it.

We thus find that the family, as the basic unit of social organisation, is likely to outlast the forces tending to destroy it. A stable family life is necessary not only in the interests of society, not only for the happiness and moral development of the husband and the wife, but also for the proper growth and development of future generations. Conditions and forces which tend to shake the stability of the family should be countered and removed in the interests of the society and the individual. If these basic facts are admitted, chastity becomes a value of the highest social importance to be safeguarded at all costs.

And from this conception and pattern of family life, the mutual rights and obligations of men and women can be determined with more scientific precision and greater justice than from an abstract conception of equality which does not keep in view the practical requirements of family organisation. Islam has built its system of rights and obligations for men and women not on a vague and abstract conception of sex equality but on a doctrine of basic sex equality qualified by actual biological sex differences and the practical needs of a stable family organisation. With this background in view, we proceed to discuss the rights and obligations of the female sex as defined by Islam.

In order to ensure a happy home and a really stable family life, Islam has assigned to marriage the status of a contract dissoluble if ,either party develops grievances against the other leading to a final and irrevocable break in their mutual relations.

It is not as in Christianity, a sacrament indissoluble except by a difficult process and under very extraordinary circumstances. This may appear, at first sight, to be a factor operating against family stability, but in fact it is deșigned to safeguard it.

There is really no virtue in keeping two persons tied together to save appearances, when their relations have deteriorated beyond all hope of reconciliation. An unhappy marriage resulting in interminable quarrels fails to realise the primary object of the union which brought the partners together, besides increasing the probability of illegal sexual relations outside marriage. It also tells upon the health and education of children. It is, therefore better both socially and morally that the husband and the wife should be allowed to part with each other if the breaking point has been reached in their mutual relations. Therefore, marriage in Islam is not indissoluble but a kind of contract in which specific rights and obligations may be undertaken besides those already implied in marriage. These rights are justifiable in a court of law.

It is open both to the husband and the wife to enter into agreement prior to marriage on matters which they consider important for the regulation of their future relations. Such agreements shall be parts of the marriage contract and adjudicable in law-courts, provided they are not repugnant to the basic rights and obligations of husband and wife as stated by Islam. Thus, Umar, the Second Caliph, says: 'When a person marries a woman and the woman stipulates that she would not be taken out of the town or city of her residence, it is necessary for the husband to abide by the stipulation' (Tirmidhi, p. 385).

Imam Ahmad and Imam Shafii also hold the same opinion. But Ali, the Fourth Caliph, says:,' The conditions laid down by God take precedence over the, conditions set by man,' which means that, in his opinion, such a condition is repugnant to the basic terms of marriage. Sufyan Thabri and other scholars of Kufah also hold the same opinion. Whatever the differences among the scholars on this point, they relate to the point whether this particular stipulation is or is not repugnant to the basic terms of marriage contract as defined by Islam. There is no disagreement on the point whether a woman can insist on inserting terms of her own in the marriage contract. All are unanimous that she holds this right. Thus, the author of *Nail al-Autar* (Pt. VII, p. 64) says: 'The wife can lay down conditions prior to marriage relating to her way of living, her food, house and dress, according to the social status of the husband and that her just rights shall not be whittled. Similarly, the husband can lay down these conditions: that the wife shall not go out from home without his permission, that she shall not refuse sexual intercourse with him and shall not use his property and possessions except by his permission.'

Just as a man can stipulate that his wife shall not go out except by his permission, it is open to the woman to insist that she shall not be prevented from going out of her home on suitable occasions or for her economic or social needs, so long as this action does not disturb the work of her husband or the proper upbringing of the children. All these matters come within the scope of the marriage agreement, but since some of them are not easily justifiable, much depends on the actual relations of the husband and the wife after marriage and their mutual understanding. All these things show that the wife does not lose, under Islam, her separate legal personality, but retains full possession of it. She can sue her husband in a law-court if the implied or express terms of the marriage contract are violated by the husband.

This is in direct contrast to the position of woman under Christianity. Professor Mansfield, writing in his book, *The Legal Rights, Liabilities and Duties of Women*, states: 'The first great principle of Scripture, the unity of husband and wife, is repeated by the law. They are, in law, one person. Upon it, as observed by Blackstone, depend nearly all the legal rights, duties and disabilities acquired by marriage.' The English Common Law, as interpreted by Blackstone, whose commentaries governed actual legal decisions both in England and America for a very long period, assigned the same position to a wife in relation to her husband. It was only with the greatest difficulty and by resorting to parliament any legislation or equity courts that the wife was able to secure a few rights over against her husband. From a strictly legal viewpoint, the position of women among the Muslims has been really enviable when compared to that of their counterparts in the Western countries.

In order to safeguard the economic position of women after the marriage, Islam has made it legally obligatory on the husband to pay her a reasonable amount as dower. The amount to be fixed, as dower depends on the agreement between the two parties, but, in any case, the object is to strengthen the financial position of the wife, so that she is not prevented, for lack of money, from defending her rights. The Quran says:

> And give women their dowries as a free gift, but if they themselves be pleased to give up to you a portion of it, then eat it with enjoyment and with wholesome result. (iv. 4)

> And if you wish to have (one) wife in the place of another and you have given one of them a heap of gold (as dowry) take not anything from her; would you take it by slandering (her) and (doing her) manifest wrong? (iv. 20)

No marriage can be regarded as legally valid, according to Islam, for which dowry has not been stipulated. If the amount of dowry is not fixed, the wife is entitled to proper dowry (*mehr-i-mithl*), even if the marriage was contracted on the express condition that she should not claim any dowry. In determining what is 'proper' dowry, regard is to be had to the amount of dower settled upon other female members of her father's family such as her father's sisters. The following tradition of the Prophet stresses the importance attached to dowry in Islam:

Ibn Umar reported that the Prophet of, Allah forbade

> shighar and shighar is a man's giving his daughter in marriage on condition that another would give his daughter in marriage to him and that there should be no dowry between them.

Another tradition collected by Abu Daud and Nasai says:

> Alqamah b. Masud reported that he was asked about a man who married a woman but did not fix any dowry for her, nor had he any intercourse with her till he died. Ibn Masud told her: Fix the equivalent dowries of his women, neither less nor more. And there is the period of waiting for her and there is her share of inheritance for her (from her husband's property), then Maqal b. Sinan got up and said: 'The Messenger of Allah decreed in case of Barwaah bint Washiq (a woman belonging to us) just as you have decreed.'

Regarding the amount of dowry to be fixed, Islam has given a wide, latitude to men and women. It can be as low as possible or as high as the parties may desire. Ibn Majah and Tirmidhi report from Amir ibn Rabia that a woman belonging to the tribe of Banu Fazarah married a man for a pair of shoes. The Prophet asked her whether she was really happy over that much dowry. She replied in the affirmative, whereupon the Prophet made no objection.

> According to Abu al-Jafar, it was the opinion of Umar, the Second Caliph, that the dowry should not be fixed at a very high rate, for if this had been a point of honour and pleasing in the sight of God, the Prophet too would have acted accordingly, but he did not fix more than a hundred and twenty-five dirhams of dowry for his wives and daughters (Tirmidhi, p. 132). Umar's opinion was, however, challenged by a woman who said: Umar, you have no right to impose such restrictions, because the Holy Quran says that men

> should not take back anything from their wives if they intend to divorce them, even if they have given them a heap of gold. This shows that God allows even a very high rate of dowry. Umar replied to her saying that she was right and that he had made a mistake himself. (Nafl-al-Autar by Shaukani).

The amount of dower may be fixed either before or at the time of marriage or after marriage, and can be increased after marriage. A contract of dower can be made by a father on behalf of his son, if the latter is a minor. The wife may remit the whole or part of dower. Such remission is valid though made without consideration. If the dower is not paid, the wife and, after her death, her heirs may sue for it. The wife may refuse to live with her husband and admit him to sexual intercourse so long as the dower remains unpaid. If the husband sues her for the restitution of conjugal rights, before sexual intercourse has taken place, non-payment of dower is a complete defence to the suit, and the suit will be dismissed.

If the suit is brought after sexual intercourse has taken place with her free consent, the court can issue a decree for restitution conditional on payment of the dower, to the extent only of a share of the dower debt proportionate to his share of the estate. When a widow is in actual possession of the property of her deceased husband, she is entitled as against the other heirs of her husband and as against the creditors of her husband, to retain possession of the property until her dower is satisfied. The fact that a widow is in possession of her husband's property under a claim for her dower is no bar to a suit against the other heirs of her husband to recover the dower debt, but she must in such a suit offer, to give up possession of the property.

Further, to secure a strong economic position for women, Islam has given them full property rights. A daughter gets half the share of property allotted to the son, half of the entire property of her father if there is no other son or daughter; and if there is more than one daughter but no sons, the daughters share among them equally two-thirds of the entire property. A widow is entitled to one eighth of the property left by her husband, but if there are no children by the marriage, she receives one-sixth. No distinction is made by Islam between movable and immovable property.

The whole, including both kinds, is distributed to the heirs in their fixed proportions. It may be said that by giving the daughter half the share of a son, Islam has let down the position of women, but it should not be forgotten that a woman may also receive dower and property from her husband in which case her inequality is more than compensated for. Moreover, there is no obligation on a wife to sustain her husband economically, while the husband is under a legal obligation to provide for his wife. Thus, the inequality of women in the share of inheritance is matched by a corresponding increase in the economic burden of men, which makes the two sexes equal in respect of their economic rights.

One of the most essential factors of a happy marriage is the right of free choice by either party. Islam has given this right both to men and women. The Prophet insisted on a number of occasions that a person wishing to marry a woman should have a look at her before finally consenting to marriage. Thus, Abu Hurairah reports: 'A man came to the Prophet and said, "I intend to marry a woman of the Ansar." He said, "Have a look at her, because sometimes there is something defective in the eyes of the Ansar." Jabir reports that the Prophet said: 'When one of you seeks a woman in marriage and then if he is able to have a look at one he wishes to marry, let him do so' (Abu Daud). Mughira b. Shubah reports: 'I sought a woman in marriage. The Holy Prophet asked if I had seen her. "No," said I. He said: "Then look at her, because it is more proper that love should be cemented between you."

The jurists agree that this right to have a look at the prospective partner is equally eligible for the members of the female sex. According to Imam Abu Hanifah, it is lawful to have a sight of the bride and the bridegroom. Imam Malik holds that it is lawful with the permission of the bride. Imam Shafii and Imam Ahmad are of the opinion that a look at the prospective husband or wife is lawful with or without the permission of the other.

Freedom of choosing one's partner for life has been extended both to men and women. No marriage in Islam can be valid without the consent of either partner. According to a report from Abu Hurairah, the Prophet said: 'A previously married woman shall not be married till she gives her consent, nor a virgin be married till her consent is sought.' They asked: 'How shall her permission be known. He said: 'If she remains silent.' A report from Ibn Abbas, collected by Muslim, states that the Prophet said: 'A previously married woman is more a guardian for herself than her guardian and a virgin should be asked permission about herself, and her permission is her silence.' Abu Hurairah further reports that the Prophet said: 'A grown-up girl shall be asked permission about herself. If she is silent, it is her permission; and if she declines, there shall be no compulsion on her.'

The presence of two witnesses is necessary to make a marriage valid, because open declaration of marriage constitutes its soul and essence. According to a tradition of Tirmidhi reported by Ibn Abbas, the Prophet declared: 'Those women are adulteresses who marry themselves without the presence of witnesses! Umar was once told that a certain marriage had been performed with one witness only. He said that such a marriage amounted to clandestine relationship which was illegal. If he had knowledge of it beforehand, he would have dealt stern punishment to either party.

Guardianship is regarded by some as necessary for the marriage of a woman. There are some traditions in which the presence of a guardian has been made an essential condition precedent to the marriage of a girl. Thus, Bukhari gives a tradition stating: 'There is no marriage without a guardian.' This is probably meant only for minor girls. Imam Abu Hanirah, the greatest and the most popular jurist of Islam, holds that a marriage, whether of a widow or a grown-up virgin, is permissible even without a guardian. Imaṃ S̀hafii's and Imam Malik, however, hold that guardianship is necessary for the marriage of a woman.

As marriage depends essentially upon the choice of a woman, the presence of a guardian, even if not required by law, can be regarded necessary only in the sense that he undertakes to watch the interests of the minor or the grownup girl who is to be married and to see that she is not disadvantaged by reason of sex in the settlement of the terms on which marriage is contracted. This interpretation is supported by a tradition contained in Kitab at Nikah of the collection made by Tirmidhi. The tradition states: Aishah said, the Prophet of God declared: 'Marriage of a woman is invalid without there being a guardian.' He repeated this three times and said that if the husband of such a woman had sexual intercourse with her, she should receive her dower and if, after the performance of the marriage, the two quarrel, then the ruler of the Muslims is the guardian of the woman who has no other guardian.

The reference here to the recovery of dowrý and the possibility of quarrel as well as recognition of the right of the State to take up the functions of a guardian all point to the fact that the Prophet had in mind the necessity of safeguarding the interests of women by making the presence of a guardian essential. In a society which, until the advent of Islam, had been ridden by sex inequality and where women had been treated as mere chattel, it was always possible, despite the teachings of Islam, that a single woman without a guardian or a patron should find herself at a disadvantage in the settlement of marriage terms. So the Prophet deemed it essential that, if there be no guardian for a woman, the State should become her guardian with a view to ensuring equality and justice at the time of marriage contract and thereafter. No other interpretation is possible in view of the fact that the final say in all matters has been accorded to women themselves and not to their guardians, a fact which is attested by the authentic traditions of the Prophet himself.

That the woman who contracts a marriage, and not her father or guardian has the final choice in the matter, is proved by the following traditions which extend to women the right to repudiate a marriage forced on them through pressure, direct or indirect:

> Ibn Abbas reported that a virgin grown-up girl came to the Prophet of Allah and narrated that her father had given her in marriage to a person whom she disliked. The Prophet gave her option.
>
> (Abu Daud)

Again:

> Khansa b. Khidham reported that her father gave her in marriage, after, she became a widow. She disliked it and came to the Prophet. He annulled the marriage.
>
> (Bukhari)

A very significant' report which throws a flood of light on the complete liberty of choice and repudiation extended to women by Islam in the matter of their marriage is found in the traditions collected by Nasai. The reporter is no less a person than Aishah, the wife of the Prophet. She says, 'A girl came and stated that her father had given her in marriage to his nephew and she disliked him. I told her to wait till the Prophet arrived. When the Prophet came, I told him the full story of the girl. He at once sent for the father of the girl and inquired of him whether the facts stated were true, after which he told the girl that she was at liberty to choose or repudiate her husband. The girl replied saying that she chose to retain her marriage, And that she wanted only to know whether women had any rights in the matter.' Another tradition from the collection made by Ibn Majah states: 'Ibn' Umar says: Uthman b. Mazun left behind a young daughter. My uncle, Qudamah, married her to me, and did not even consult her. When the girl came to know of this, she disliked this marriage and wished to marry Mughira b. Shubah. So she was married to Mughira.'

All these traditions furnish conclusive proof that a girl is as free in Islam as a boy to choose or repudiate her partner and that the Prophet's insistence on there being a guardian before a woman can be married was intended to safeguard her position and rights in a society which was not yet completely free from the dominance of the male sex and in which a lonely woman ran a chance of being outwitted by clever men and left without the necessary protection.

The legal equality of men and women in Islam is a fact which has never been in dispute among the Muslims. There is no legal right belonging to man for which a corresponding female right cannot be cited. But the ideal of sex equality or any other kind of equality cannot be wholly given effect to by the law. Specially is this true of the relations between husband and wife which in their very nature refuse to be covered and guided wholly by legal injunctions and principles. Real equality between the sexes depends much more on social opinion and national traditions than on legal commands.

Even in Western countries where the claim for complete equality between the two sexes has been pressed to extremes, formidable difficulties have been experienced by legislators to translate the ideal into the actual. Mary Beard, after giving a detailed account of the attempts made in America to give equal property rights to men and women, mentions a long list of legislative failures to give effect to the principle of equality. The following extract from her book, *Woman as Force in History*, will give the reader an idea of the intricate and evasive nature of the ideal of sex equality. Writing about the legislative changes made in America with respect to women's property rights, she says:

> A Married Women's Property Act was, therefore, simple in principle. But in application the terms of such an Act were difficult to draw. Despite the theory of independence and equality which was supposed to furnish guidance in drafting the Act, law reformers and lawmakers actually confronted a paradox: The wife is to be treated as if she is a single woman in respect of her property, but in marital relations she has obligations not assumed by single women and is no more of a single person than her husband is; for both are entangled in a network of duties not imposed on single persons. Is the wife free to use her property as she pleased while the husband is in straits to support her and their children? In what, if any, circumstances is the wife to be under obligation to support the family in part or whole? Is the owner of the home, whether husband or wife, to be allowed to sell it at will, without the consent of the other party to the marriage contract, and turn the family out of it? These and a hundred other questions taxed the adroitness of law-makers and were answered by men and women in many different ways. No mere declaration of equality could dispose of them in a few words. At no time or place did it prove possible to write one Married Women's Property Bill which could settle all these questions.

The same writer goes on to say:

> In their efforts to clear away anachronisms and to bring the law abreast the advance in civilization, legislators did not, indeed could not, treat a man and a woman who had chosen to marry and bring children into the world as if they were perfectly free and entitled to be wholly whimsical with their respective properties and earnings, without regard for obligations due to each other. Nor could legislators overlook the rights of their children, their creditors and their more or less distant relatives. All lawmakers recognized the fact

> that husband and wife had to surrender some freedom by virtue of their very marriage contract. How much and what kinds of freedom? ... On the point of how to realize the ideal of equality, men differed and women differed and provisions of law running into hundreds of pages reflected their doubts, uncertainties and aspirations.

Furthermore, after statutes were enacted, the application of the principles in them to human controversies which arose in law and equity, led to a positive risk of variations. The more general the principles, the more difficult it was for men and women as litigants and for courts as tribunals of adjudication to agree on the meaning of principles as governing concrete cases. Especially is this true of novel cases not specifically contemplated or provided for in the written laws. And novel cases were and are perennial and striking features of life and law.

How far Married Women's Property Acts and kindred legislation fell short of covering in concrete anticipation the numerous problems that arose under them is indicated by the following types of questions raised and adjudicated in various jurisdictions of the United States after the process of abolishing common-law doctrines had been started. In order that the readers may decide for themselves, if they can, how these questions should have been answered under the theory of separate property rights and equality, the answers given to these questions by the judges in affirmative opinions, negative opinions, and diversities of opinions, are left to the readers' imagination.

Does the Married Women's Property Act relieve a husband of obligation to support his wife, even if he has become bankrupt and she is earning money?

If the wife leaves the husband without good reasons and returns home voluntarily at a later date, is the husband to pay the bills which she had incurred for her support during her absence?

Can the wife lawfully waive the husband's liability to support her with a view to helping him pay his debts to creditors?

If the husband employs his wife at wages otherwise payable to someone else, may she be deprived of the money or the property in which it is invested on the ground that it is actually her husband's?

May the wife take her separate property, enter business, and, without his consent, compete with her husband's who is legally liable for her support?

Where under a new statute the husband is forbidden to use even gentle force to restrain his wife, may he lawfully restrain her from committing a crime?

If the husband carries on a gambling business in his wife's house, may she be liable for his crimes committed therein?

There are a thousand other questions likely to arise in the married state to show the limitations of law in governing husband and wife relations. Even if perfection in legislative acts were possible and the marital relations of men and women could be placed on a footing of full equality, that would not automatically ensure actual equality in day-to-day relations. Human relations in general and marital relations in particular are governed and regulated far more by customs, traditions and the spiritual and moral outlook of human beings than by legal enactments and commands of the sovereign. Law alone is an insufficient guide and measures in gauging the extent to which a civilisation gives effect to the ideal of sex equality. To understand in full the attitude of a community towards the relations between the two sexes, we must look to its general moral teachings, as distinguished from legal provisions. Let us judge Islam from this angle and see how far it adds to the social dignity of women and ensures their equality in its social precepts, moral principles and spiritual directions.

In stating the general principles according to which marital relations should be regulated, the Quran had laid particular emphasis on love and compassion as an essential ingredient of married life:

> And one of His signs is that He created mates for you from among yourselves that you may find quiet of mind in them and He put between you love and compassion. (xxx. 21)

With a view to dispelling the false idea that men are inherently superior to women, the Quran emphasises that differences of race, tribe, sex and nationality do not disturb the fundamental equality of mankind:

> O you men! surely We have created you male and female and made you tribes and families that you may know each other; surely the most honourable of you with Allah is the one among you most careful (of his duty). (xlix. 13)

The same breadth of outlook is reflected in those verses of the Holy Quran which deal with the more concrete problems arising out of marital life. In regard to the treatment of wives whom their husbands wish to divorce, the Quran says:

> O believers! it is not lawful for you that you should take women as heritage against their will and do not straiten them in order to take from them a part of what you have given them, unless they are guilty of manifest indecency; and treat them kindly; then if you hate them, it may be that you dislike a thing while Allah has placed abundant good in it. (iv. 19)

> But when you divorce women, and the time for sending them away is come, either retain them with

> generosity, or put them away with generosity, but retain not them by constraint so as to be unjust towards them He who doth so, doth in fact injure himself. (ii. 231)

Generosity in the relations between husband and wife has been emphasised again and again:

> But if you divorce them before consummation and have already settled a dowry on them, ye shall give them half of what ye have settled, unless they relinquish or he should relinquish in whose hands is the marriage tie; and it is nearer to piety that you should relinquish; and do not forget to be generous between yourselves: surely Allah sees what you do. (ii. 237)

After a woman has been divorced, no motive remains for the husband to treat her kindly, but the Quran insists on kindly and generous treatment so long as there subsists the weakest tie among the partners:

> Lodge them where you lodge according to your, means, and do not injure them in order that you may straiten them; and if they are pregnant, spend on them until they lay down their burden; then if they suckle for you, give them their recompense; and consult among yourselves and act generously, and if you disagree, another woman shall suckle for him. Let him who has abundance spend out of his abundance, and whoever has his means of subsistence straitened to him, let him spend out of that which Allah has given him. Allah does not lay on any soul a burden except to the extent to which He has granted it. (lxv. 6-7)

The same generosity towards women is enjoined by the Prophet in his traditions. A report from Abu Hurairah says: 'No believer should be angry towards his wife. If some of her qualities are displeasing, there will be many other qualities worth appreciation' (Nail al-Autar, p. 125). Aishah, the wife of the Prophet, reports: The Prophet of God said: 'The best of you is he who is good to his wife' (Tirmidhi).

On the occasion of his last pilgrimage, the Prophet advised the Muslims to treat their women kindly and added: 'You have no more rights against them except that if they are guilty of manifest lewdness, you can ask them to leave your beds and strike them softly; if they improve their conduct, do not leave them helpless, because there are some rights for you over against them and some rights for them over against you. The duty of a woman is that she should not allow anyone to enter your house whom you dislike, nor spoil the bed which is your preserve and the duty of a man is that he should feed, clothe and treat his wife generously' (ibid.).

According to a report from Abdullah b. Umar, the Prophet declared: 'The whole world is a thing to be made use of and the best thing in the world is a virtuous wife' (Muslim). On his deathbed, the Prophet's last words related to the duty of offering prayers and safeguarding the rights of women and, slaves. About women he said: 'Women are like prisoners in your hands and you have taken them on trust from God and the word of God has made their private parts lawful for you; so be careful towards the treatment of women.' On another occasion the Prophet is reported to have declared: 'The Angel of God advised me so many times about women that I became convinced that it is not lawful for a man to divorce his wife, except when she commits adultery' (Irshad al-Muhtaj, Huquq al-Azwaj). A report from Bahz b. Hakim states: 'I inquired of the Prophet about his teaching in respect of women.

He replied: "Feed them as you feed yourselves, clothe them as you clothe yourselves and do not beat or scold them' (Kanz al-Unimal). According to Aishah, the Prophet's wife, he said about women: 'They are like pleasing roses,' meaning thereby that their grace and tenderness deserve special regard from men (ibid.). In regard to domestic duties, Islam has relieved women of all manual drudgery.

According to strict Islamic injunctions, it is not obligatory for a woman to cook the food for her husband or children, or to wash their clothes or even to suckle the infants. A woman may refuse to do any or all of these things without this being made a ground of legal complaint against her. If she undertakes these duties out of her regard for the husband, it is an act of sheer grace. It is reported that a man once came to Umar, the Second Caliph, with the intention of bringing to his notice certain complaints which he had against his wife.

When he reached the door of Umar's, house, he heard the Caliph's wife railing against him. Hearing this he went back as he thought that the Caliph was himself in the same predicament and could, therefore, be hardly expected to set matters right for him. Umar, coming out of his house, saw the person going back. So he called him out and inquired as to the purpose which had brought him to his house. He said that he had come to him with some complaints against his wife, but turned back on finding that the Caliph himself was subject to the same treatment from his wife.

Umar said to him that he patiently bore the excesses of his wife, because she had certain rights against him. 'Is it not true that she cooks my food, washes my clothes and suckles my children, thus relieving me of the necessity of employing a cook, a washerman and a nurse, although she is not in the slightest degree responsible for any of these duties? Not only that, I enjoy peace of mind on amount of her and I am protected from committing the sin of adultery. In view of all these advantages, I put up with her excesses. You should also do the same.'

In regard to the authority of men and women in their respective spheres, the following tradition of the Prophet shows the status enjoyed by women under Islam:

> Man is the ruler in his home. He will be held responsible for the conduct of his dependents, and woman is the ruler in her husband's home. She will also be held responsible for the conduct of her dependents. (Bukhari)

This tradition makes the wife co-equal of her husband in home affairs. She is as much responsible for the conduct of domestic affairs; as the husband. Only in larger matters affecting, the total welfare of the family, the husband is given a degree of superiority, since two coordinate authorities with equal powers are likely to lead to clashes and conflicts such as may destroy the balance and poise of family life.

A Social Bond : Marriage in Islam is regarded as a strong bond and a total commitment to life, to society and to being a respectable human. It is a promise that the married couple make to one another and to God. This undertaking on the part of the married partners would allow them to find mutual fulfilment and self-realisation, love and peace, comfort and hope. This is because marriage in Islam is essentially a righteous act and an act of complete devotion. As such, celibacy is discouraged not only for men, but for women as well. This is in consideration of the fact that their needs are equally legitimate and valid.

Islam views marriage as a natural course for women in the same way as it is for men, and probably even more so, in view of the fact that marriage guarantees women some form of economic security. It must be stressed here that this benefit for women is in no way an indication that marriage in Islam is sheer economic transaction. Indeed, the economic factor is the least aspect of the whole enterprise; the emphasis has been always on the religious qualities of the spouses.

From the collective point of view the most significant benefit is of course procreation, but not just the physical perpetuation of the human race; rather, the institution of marriage ensures that this procreative function will be both sanctified and orderly, not vulgar and chaotic. From the specifically religious point of view, having children entails the following: the realisation of God's desire, the fulfilment of the Prophet's call to marry and increase his followers' number; gaining the fruit of a child's prayer.

Muslims believe that when parents die and leave a child, his prayer would benefit the dead parents. However, if the child dies before his parents, he would make intercession on his parents' behalf. Fulfilling one's sexual desire is another important aspect of marriage. Marriage, from the Islamic viewpoint, helps control sexual passion and channel it in the right direction. Also, it functions as a shield against committing adultery and fornication, both of which are forbidden in Islam. Marriage, moreover, brings peace and tranquillity of spirit and implants love and compassion between the married partners. These are great supports for one's worship of God. Intimacy between spouses is viewed as catalyst for the development of their souls.

In other words, the intimate relationship that develops between a husband and wife is crucial for relieving the heart from its burdens and thus enables the mind to better focus on accomplishing the Divine requirements. Al-Ghazzali beautifully explains this point in the following account: 'The third benefit of marriage is that the heart finds ease through intimacy with women, because of sitting and joking with them. This ease then becomes the cause of an increase in desire for worship. For diligence in worship brings weariness, and the heart contracts. But ease acquired in this way brings back the heart's strength. Ali said, 'Do not remove rest and ease completely from the hearts, lest they become blind'. It sometimes happened that the Prophet was overcome by such tremendous unveilings that his bodily frame was not able to tolerate it.

The marital link helps the partners to work together and cooperate amicably in the management of the domestic affairs of their house; hence sufficient time could be spared to meet the Divine commandments. Therefore, the Prophet is reported to have advised his followers to choose the right spouses who would help them attain Divine blessings.

Marriage, in addition, is seen as an opportunity to develop for oneself a good and sound character as a result of the added family responsibility which both spouses have to endure during their married life. Hence, success in carrying out family commitments (which are equally regarded as divine duties) would ensure Divine reward. The Prophet said 'A man will be rewarded for what he spends on his wife, even for putting a morsel of food into her mouth'.

Also, 'Whoever performs his prayers correctly, and spends on his children in spite of his modest means, and does not speak ill against others, will be in paradise as close to me as these [two fingers of mine]'. Finally, marriage ensures social stability and a dignified form of living for both partners (the husband and the wife), probably even more for women since it guarantees their rights both as wives as well as mothers (of course alongside their fights as individuals).

Since Islam takes marriage seriously, its concern has been always to ensure that the marriage bond stays relatively stable and durable. To achieve these goals, it has laid down certain rules and regulations to meet these objectives. First, the couple have to be of proper marriageable age; also, there should be no discrepancy between their ages. It must be stressed that the claim by some scholars that the groom has to be always senior in age so as to ensure a healthy marriage relationship has no religious grounds and in practical terms does not make any sense. In fact, it contradicts the practice of the Prophet, two of whose wives (Khadijah and Sauda) happened to be older than him; despite this, the record shows that they lived in peace and harmony.

Second, there should be a degree of compatibility between the two partners in terms of social status, educational standards and physical attraction (again the claim by some scholars that the bride has to be more beautiful and more attractive than her groom is a fallacy). Third, the dowry of the bride should be of a reasonable level: neither too high, which could cause hardship for both of them, nor too low which might give the impression that the bride is of no worth. The dowry which is in its essence a gift from the groom to the bride-should be affordable and manageable so as to ensure satisfaction and happiness on both sides. Fourth, the consent of the couple is crucial for the stability and durability of the marriage. Both have to enter into the wedlock with free will and without coercion.

Compelling the couple (or even just one of them) to contract an unsatisfactory union would be detrimental to the interest of both sides and could lead to a disastrous end. Fifth, the prospective partners have to be pious and of good moral conduct. Both have to be kind, sympathetic, considerate, patient and loving, caring to one another; this encourages peace and harmony in domestic life. Sixth, the two parties have to declare, from the beginning, their intentions to keep the marital bond as permanent as humanly possible. This commitment requires that the marriage contract should be free of any hidden agenda such as casual or temporary unions.

Islam is against all marriages that have been described as experimental, casual and temporary. In a clear statement, the Prophet outrightly denounced those men and women who enjoy the frequent change of marital partners and warned against their unacceptable behaviour. Having stated the importance Islam lays on the permanency of marriage, it is essential to stress that in Islam there is no concept of 'indissoluble' marriage.

Although Islam endeavours to keep the marital link stable and intact, this does not mean that the wedlock cannot be brought to an end if there are compelling circumstances. Indeed, Islam recognises that if the marriage is not working, it is in the interest of both sides to terminate it on good terms. Hence, divorce in Islam is a legitimate act, although it is discouraged by the Prophet. Islam, as we know, encourages both men and women to marry. Just like a man, a Muslim woman (virgin or non-virgin) has the freedom to propose to a man of her liking, either orally or in writing (I wonder how many Muslim women these days would dare to initiate an oral proposal, let alone put it in writing!).

The Muslim woman has the freedom of marital choice: she is at liberty to choose her prospective husband, look at him and get to know him without coercion on the part of the father or other relatives. If force or pressure takes place, she has the right to appeal to the court to redress the wrong. Her consent is essential for the validity of the marriage contract.

The Prophet is reported to have made the following statements: 'A previously married woman shall not be married till she gives her consent, nor should a virgin be married till her consent is sought'. 'A previously married woman is more a guardian for herself than her guardian, and a virgin should be asked permission about herself, and her permission is her silence'. 'A grown-up girl shall be asked permission about herself. If she is silent, it is her permission; and if she declines, there shall be no compulsion on her'.

According to Islam, a divorced or widowed woman has the right to remarry without any shame or denunciation. In fact, the Quran allows the betrothal of a divorced or widowed woman even during her period of transition (idda). 'It shall be no offence for you openly to propose marriage indirectly to such women or to cherish them in your hearts. Allah knows that you will remember them. Do not arrange to meet them in secret and, if you do, speak to them honourably. But you shall not consummate the marriage before the end of their waiting period. Know that Allah has knowledge of all your thoughts. Therefore take heed and bear in mind that Allah is forgiving and merciful'.

Neither age nor previous marriage would impede a woman

from contracting perfect matches. Many are the examples which can be cited from the early Muslim community during which women were, very often, re-married after they were divorced or widowed, and this was done without stigma or discredit. Take, for instance, Umm-Kulthum bint Uqba, an early convert from Mecca. She emigrated to Medina in defiance of her family, who tried to force her to return to Mecca, but to no avail. She stayed in Medina and married her first husband, Zaid bin Harith. When Zaid was killed in one of the battles she contracted a second marriage with Zubayr bin al-Awwam. Zubayr was rough with her, so she decided to part with him. After the separation, she married Abdul Rahman bin Auf, her third husband, and bore him two sons.

Upon Abdul Rahman's death, Umme Kulthum once more contracted herself into marriage, to her fourth and final husband, this time with the conqueror of Egypt, Amr ibn al-As. She stayed with him until she passed away. Atika bint Zaid is another good example. She was a woman of exceptional abilities who had managed to contract four marriages during her lifetime. Her first husband was Abdullah ibn Abu Bakr, son of the first Caliph Abu Bakr. He died, leaving her a fortune on condition that she would not re-marry. For a while she was content with the idea of living a celibate life, but later she decided to go against his wish and not to spend the rest of her life alone; hence her decision to accept Umar ibn al-Khattab, the second Caliph, as her second husband. When Umar was assassinated in 642 she married her third husband, Zubayr ibn al-Awwam. After his death in 656, she took her fourth husband, Hussain ibn Ali, son of the fourth Caliph Ali; by this time she was around forty-five years old.

Marriage in Islam requires a contract between two equal partners. Hence in Islamic terms, the woman is to be a subject rather than an object in the marriage contract. The contract, in sum, is a legal written document between two adults, which entails an offer by one partner and an acceptance by the other in the presence of two witnesses. The Qadi, or official, usually solemnises the marriage in a mosque or court or any other location.

The consent of the prospective wife is crucial for the effectiveness of the marriage contract. Any force or blackmail on the part of the relatives would automatically render the contract invalid. The bride, moreover, has the exclusive right to stipulate her own conditions in the contract. These conditions include mainly (though not exclusively) such issues as marriage terms (the right, for example, to have a monogamous relationship whilst she is still living with her husband) and divorce terms (the right, for instance, to dissolve the marital bond at her own initiative if she deems it necessary). In addition, dowries-one initial and another deferred in case of divorce-must be specified and written down and they should be of substance. The dowry (or Mehr, in Islamic terms) belongs to the wife; it is her exclusive right and it should not be given away, neither to her family nor to her relatives. The Quran says 'Give women their dowry as a free gift; but if they choose to make over to you a part of it, you may regard it as lawfully yours'.

When the marriage is consummated, the couple assume a new relationship: that is, a husband-wife relationship. It is a kind of reciprocal and interdependent relationship. The Quran says 'And of His signs is that He gave you wives from among yourselves, that you might live in tranquillity with them, and put love and kindness in your hearts. Surely there are signs in this for thinking people'. The verse implies that in a marriage bond the two partners are a comfort to each other. They should find and enjoy peace and tranquillity in each other's company and be bound together not only by a sexual relationship but also by love, compassion and mercy. As such, both have to demonstrate mutual care, affection, respect and be prepared to make sacrifices.

There should be no servility on the part of either side, for they are two equal partners in a healthy, loving and caring relationship. The Quran eloquently illustrates this equal partnership in the following statement: 'They are an apparel to you, as you are an apparel to them'. The verse explains that just as a garment covers a person completely and provides him/her with warmth, protection and decency, in the same way a husband and wife provide each other with the necessary warmth, comfort, intimacy and protection.

The realisation of these principles in actual life depends, mainly, on the way both partners react to each other.' In this context, the Quran expects them to behave in the best manner toward each other. The husband, on the one hand, is commanded to treat his wife gently and with kindness, affection and consideration. The Prophet said 'The best of you is the best of you to his wife, and I am better than any of you toward my wife'. He is to deal with her with dignity and in an equitable manner, not to hurt or injure her feelings. He is to show her that he loves her, appreciates her good qualities and he is to give her the impression that he needs her and depends on her to attain happiness in life. Also, he is asked to ensure that his tasks as husband and father are fulfilled to the utmost. Besides, the husband has to meet his legal responsibility to provide full maintenance of the wife: a task which he has to accomplish with good cheer and gladness.

The wife, on the other hand, is similarly required to reciprocate in kindness towards her husband, treat him with respect, admire his good qualities and express her love and affection to him. Also, she is called upon to ensure that her duties as wife and mother are performed to the best of her abilities. To maintain a happy conjugal relationship, both partners must be loyal, honest, direct, and trustworthy. They should be thoughtful, sympathetic and sensitive towards each other's feelings; in particular, they must avoid raising each other's suspicions and jealousy and try to maintain their integrity as husband and wife, united together in a matrimonial link.

Concerning their sexual intimacy, both must be pleasing and receptive. They should endeavour to attain and give maximum gratification.

Moreover, in order to keep the marital link intact, stable and healthy, both partners have to demonstrate their willingness to share the burden of looking after the welfare of the family. They must share the ups and downs of married life, be prepared to make sacrifices, pay attention to each other's point of view, consult each other and adopt joint decisions on important matters that affect the entire family. These joint decisions have to be delivered or enforced by the husband since, in Islam, he is the head of the family. This is based on the following Quranic verses which give the husband the right to be in charge of the family: 'Women shall with justice have rights similar to those exercised against them, although men have a degree above women. Allah is Mighty and Wise'. 'Men have authority over women because Allah has made the one superior to the other, and because they spend their wealth to maintain them'. These verses were and still are a source of much discussion and debate throughout the Muslim world, generating a host of different interpretations. These interpretations range from liberal to moderate to conservative.

Our view in this context is that the headship of the husband should on no account be a license for dictatorship; it should entail no absolute freedom on the part of the person in charge; if the husband misuses or abuses his status, the wife has ' the right to interfere to rectify the situation. After all, the whole issue of being a chairperson is to ensure the smooth running of the family. Any neglect on the part of the husband to fulfil the task which is designated to him justifies his replacement by the more able person (the wife).

However, God-conscious pairs would always act responsibly because they are aware of their commitments to God as well as to each other. Also, because they are conscious of the fact that if they live up to their promises and act rationally in their married life they would invoke God's pleasure, hence making their lives a perpetual joy and paradise. But, sadly, this kind of paradise, envisaged by the Quran and practised briefly during the Prophet's time, has hardly ever been realised.

In fact, the case has nearly always been the reverse. Slowly but surely, attitudes towards women and marriage changed. The Quranic principles which bestowed honour, dignity, kindness and respect on women were gradually eroded and went into limbo. Customs, rather than Divine laws, shaped and continue to shape the social fabric of society and govern people's attitudes towards women and marriage. The outcome has been a steady deterioration in the status of women as far as their marital rights are concerned. Take, for example, the right to initiate a marriage proposal. This has been completely abandoned: not even in her wildest dreams would a woman dare to propose orally or in writing. The disappearance of this early practice has been so total that most women, even educated ones, are not aware of its existence, let alone practise it. The right to exercise her choice in selecting a marriage partner has, in most cases, been forgotten.

Most marriages that currently take place in Muslim societies are arranged unions, during which force and intimidation are quite often employed to obtain the girl's consent. Moreover, her freedom to sign the marriage contract has been considerably curtailed. The majority of Muslim marriages nowadays are contracted through agents (guardians, especially on the part of the woman), very often a male member of the family (father, brother, or uncle), who formalises and signs the contract on her behalf. In doing so, her opportunity and right to negotiate marriage and divorce terms are deliberately denied.

In most cases, a woman is subjected to considerable pressure to avoid stipulating in her marriage contract a divorce right or any other rights which might be viewed as a constraint on the freedom of the husband. If she did so, the social pressure on her would be so tremendous that in the end she would be obliged to give up, otherwise she would be accused of endangering the whole enterprise. Divorce has become a stigma and women are always regarded as being culpable.

The prospects for a non-virgin (divorcee or widow) getting remarried is dim. Indeed, in many cases they are forced to spend the rest of their lives cherishing the memories of their dead husbands and serving the male members of their own families. Within the context of a husband-wife relationship, authoritarianism and dictatorship have replaced the ideal and equal partnership advocated by the Quran.

The husband assumes the role of ruler, superior, controller, oppressor and master, while the wife, on the other hand, is reduced to a slave, a captive, a low, inferior and submissive creature. Listen to what the so called Council of Ulama (that is, people with knowledge about Islam) of South Africa has to say about the relationship between the two spouses: 'She (the wife) should mould herself to wholeheartedly submit to his whims and fancies. His likes must become her likes and his dislikes, her dislikes. She should step out of her way to comfort him and to console him in his worries and distress.

Her wishes and desires are subservient to his wishes and orders.... After all (God) has created her for her husband's comfort and peace'. The Council goes on to say 'The Shariah has accorded the husband the highest degree of authority over his wife. Likewise it will transpire that the wife has to offer the higher degree of submission to her husband... with humility and patience she should tolerate his shortcomings and even his injustice... men are the rulers of women and they have a superior rank... (as such) it is the husband's right and role to dominate and dictate (and) it is the duty of the wife to submit and serve. The wife should understand that she can never conquer her husband by confrontation and seeking to set herself up as his equal or superior'.

Concerning the financial arrangements between them, the

Council stresses: 'It is significant that in spite of the wife remaining the sole owner of her wealth... (she is encouraged) to put her wealth at his disposal and pleasure'. What about his money? 'She should not attempt to appoint herself as the controller of his finances. It is none of her business on whom her husband spends his wealth'. What if the husband fails to perform his duties properly?

The Council emphasises: 'She must not adopt a legal stand and a technical attitude, demanding from her husband perfect and total fulfilment of her legal rights.... The wife has to remember that despite her husband's failure to fulfil his duties to her, she is under... obligation to obey her husband.... obedience to the husband will ensure the everlasting happiness... for her'.

The mutual responsibilities on both sides to demonstrate to each other their loyalty, honesty and respect have become exclusively the wife's domain and obligations. The husband has been deliberately left out of the equation. So whether he is honest and loyal or a cheat it does not matter. What matters most (and this is important to him and to the male-dominated society) is the faithfulness and loyalty of the wife. There is no question of reciprocity between them in this matter. The emphasis has always been on the wife, as if she is a creature with no control over her sexuality.

The word 'divorce' 'traces its origin back to the Latin derivative and conjures up the splitting of a unit, the permanent physical separation of the spouses', while the Arabic word '*talaq*' is derived from the verb *itlaq* which means to set loose, set free or to leave. Talaq, therefore, within the context of the marital link means to terminate the bond created by a marriage contract.

In every society there are ways and means which allow the marital link to be dissolved if it fails to fulfil its objective. The reasons for the dissolution of marriage are, generally speaking, common and almost universal. They apply to human society irrespective of time, place or level of civilisation from the unavoidable death of a spouse or involuntary barrenness to the trivial cooking mistake of burning the husband's food or putting too much salt in it, not to mention the man's arbitrary dislike of his spouse or capricious preference for another woman who seems more pleasing to him. So the termination of marriage is sometimes inevitable and no system can afford to ignore this reality, otherwise it is doomed to failure.

Any system which insists on the indissolubility of marriage and overlooks the fact that under exceptional circumstances the dissolution of the family becomes a necessity is static, impractical and does not respond adequately to human needs. A system under which marriage is indissoluble would inevitably lead to the abuse of marriage, because people will always find ways around it, hence defeating the whole purpose which the system stands for in the first place.

In principle, Islam regards marriage as a lifelong commitment. However, sometimes there do arise situations wherein marriage ceases to fulfil its purpose. Hence, divorce can be invoked by either side or both of them in order to accommodate the realities of an unsuccessful marriage. It, must be stressed that divorce can only be exercised as the last resort after all efforts for reconciliation between the spouses are exhausted. Therefore, in Islam divorce is considered a necessity if the married partners are not happy. However, divorce is heavily disapproved of and discouraged.

The Quran discourages divorce in the following verses: 'And (remember) when you (Muhammad) said to the man (Zaid, Muhammad's adopted son) whom Allah and yourself have favoured: keep your wife and have fear of Allah'. In this verse there is an implicit disapproval of divorce.

In other verses the Quran clearly discourages Muslims from having recourse to a hasty divorce, even though they might be dissatisfied with their marriage partners. 'Treat them with kindness; for even if you do dislike them, it may well be that you may dislike a thing which Allah has meant for your own good'.

The Quran not only discourages divorce, but it prohibits the slandering of one's wife in order to take back her dowry 'If you wish to have a wife in the place of a (divorced) one, do not take from her the dowry you have given her even it if be a talent of gold. That would be improper and grossly unjust; for how can you take it back when you have lain with each other and entered into a firm contract?'

Divorce was also discouraged by the Prophet, who is reported to have said: 'Of all things licit, the most hateful to God is divorce,' Also: 'Let not the faithful man hate the faithful woman; if he dislikes some of her habits, he may like others.' Ali, the son-in-law of the Prophet, said, 'Marry and do not divorce your wives, for divorce causes God's throne to tremble.' These disapprovals notwithstanding, Islam concedes the possibility of divorce as the lesser of two evils when the alternative is a disastrously unhappy marriage and it devotes much attention to dealing with it both in the Quran as well as in the Sunnah.

There are many causes for divorce. If the spouses discover that they are incompatible because of their ideas and opinions, their modes of behaviour and their temperaments, then they should resort to divorce. The conflict and tension that would inevitably arise as a result of their incompatibility would certainly give rise to ill feeling and contempt between the spouses. This would adversely affect not only the couple but their children as well as their relatives and closest friends. As a way out of this difficult situation, Islam therefore prescribes divorce.

Furthermore, spouses locked forcibly in an unhappy union would surely be forced themselves—in an attempt to satisfy their sexual urge—to seek sexual intimacy outside the marriage tie, hence falling into the trap of committing adultery, which is forbidden in Islam. To prevent partners from indulging in such indecency, Islam allows the couple to be divorced so that they can go their own separate ways.

Divorce is also granted if the husband is impotent. Divorce, moreover, can take place if both spouses or one of them suffers a serious disease that renders the continuation of the marital relation either impossible or unsafe, or if the husband is put in prison for a long time or fails to support his wife.

In order for the divorce to be effective and valid, the person who is performing it has to be adult (*baligh*), sane (*aqil*), free from any confusion or coercion and full of clear and good intentions (*qasid*). In addition, the witnesses have to be reliable, trustworthy and of good conduct.

Divorce in Islam is one of those issues which has generated considerable controversy and debate among Muslims and non-Muslims alike; this is probably because it has been grossly abused by Muslims and certainly misunderstood by both Muslims and non-Muslims.

Islam is against divorce and is strongly in support of the family unit: hence, both spouses have to do their utmost to build up a strong and harmonious marital relationship. If, however, tension arises between them, they should not rush into a hasty divorce. First, they should try and make some serious efforts to save their marriage. For example, they should attempt to stand the causes of their differences and try to solve them in a private and amicable way. If this proves to be unsuccessful, then they are advised to ask representatives, one from each side, to mediate and try to restore peace between them.

The Quran says, 'If you fear a breach between a man and his wife, appoint an, arbiter from his people and another from hers. If they wish to be reconciled, Allah will bring them together again-Allah is Knowing, Wise'. The arbiters have to be close to the parties involved and command their trust and respect. They should conduct their task impartially and discreetly. Also, they should try and settle the differences between the spouses without publicity; they should especially attempt to avoid the embarrassment of revealing such issues that might be regarded (by the married partners) as very private and intimate. The decisions reached by the arbiters are binding on both spouses. However, if one or both of them refuse to abide by them, then the rulings have to be enforced by the court.

The Quran clearly protects the right of the woman in this matter. By insisting here that two arbiters one from the side of each party (the husband as well as the wife) have to be called to investigate the matter between them peacefully and objectively, it has in fact put the interests of the wife on an equal footing with those of her husband, by giving her the opportunity to present her case and viewpoint before the arbiters. This is surely a fair and just way to deal with divorce matters because it takes into consideration the interests of both sides. More importantly, it protects the weak (the wife) from being abused by the strong (the husband), an outcome which all too frequently occurs in our society these days. For example, it prevents the husband from arbitrarily divorcing his wife without any due consideration for her mental or physical well-being, a practice very often used by the husband to punish his wife in contemporary Muslim societies.

In light of the above it would seem sensible to favour and recommend the adoption of this orderly divorce process by the judicial systems of all Muslim countries for it is simple, civilised and, most importantly, authentically Islamic: it has been described and recommended by the Quran. So, it is not something foreign or alien to Islam; on the contrary, it is an integral part of the Islamic tradition. Indeed there are many examples in which divorce cases were judged according to this procedure in early Islamic history.

For instance, it has been reported that during the reign of

the fourth Caliph Ali (son-in-law of the Prophet), a man and his wife approached him complaining about each other's behaviour and stating that there were gross differences between them that had made their lives miserable. Ali immediately acted as Judge and asked for representatives from both sides to be despatched to him. Upon their arrival, he commissioned them to look into the matter carefully and decide whether there would be any possibility of making peace between them.

Also, he reminded them of their responsibility and sacred duty to handle the case with tact, due consideration and impartiality. He told them that if they sensed that there was a chance that they could be reconciled then they should spare no effort in doing so, otherwise they had to be separated with honour and in dignity. When the arbiters reached a decision, Ali made it legally effective by forcing the spouses to abide by it.

If the arbiters realise that there is a good chance for patching up things between the spouses, they are encouraged to do so, but if they think otherwise, the partners have to be allowed to go their own separate ways. It is most unfortunate that such a humane understanding of the verse and such a civilised practice of it failed to materialise throughout most of our Islamic history. For one reason or another, both the jurists as well as the rulers decided to ignore and shelve it.

Nevertheless, there were a few scholars who continued to stress the importance of utilising the directions contained in this verse and use them as guidance to promote legal or judicial divorce systems in the Muslim world. One of the most respected Egyptian scholars, Muhammad Abduh, advocated such reform.

In his book *Women and Islam*, Abduh explains as follows:

> The call in this verse if you fear a breach between a man and his wife, appoint an arbiter from his people and another from hers is a general, not specific, one. It cannot be the responsibility of every person or

every group of people in society. Therefore, there are two opinions among the interpreters: one says that the call is directed to the people who are concealed with the general affairs of the Muslim people, namely the rulers or representatives who are responsible for their overall well being. Both opinions are right, for the first one allocates the responsibility of looking after the interest of the people in the bands of the representatives who have to endeavour to do their jobs properly, while the second one assigns the duty to the general public who have to team up and be cooperative with one another.

As far as the representatives are concerned, Abduh explains that there are two different views: one sees that the arbiters as mere mediators with no legal authority, while the other insists on regarding them as judges with legal power to enforce their decisions. Concerning the part which states, 'If they wish to be reconciled, Allah will bring them together again. Allah is, Knowing, Wise', Abduh interprets it thus: this part means that, God favours peace and harmony between spouses and wishes that they would be reconciled, because of the emphasis Islam lays on the family unit in society. As such the arbiters are exhorted to ensure that peace can prevail between them. However, if the arbiters fail to bridge the gap between the couple, they are not to blame.

Abduh then introduces his own version. He says: 'when conflict erupts between husband and wife and proves difficult to solve amicably, the spouses are advised to take the matter to the judge of the county. The judge here has to appoint two mediators-one represents the wife while the other acts for the husband. Both representatives have to be of good character and highly respected people. The judge, after briefing them, has to send them to the spouses in an attempt to solve the dispute. If the arbiters' efforts culminate in success, then it is good news. But if they fail to bring the two spouses together again, then they have the legal power to divorce them. The representatives, after completing their mission, have to report to the judge and the judge has to enforce their decision.

It must be stressed here that the mediators—when they decide on separation have to give only one revocable divorce, so that time may be given to the spouses to reflect on their situation before final separation can take place.' Abduh's view on the judicial process of divorce found acceptance among the reformers in some Muslim countries who thought that improvement in this area was badly needed because the unlimited power of the husband to repudiate his wife was grossly abused, hence making the lives of many Muslim women unbearable. His view was, therefore, incorporated into their legal systems and helped them to introduce such reform. Tunisia, for example, was one of a few Muslim countries which decided to introduce legal, reform based on Abduh's view on judicial divorce.

The Tunisian reformers argued that; 'In the case of discord between spouses, the Quran orders the appointment of arbitrators-yet what more obvious case of discord between spouses is there than a pronouncement of repudiation by the husband? And who is then better qualified to undertake the necessary function of arbitration than the official tribunals? On this ground, therefore, the right of a husband to repuditate his wife extra judiciously, was abolished.'

Thus, all divorce actions were prohibited, henceforth taking place outside, the domain of the court. The introduction of such reform has heralded two things. Firstly, it has empowered the court with an unrestricted power to compensate the wife for any injury endured as a result of the divorce; secondly, it ensures that both spouses are treated on an equal basis in this regard.

The Quran deals with divorce issues in another verse which states:

> Divorce may be pronounced twice, and then a woman must be retained in honour or allowed to go with kindness. It is unlawful for husbands to take from them anything they have given them, unless both fear that they may not be able to keep within the bounds set by Allah; in which case it shall be no offence for either of them if the wife ransoms herself.

In this verse, God explains that divorce may be pronounced twice, during which period reconciliation can take place; hence it is a revocable type of divorce, since the couple can still resume their marital life if they wish to do so.

However, a third pronouncement would lead to irrevocable divorce, after which the spouses cannot remarry, unless the woman marries another person first and that person also divorces her. In this case, she is allowed to remarry her former husband if she desires to do so: 'If a man divorces his wife, he cannot remarry her until she has wedded another man and been divorced by him; in which case it shall be no offence for either of them to return to the other, if they think that they can keep within the limits set by Allah. Such are the bounds of Allah. He makes them plain to men of understanding.'

Divorce must be pronounced when the wife is in a state of purity (*tuhr*), otherwise it is regarded as invalid. The reason for not allowing the husband to divorce his wife during the state of impurity is that the husband is physically separated from her and this might induce him to press ahead with the separation. While if she is in a state of purity, he is physically close to her and in this case he might be persuaded to reconsider his decision.

Anyway, if divorce takes place, the wife has to observe *idda* or the waiting period. This lasts for three months, during which time sexual intercourse is not allowed between the spouses. By the end of this waiting period, the separation becomes final and legally effective. The reason for making the waiting period obligatory is to ensure the achievement of the following: first, to give the spouses more time to reconsider their attitudes and resolve their differences; second, to determine whether or not the wife is pregnant, for if she is expecting a child there is always a good chance that the spouses might be willing to effect a reconciliation.

Both spouses are encouraged to recognise and respect each other's rights, after the separation. In particular, the Quran exhorts the man to be considerate and kind to his former wife. Also, he is enjoined to act with due care and not allow her to be thrown out of her house. He must ensure that she may stay, if she wishes, with respect and dignity. Moreover, he should properly maintain her and give her sufficient support. Here, it must be noted that there are differences of opinion among scholars regarding the maintenance of divorced women. Some recommend that a divorcee is entitled to sustenance, which includes both the dowry as well as a financial allowance, whilst others insist that the payment of her maintenance should only continue for the period of idda, which is not more than three menstrual cycles.

Under Islamic Law, the marriage contract may be dissolved in three ways: first, the death of one of the spouses; second, by act of the husband or the wife or both of them; third, through Judicial process or a decree of court. The dissolution of the marriage contract by the husband is called Talaq (divorce), which is usually translated as repudiation. It can be done unilaterally by the husband without his having to produce any reason. This form of divorce or *talaq* has been classified (by the jurists) into three main types:

Talaq al-Ahsan: This is the most approved form of repudiation. In this kind of Talaq the husband has to pronounce one single divorce during *tuhr* or the period of purity of the wife. Then he must abstain from having physical contact with her during the waiting period. This form of repudiation is revocable. For the husband can, before the end of the idda, revoke the divorce and resume the conjugal relationship. It must be noted here that the approval of the wife is essential in this context. The husband cannot force her back, even if he regrets divorcing her. She must first give her consent before the couple can resume their matrimonial relations. In order for him to signal his intention to retain her, he may express this desire either explicitly or implicitly. The former is the preferred one, and is usually done by pronouncing the revocation of the repudiation. If, during the waiting period, one of the spouses dies, the other can still inherit the estate. If the husband allows the waiting period to elapse without reclaiming his wife, the repudiation becomes irrevocable or absolute (*bayan*).

Talaq al-Hasan: This is a less approved form of divorce. Here the husband repudiates his wife three successive times over a period of three months, once each month during the period of tuhr. As with Ahsan talaq, the husband can revoke his divorce after the first or second repudiation, but after the third repudiation the divorce becomes absolute (bayan). The only difference is that the wife cannot remarry her former husband until she has first married someone else and then dissolved that marriage. The reason for adding this condition is to prevent a hasty repudiation on the part of the husband.

Talaq al-Bidah: This is the least approved method of divorce in the Muslim world but, unfortunately, it is the most widely used. It is highly condemned by women and civilised men and regarded as sinful. Nonetheless, it is considered legally effective once it is pronounced. This form of divorce is effected by three repudiations, which may be pronounced at any time (not merely in clean periods) and without definite intervals'.

It is an irrevocable form of talaq and the husband can only remarry his ex-wife after she has contracted a new marriage with a second man and dissolved that marriage (after proper consummation). Bidah divorce lacks any Quranic support. Also, it was strongly denounced by the Prophet, who is reported to have reacted angrily when he heard that somebody had divorced his wife by the triple pronouncement of talaq in a single sitting and said 'How would you play with the book of Allah while I am alive and amidst you?' He then ordered the man to take back his wife. Nonetheless, this innovative divorce acquired legitimacy under the reign of the second Caliph Umar, who decided to make it legal in an attempt to prevent any careless use of the formula. However, his efforts in this context proved to no avail as his decree eventually produced counterproductive results. Since then it has remained lawful and legally effective among Sunnis (the Shia do not recognise this type of divorce), and men have continued to make use of it to their own advantage. We are therefore strongly in favour of banning it outright. It is a bizarre and odd practice; most importantly, it is very degrading to the dignity of Muslim women.

The great jurist, Ibn Taymiyyah, was against it. He stated that the erratic use of such a practice (triple pronouncement on a single occasion) was invalid and had no impact on the statutory position of a marriage. His aim was to protect women, as he thought that they were victimised by such a ruling (Umar's validation of Bidah divorce). It is a shame that his position has been forgotten and disregarded in contemporary Muslim societies.

The dissolution of marriage by the wife takes two forms:

> Talaq al-Tawfid, (or delegated divorce.) In this form of divorce the husband, at the time of marriage, agrees to delegate to his wife the power of pronouncing the talaq, thus allowing her to dissolve the marriage contract. It must be stressed here that once the husband consents to give his wife the right to divorce him, he is no longer in a position to reclaim it. Tawfid divorce is indeed a powerful weapon in the hands of the wife, since she can easily use it if the conditions in the marriage contract are violated by the husband.
>
> Khula, also called ransom by some jurists Here, the

wife initiates the divorce, but the husband has to agree to free her in return for repayment of part or all of the dowry or mehr. A woman, seeking khula, however, may lose her right to maintenance during the waiting period. Women's right to khula was acknowledged and respected during the early Islamic era; they were very often allowed to exercise it without fear or intimidation. For a woman to request khula she does not have to quote any specific reason; the fact that she is unhappy with her husband would be enough to grant her separation under khula.

Divorce through mutual consent is usually called *Mubaraah*. This form of divorce centres around an agreement between spouses to release each other from the marital link with no exchange or payment on either side.

The final method of dissolving the marriage contract is through a judicial process, at the instigation of either the wife or husband.

This can be obtained in the case of (a) Lian and (b) annulment.

Lian: It is the divorce by oath and it occurs when the husband accuses his wife of committing adultery without evidence. The court, after studying the case and hearing particular oaths from both spouses, would issue a decree allowing the marriage to be dissolved. This form of separation is irrevocable and the partners cannot remarry each other again.

Annulment: The annulment of the marriage takes place when the wife lodges a complaint against her husband on the basis of the following: impotence, failure to fulfil the marital obligations, maltreatment, insanity and any other causes which might justify the annulment of the marriage.

Women's Rights

Men have been exhorted to marry women of their choice and liking, provided they do not transgress the prescribed limits. There are some women with whom it is unlawful to marry. Some are near relatives and some belong to other religions. Except these women, man has the freedom to select from among other women. The women also enjoy the same right of choice. There is no pressure or compulsion to marry a particular man or woman. Everyone who has a grain of common sense knows that at the time of purchasing a thing costing even only a few pennies, we make sure of our full satisfaction as having made a good bargain. Who can then advise anyone to marry in haste without proper investigation? It is obvious that the thing upon which depend the lives of two people, who are strangers, cannot be taken lightly.

Islam which is a harbinger of justice and peace for the oppressed and downtrodden humanity and their greatest supporter, does not at all tolerate that the rights of the rightful people should not be restored to them. It aims at curbing tyranny and oppression with an iron hand. So the Holy Prophet (peace and blessings of Allah be upon him) declared that all sorts of persecution should be ended. He did not leave any aspect of life untouched and issued reforms in conjugal life as well. He safeguarded the rights of the downtrodden and trampled humanity by holding back the hand of the tyrant so that the husband and wife could lead a happy and fulfilled life, the real purpose of marriage.

It would be better if the rights and obligations of the husband and wife are determined in the light of the teachings of Holy Quran and the Sunnah. Both the husband and wife enjoy full rights. The only restriction on them is that none of them should transgress the limits imposed by Allah.

Islam has, within prescribed limits, given priority to the opinion of the men and women who are going to be married in the matter of the selection of a spouse. Their opinion must be sought. Before the advent of Islam, the parents or guardians wedded their daughters to men whom they did not like, by exerting undue pressure upon them, thus committing tyranny and oppression on them. Especially, the orphan girls were subjected to the worst oppression.

History bears ample proof of the fact that in the Days of Ignorance, the condition of women was most miserable. The poor creature was condemned to be a moveable property which had been bought by a man on payment of dower. After the death of her husband, the heirs considered her as their personal property and perpetrated all sorts of tyrannies on her. Islam eradicated this evil.

Just as every wise man and woman are free to decide their worldly matters after attaining puberty, similarly in the matter of marriage, Islam has given them freedom to give their proposals. Parents and other relatives can give them suitable advice, as they should, but they should not pressurise the boy or girl. The men and women going to be married should act upon the advice of their experienced and loving parents and relatives, but according to Islam, their advice is not binding on them.

> It is far from the truth to say that in Islam women are helpless, dumb creatures. Islam has given them freedom of choice like men. In contracting marriage, the consent of a woman, attaining the age of puberty must always be sought. The Holy Prophet (peace and blessings of Allah be upon him) has said: 'A divorcee or a widow must not be married until she is consulted and a virgin must also not be married until her permission is sought.' (Bukhari)
>
> In another Tradition the Holy Prophet (peace and blessings of Allah be upon him) said: 'A woman who has been previously married (Thayyiba), has more right to her person than her guardian. And a virgin should also be consulted and her silence implies her consent.' (Muslim)

A further probe into the above Ahadith would affirm the fact that women are not helpless but they have been given the freedom of choice by Islam and without the consultation of a woman, the marriage of a woman with any man is not permissible. Thus, consent of a woman is an essential condition of marriage and it must be obtained in all circumstances.

It is the duty of a guardian that he should first consult the woman, attaining the age of competency, regarding her proposed marriage and then begin the negotiations. Islam ordains that both the parents and guardians of a girl should seek permission from her before marriage.

But where Islam considers the permission and consent of the woman as an essential condition of her marriage, it does not do so at the cost of her sentiments of modesty and chastity. So if she is a virgin her silence implies her consent, but in the case of a woman previously married (divorced or widowed) explicit consent from her is necessary. Some scholars are of the view that it is more appropriate that it should be made clear to a virgin.

A Hadith narrates the incident of a Sahabia, Hadrat Khansa bint Huzam (Allah be pleased with her) that her father married her to a person whom she did not like. She came to the Holy Prophet (peace and blessings of Allah be upon him) and submitted a petition which was accepted by him, and he revoked the marriage.

Hadrat Abdullah bin Abbas (Allah be pleased with him) reported that a woman came to the Holy Prophet (peace and blessings of Allah be upon him) and said: 'My father has married me to a person whom I do not like.' The Holy Prophet (peace and blessings of Allah be upon him) authorised that woman to accept or revoke the marriage.

According to an incident narrated by Buraida (Allah be pleased with him) a young woman came to the Holy Prophet (peace and blessings of Allah be upon him) and said: 'My father has married me to my cousin whom I do not like.' Thereupon the Holy Prophet (peace and blessings of Allah be upon him) gave her permission to adhere to or revoke the marriage contract. Hearing this the woman heaved a sigh of relief saying: 'I have already given my consent to what my father has done, but what I want to impress upon women is that a father has no right to give the hand of his grown up daughter without her consent.'

Abdur Rahman bin Yazid and Majma' bin Yazid (Allah be pleased with them) narrated an incident. A person, namely Khuddam, married his daughter to a person whom she did not like. She came to the Holy Prophet (peace and blessings of Allah be upon him) and expressed her disgust. He (the Holy Prophet) (peace and blessings of Allah be upon him) revoked the marriage contracted by her father and then she married Abdul Baya bin Abdul Mundhir (Allah be pleased with him).

The above Ahadith bear ample testimony to the fact that it is not permissible to put pressure on a grown-up lady in the matter of marriage, but that she reserves the full right to select her husband. The sum and substance of what we have said above is that the real aims and objects of marriage i.e., morality and chastity, love and affection and multiplication of the human race should always be kept in view.

The guardian and the father possess the right to get a girl, who has not yet attained the age of puberty, married to someone; but the right of the father is more essential as she cannot, in that case, exercise her option or choice on attaining the age of puberty.

However, marriage is an important matter. It should be arranged after thorough investigation. The parents and guardians should satisfy themselves to the possible extent and those who are going to be tied in wedlock should also feel contented.

Another point worth thinking about is that nowadays people

do not consider it necessary to consult their parents and guardians. No doubt, the like and dislike of a person proposed for marriage is the primary factor, but the heart and passions should not be allowed to overrule the mind and one should be vigilant and not lose one's sense. Besides, in the gratification of the sexual instinct, marriage entails responsibilities which one owes to one's family, society, country and nation. One should not be concerned with one's present state only, but should also keep the future in view. It is, therefore, quite necessary to consult elderly people as they possess more experience of life. If there arises a dispute, the choice of the woman should be given priority.

Now the question remains of the case of dispute between a guardian or father and a woman going to be married; how should the matter be decided? Certainly, the verdict will be in the favour of the woman, and according to the Shariah, priority will be given to her opinion as it is she who is going to be married and the matter pertains to her modesty and chastity. The guardian is not being married nor is he to shoulder the responsibility of marriage. Then how is it that the opinion of the woman should be overlooked? There are incidents and clear decisions of the time of the Holy Prophet (peace and blessings of Allah be upon him) that he gave preference to the opinion of the woman. He revoked the marriage contracted by the father, but did not decide against the woman. It has been said in the Holy Quran:

> "When they reach their term, place not difficulties in the way of their marrying the husbands of their choice if it is agreed between them in kindness." (2:232)

In the matter of marriage, the woman has the right to decide according to her sweet will. The woman is also human, she possesses intellect and wisdom. She is not a helpless creature unable to decide any matter of her own accord.

From the above we are bound to arrive at the conclusion

that coordination between the guardian and the woman is essential for arranging the marriage smoothly. The views of Hadrat Maulana Kashmiri on this subject are worth reading. Here we shall give only the gist thereof: In the case of the matters concerning the people, the Shariah has given the right to both the parties. One should decide keeping in view all the Ahadith. One-sided decisions can be wrong. For instance, in the case of Zakat, the matter pertains to both the payer and the payee. So far as the payer is concerned, there is a clear Hadith that if any collector of Zakat comes to him for Zakat, he should please him by giving to him what he demands. If he does justice, the reward will be for him and if he commits injustice, he will be liable to punishment. The excellence of Zakat is that the collector should go back cheerfully.

It has been narrated in a Hadith that the people complained to the Holy Prophet (peace and blessings of Allah be upon him) against the collector of Zakat. He said: 'Please him and give him what he asks for.' Thereupon they asked: 'O' Allah's Messenger, even if he commits injustice?' He answered: 'Yes, in that case too!' On the other hand, the payee has been admonished: 'Beware against taking the best of the wealth of the people. Be afraid of the outpourings of the heart of the oppressed as there is no barrier between him and Allah.'

Now, ponder over both the Ahadith. According to the instructions of the Holy Prophet (peace and blessings of Allah be upon him) the collector of Zakat should be given what he demands even if he commits injustice. On the other hand, the payee has been warned to receive what the payer gives him justly and should not be arrogant. Similar is the case of husband and wife. On the one hand, the wife has been ordained to please her husband and a stern warning of being thrown into the Fire of Hell has been given for misbehaviour on her part. And on the other hand, it has been said that the perfect in Faith among you is the one who is of good manners and who is the best in behaviour towards his wife.

The same is the case of the woman and her guardian. It is impressed on the woman that the guardian possesses the right in respect of her marriage and without his consultation the marriage contract is not complete. On the other hand, it is said to the guardian that the woman has more right to her person than him and he has no right to intervene.

What can be concluded from the above Ahadith is that both are responsible and that the marriage should not be contracted without each other's consultation. The woman should, as far as possible, give due regard to the opinion of the guardian and the latter must seek the former's consent. Neither is the guardian allowed to deprive the woman of her legal right nor should the woman bring disgrace to the fair name of her family and guardian. In any case, the guardian has no right to put pressure. It is, however, preferable that he should give advice. If the girl is a minor, the guardian can exercise his will. As is evident from the Quran and the Sunnah, in the event of a dispute between the woman and the guardian, priority will be given to the opinion of the woman.

The views of Maulana Kashmiri are most reasonable and practicable in so far as social problems are concerned. He is aware of the implication of Allah's Prophet's directives. He is fully conversant with the significance and style of the Ahadith.

While explaining this point, Shah Wali Ullah also supports the above view, though his style is distinct from Maulana Kashmiri's. He says:

> 'Merely the opinion of the woman is not sufficient for the purpose of marriage It is only men who can solve difficult and knotty problems. Moreover, in the matters covering marriage the proposal by a woman is considered as arrogant and as an act of immodesty on her part. The intervention of a guardian is therefore, necessary to make a distinction between love-affair and marriage and to give due publicity to the proposed

marriage. The woman, therefore, should consult the guardian, but the latter has no right to get her married to a person without her consent as the matter pertains exclusively to a woman. The benefits or loss occurring out of this marriage will have to be faced by her alone. So her consent must be sought.'

Imam Nawawi, who belongs to the Shafii school of thought, is also of the view that the opinion of the woman has preference to the opinion of the guardian. He has written:

> 'The right of a woman has priority over the right of a guardian. If a guardian intends to marry a woman to a relative and she is not inclined, she cannot be pressurized. If she desires to marry with a relative and the guardian is not inclined, pressure will be exerted on the guardian. If he is adamant, the Qadi will get her married. This affirms the view that priority is to the right of a woman and this practice is in vogue.'

It is evident from what we have said above that in Islam a woman is not quite helpless in the matter of marriage but her consent must be obtained before the guardian arranges her marriage. If a woman refuses to marry a person, she should not at all be forced to do so. Peace and harmony, the foremost aims and objects of marriage cannot be achieved in the case of the unwilling marriage of a woman. The rules and regulations pertaining to divorce and Khula have been framed for this purpose.

It has been mentioned in "Masbut" that at the time of Nikah the consent of a woman must be sought. It is just possible that the woman may have some defect or disease due to which sexual intercourse is not possible or the woman may like another man. If she is married to a person whom she dislikes, she will never be able to live amicably with him.

After the woman, comes the question of the opinion of the

man. Here too, the consent of the grown-up man, going to be married, must be sought. Since man is not helpless, this matter needs no detailed discussion, rather it is advisable that he should give due weight to the opinion of his elders and should not ignore them saying: 'This is my personal matter in which the elders have no right to intervene.' In the matter of marriage the views of experienced people and those who have deep human insight count much. It is an obvious fact that young men do not possess the wisdom and prudence of elderly people. In the former case sentiments and passions only play a part.

> Now we come to the point as to what should be the criteria for the selection of a woman. According to the Shariah, the chastity and piety of a woman should be given top priority at the time of selection. A person may marry an ordinary woman or a rich and wealthy lady or a woman of high descent or one for the sake of her beauty, but her piety and moral character must always be kept in view. The Holy Prophet (peace and blessings of Allah be upon him) has observed: 'Marriage with a woman is contracted for the sake of four things: for her wealth, for her descent, for her beauty and for her piety, but you should succeed (marry), for piety.' (Bukhari)

A man chooses a woman for the sake of four things. Sometime he chooses for the sake of her wealth only. He thinks that if the woman possesses property or a grand building, he would lead a luxurious and comfortable life and would be relieved of a large number of worries. He does not care to ponder over the virtues of piety and chastity, in his haste. He is not aware that by marrying a rich woman, he would be deprived of the real pleasure and happiness of marriage, as in that case his wife would rule. He would not feel any pleasure in seeing the furniture and other household goods which have not been purchased by his hard earned income nor would he be glad to see his gaily dressed children after losing his respect and honour in the eyes of his wife. His status or position would be that of a manager or organizer, if his wife is of good behaviour. If, God forbids, the wife happens to be arrogant, she would annoy and taunt him at every moment. The children of that wife would also not pay due respect to their father. If the husband intends to admonish his wife for any mistake of hers, it would come to a fight. Under the above circumstances what pleasure and happiness would exist in his life? The Holy Prophet (peace and blessings of Allah be upon him) has observed: 'Do not marry women for the sake of their wealth. Just possible their wealth makes them arrogant.' (Ibn Majah)

Sometime a man chooses a woman of high descent even if she is deprived of any personal ability and virtues. If she is of high descent but lacks piety, she would be proud and arrogant and would not remain within limits. This kind of behaviour is almost intolerable for a man. It does not mean that one should not attach importance to the race and descent of a woman, but it should not be the only consideration. These things have no value if the woman has no personal ability and is not pious and chaste. Islam holds piety and chastity in high esteem and these virtues are far more important in the eyes of Islam than race and descent. The Holy Prophet (peace and blessings of Allah be upon him) said: 'A woman may be married for four reasons: for her property, her status, her beauty and her religion; so try to get who is religious.' (Sahih Muslim)

The other Ahadith also support this view. Once the Holy Prophet (peace and blessings of Allah be upon him) said:

'Wherever they may be and whosoever they may be, my followers are pious.'

According to some people, beauty is the only consideration for the selection of a woman. She must have appealing looks, attractive, wide eyes, fair complexion and a proportionate body. She should be of gay disposition and pert and coquettish. She must be aware of the etiquettes of the modern society and way of life.

> But they do not take any trouble to think that the above qualities do not count much if she is lacking in ability and good manners. Mere beauty is not everything. If she is deprived of other virtues, the beauty would become an evil. It would make her proud, flirtatious and arrogant. She would become haughty and extravagant. Other people would try to allure her. The holy Prophet (peace and blessings of Allah be upon him) has said about this kind of beautiful woman: 'Do not marry women merely for their beauty. It is most probable that their beauty may prove disastrous.' (Ibn Majah)

The Holy Prophet (peace and blessings of Allah be upon him) has, therefore, made piety and chastity the real criteria for the selection of a woman. Wealth, beauty, race and descent of a woman are not the real virtues. The person going to be married must see the personal ability and intelligence of a woman. The Holy Prophet (peace and blessings of Allah be upon him) has said: 'Do not marry a woman merely for the sake of her beauty and wealth.'

> In the matter of marriage, preference should be given to chastity and piety. A black but pious woman is better. The Holy Prophet (peace and blessings of Allah be upon him) has said: 'But marry women on the basis of religion and piety.' (Ibn Majah)

There is no denying the fact that a religious and pious lady is always solicitous for the welfare and comfort of her husband and discharges her household duties efficiently and carefully. Such a woman is not unduly proud. She takes the utmost care in bringing up and educating her children. She does not pick up quarrels with the neighbours, relatives and other people. The people rely on her and respect and honour her. She enhances the honour and prestige of her husband.

The Holy Prophet (peace and blessings of Allah be upon him) has observed: 'Whosoever achieves four things, is successful in this world and in the Hereafter: A heart which is grateful, a tongue which remains busy in Dhikr (commemorating the name of Allah) a body which shows patience, and a wife who abstains from sins and guards her chastity.'

Once the Holy Prophet (peace and blessings of Allah be upon him) said: 'Marry a woman who has excellent faith in Allah and who is helpful in making the life successful on the Day of Resurrection.'

> ***Indifferent Attitude :*** Should the people adopt an indifferent attitude towards moral conduct and behaviour, devoting their all out attention to worldly pomp and show and exterior beauty, what would become of this world? A storm of evil and wickedness would rage and destroy the peace and harmony of this world. The respect and honour of everyone would be at stake. A large number of women could not get husbands and would be tempted to wickedness and debauchery as someone has rightly remarked: An idle brain is the devil's workshop. While explaining this fact the Holy Prophet (peace and blessings of Allah be upon him) has observed: 'Whenever a person whose moral conduct and behaviour pleases you, comes to you, get him married, otherwise there will be a widespread evil and wickedness on earth.!
>
> (Tirmidhi)

> According to the Jurists, it is advised that the following principles should be observed while selecting a woman: 'It is better if the position of a woman is less in respect of her race and descent and wealth and property and influence, but she should be superior to the man in moral conduct, behaviour, personality and beauty.' (Dur Mukhtar)
>
> The following points should also be kept in view: The woman with whom a man is to marry should not be tall and weak and thin, nor should she be of short stature, ugly and of bad conduct. She should not be of advanced age. She should not be of easy virtue. (Shami)

In short, the woman with whom one is to marry should be suitable in every respect from the worldly point of view as well as from the religious point of view. Without this there can exist no mutual love and harmony between the husband and wife. As is evident from the Ahadith the woman should possess the following virtues:

- She should be religious and pious.
- She should share her husband's joys and sorrows and should be loyal and obedient.
- She should be chaste and honest and should manage the household affairs properly.
- She should be courteous, grateful and patient.
- She should pay attention to the needs of her children and should be kind to them and be healthy.
- She should love her husband and be a bearer of many offsprings.
- She should be of a pious and noble descent and educated.
- She should be virtuous and free from vices and evils.
- While living in this world, she should remember the life in the Hereafter.

6

Comparative Study

Before discussing the human rights in Islam we would like to explain a few poin ts about two major approaches to the question of human rights; the Western and the Islamic. This will enable us to study the issue in its proper perspective and avoid some of the confusion which normally befogs such a discussion.

Western Ideology

The people in the west have the habit of attributing every good thing to themselves and try to prove that it is because of them that the world got this blessing, otherwise the world was steeped in ignorance and completely unaware of all these benefits. Now let us look at the question of human rights. It is very loudly and vociferously claimed that the world got the concept of basic human rights from the *Magna Carta* of Britain; though the *Magna Carta* itself came into existence six hundred years after the advent of Islam. But the truth of the matter is that until the seventeenth century no one even knew that the *Magna Carta* contained the principles of Trial by Jury; Habeas Corpus, and the Control of Parliament on the Right of Taxation. If the people who had drafted the *Magna Carta* were living today they would have been greatly surprised if they were told that their document also contained all these ideals and principles.

They had no such intention, nor were they conscious of all these concepts which are now being attributed to them. As far as my knowledge goes the Westerners had no concept of human rights and civic rights before the seventeenth century. Even after the seventeenth century the philosophers and the thinkers on jurisprudence though preserved these ideas, the practical proof and demonstration of these concepts can only be found at the end of the eighteenth century in the proclamations and constitutions of America and France.

After this there appeared a reference to the basic human rights in the constitutions of different countries. But more often the rights which were given on paper were not actually given to the people in real life. In the middle of the present century, the United Nations, which can now be more aptly and truly described as the Divided Nations, made a Declaration of Universal Human Rights, and passed a resolution against genocide and framed regulations to check it. But as you all know there is not a single resolution or regulation of the United Nations which can be enforced. They are just an expression of a pious hope. They have no sanctions behind them, no force, physical or moral to enforce them. Despite all the high-sounding ambitious resolutions of the United Nations, human rights have been violated and trampled upon at different places, and the United Nations has been a helpless spectator. She is not in a position to exercise an effective check on the violation of human rights.

Islamic Philosophy

The second point which we would like to clarify at the very-outset is that when we speak of human rights in Islam we really mean that these rights have been granted by God; they have not been granted by any king or by any legislative assembly. The rights granted by the kings or the legislative assemblies, can also be withdrawn in the same manner in which they are conferred. The same is the case with the rights accepted and recognised by the dictators. They can confer them when they please and withdraw them when they wish; and they can openly violate them when they like. But since in Islam human rights have been conferred by God, no legislative assembly in the world, or any government on earth has the right or authority to make any amendment or change in the rights conferred by God. No one has the right to abrogate them or withdraw them. Nor are they the basic human rights which are conferred on paper for the sake of show and exhibition and denied in actual life when the show is over. Nor are they like philosophical concepts which have no sanctions behind them.

The charter and the proclamations and the resolutions of the United Nations cannot be compared with the rights sanctioned by God; because the former is not applicable on anybody while the latter is applicable on every Believer. They are a part and parcel of the Islamic Faith. Every Muslim or administrators who claim themselves to be Muslims will have to accept, recognise and enforce them. If they fail to enforce them, and start denying the rights that have been guaranteed by God or make amendments and changes in them, or practically violate them while paying lip service to them, the verdict of the Holy Quran for such governments is clear and unequivocal:

> "Those who do not judge by what God has sent down are the disbelievers. (*Kafirun*)" (5:44).

The following verse also proclaims: "They are the wrong-doers *(zalimun)*" (5:45), while a third verse in the same chapter says: "They are the perverse and law-breakers *(fasiqun)*" (5:47). In other words this means that if the temporal authorities regard their own words and decisions to be right and those given by God as wrong they are disbelievers. If on the other hand they regard God's commands as right but wittingly reject them and enforce their own decisions against God's then they are the mischief-makers and the wrong-doers. *Fasiq,* the law breaker is the one who disregards the bond of allegiance and *zalim* is he who works against the truth. Thus all those temporal authorities who claim to be Muslims and yet violate the rights sanctioned by God belong to one of these two categories, either they are the disbelievers or are the wrong-doers and mischief-makers. The rights which have been sanctioned by God are permanent, perpetual and eternal. They are not subject to any alterations or modifications, and there is no scope for any change or abrogation.

Other Thoughts

The zissue of the fundamental rights of man in fact involves a proper understanding of the position of man in the universe, the purpose of his life, the nature of his relationship with the society and the State and also the reality behind the creation of this universe and its beginning and the end. What the human rights are cannot be understood until it is ascertained what really is the position of man in this universe. The question of rights, so to say, is directly linked to that of the status and position he occupies. Without a realistic knowledge of the position of man or in the absence of a definite idea about it, we cannot determine his rights.

Western Concept: To solve these basic problems concerning human life, guidance could be had from revealed faiths only, since we have no other reliable source of knowledge in this behalf. But when man overlooked the source of revealed knowledge and tried to seek answers to these vital questions with his wits alone, he started stumbling and falling in the labyrinths of guesses and conjectures and the valleys of ignorance. These facts were beyond the grip of experiences and observations based on senses. Recorded history, which came into existence hundreds of thousands of years after the beginning of human life on this globe had to offer little material from its record to assist him gain access to these facts, in this pitch dark atmosphere totally devoid of the light of revelation when an intellect unaware of the realities tried to solve these intricate problems of life, the first and the greatest difficulty that confronted man was where to begin to tackle this problem.

Since human intellect had no established facts on which to base its arguments, it had of necessity to begin with these ideologies and theories (hypotheses) as the basis of talks and discussions. In this way, man's intellect removed its difficulty by discussing serious issues on the basis of unreliable information and based on guesses and conjectures, but failed to offer a satisfactory solution of the problems facing humanity. Then thoughts and theories presented by the intellect being ambiguous, contradictory, disjointed and unbalanced further complicated these problems. And thus humanity got more and more entangled in a whirlpool of ignorance and absurdities. It is to point out this shortcoming of intellect that Quran says:

> "Wert thou (O Muhammad!) to follow the common run of those on earth, they will lead thee astray from the way of God, They follow not but an opinion and they do but guess." Al Quran VI:116.
>
> Say: "Have ye any (certain) knowledge? If so, produce it before us. Lo! Ye follow naught but an opinion. Lo! ye do but guess." Al Quran VI: 148

Since the journey of intellect had started in pitch dark therefore its premises have no basis. It proceeds by means of conjectures and in its attempts to solve problems creates more and more complexities. In its attempts to solve the problem of fundamental human rights, it had to lean on hypotheses and theories. The first question that confronted the intellect was whether there was any justification for these rights. On what basis certain rights be recognized for man? And if at all recognized, on what authority? Who has conferred them on man?

After much deliberation the human intellect thought out the answer to the question that since nature has itself conferred certain rights on man, therefore they must be recognized. This theory came to be called the theory of Natural Rights. An objection was levelled against it saying that this form is ambiguous and ill-defined. Nature itself has not so far been defined lucidly in a manner that there could be a consensus on it. How to determine the natural rights then? The greatest objection raised was about the legal position of these rights. The concept of rights in a society is possible only with its sanction. Without social sanction there is no question of rights.

Then in order to provide a legal sanction to these rights and to obtain the sanction of the society for them the theory of Social Contract was put forth. It was suggested that since the very existence of the State depended on it, it must be the fountain-head of the powers of the rulers and the rights of the citizens. In this way a legal justification was provided for the rights of man. But what is the historical importance of this contract? Let us see what J.W. Gough has to say about it.

The whole historical school, from Blackstone and Paley to Maine and his followers, have pointed out, what is now obvious and undeniable, that in actual historical fact states and governments were not deliberately established by contract, but developed naturally from more primitive groupings and loyalties, such as that of the family or the clan.

Professor Ilys says:

> Is the Social Contract theory wholly unhistorical? Is it a. pure fiction? Is it wholly unreal and imaginary? These questions are always answered in the affirmative and no one has yet said 'no' to their answers. The whole thing is more astounding because it has been declared that the Social Contract theory is as old as speculation itself. It has, therefore, its own history without itself being historical in any sense. By historical here we mean that in the whole history of the political development of man we do not find even a single case or instance in which the 'social contract' might have been used in the origin or the making of the state.

The question is that a theory which is so baseless that it enjoys no more respect than a fable and which the western historians have themselves unanimously declared as unhistorical; why was so much importance attached to it, and the entire superstructure of the concept of rights was built on it? Let us see what the westerners themselves have to say about it:

> The doctrine made its appearance in the 16th and 17th centuries when political theorists turned to the idea of contract in order to interpret the relationship between the individual and the community.

It means that this contract was invented to provide justification or a legal basis for their theories. J. W. Gough, stating the real worth of this contract, writes:

> For, of deeper importance than this question of terms, or even than that of the truth or falsehood of the contract theory itself, is the principle which contractarians were ultimately striving to uphold.

If the phrase 'social contract' is to be retained, then, it had probably best be interpreted as an abbreviation for the Idea that political obligation involves a relationship analogous to contract.

This, I think, is the maximum that can be conceded to the contract theory.

For, as an historical theory the contract has now long been discredited, and its more recent adherents have wisely confined themselves to the claim that a contract is the philosophical basis of the State. This claim itself has taken various forms. It may be argued, as by Kant, that the contract, though historically a fiction, is valid as an 'idea of reason; and this, we saw, meant that political rights and duties should be ordered as if political obligation were founded on a contract, although really it is not.

These extracts make it very clear why the westerners, in spite of attaching no more importance to Social Contract theory than a tale, are not prepared to reject it. If they were to reject it they would be left with nothing to regularise the "rights and obligations". It was under this compulsion or helplessness that Sir Ernest Barker, supporting the Social Contract theory writes:

> There is still a case to be made for the view that the State as distinct from society, is a legal association which fundamentally rests on the presuppositions of contract.

Through the invention of this contract, justification for the fundamental rights and the powers of the state was certainly furnished, another question confronted its supporters: Who is the sovereign, the State or the people? Considering the rights and the powers, which of them enjoys supremacy?

Attempts to solve this problem were also made with the Social Contract theory as the basis, but each attempt was made keeping in view the demands and particular needs of its period. Hobbes had at heart the legal justification for the despotism of the Stuart Kings. So he drew his own picture of the state of nature prior to the Social Contract to meet the particular needs, and declaring the rulers as sovereigns made them all powerful. And the helpless people, denuded of all power, were left with no option but to unconditionally obey these despotic rulers, without complaining.

When the splendid revolution of 1688 weakened the tight grip of the despotic monarchy, and through the Bill of Rights, the rights of the parliament and the people were strengthened, John Locke felt compelled to offer a new interpretation of the Social Contract for the justification of the newly created situation. So his imagination presented quite a different picture of the State of Nature, in which human life was not "lonely, poverty stricken, worsened, beastly and short-lived, but contrary to the assertion of Hobbes it was a period of peace, good will, of mutual cooperation and protection," in which man was leading a life of great satisfaction based on freedom and equality. Locke with this background, in his new interpretation of Social Contract, divided the sovereignty between the king and the people, giving the people a little higher position, without whose consent no king could acquire the right to rule.

By the time it came to the French thinker Rousseau, since the struggle for rights and powers between the king and the people had covered a long way and had by this time entered a decisive stage, a new interpretation of Social Contract had become inevitable to energize the democratic forces and to give a final blow to the despotic rule of the kings. So we find Rousseau, keeping in view the political and social conditions of his period, presenting a beautiful picture of the state of Nature, and interpreting the Social Contract in such a way that the crown of sovereignty was taken off the head of the king and placed on the head of the people.

Since the question of Sovereignty is intimately linked with the relationship of the state and the citizens and their rights and obligations, all other political thinkers and legal experts besides Hobbes, Locke and Rousseau, also discussed it in great detail. Among them Grotius, Bodin, Austin, Bentham, Lasky, T.H. Green and Dicey deserve special mention. Commenting on the sum total of their thought Professor Ilyas Ahmad writes:

> Thus Sovereignty in Political Philosophy has been running abegging from door to door-from the one to the few and then to the many, from the individual to the community, from the minority to the majority and from majority to the minority, from the executive to the legislature and even from the legislature to the judiciary and finally from the community to the abstract conception of the state itself.

Through a study of the discussions from the theory of natural rights to that of sovereignty, it becomes evident that the entire thought content of the Western people is based on conjectures and all the theories are based on it alone. Since there is no clear concept regarding the reality about man and his position, great confusion of thought exists regarding all the basic problems of his life. Like other problems that of the determination of the fundamental rights too has been the victim of the same corruption of thought and observation.

Rights in the west do not enjoy a permanent position. They have no eternal source and criteria of a cosmic order. All the sources are either imaginary or like the law of Habeas Corpus, Magna Carta, the Bill of Rights, the French Charter of Human Rights and the ten amendments to the American constitution, are documents of a regional nature and are the product of the peculiar political and social conditions existing in Britain, France and America. There the concept of the fundamental rights has developed along with human consciousness. And these rights have been born one by one out of the agreements during the protracted struggle between the people and the king or other rulers, for the division of powers, the decision of the parliament, charter declarations and the theories put up by the political thinkers. As this struggle advanced, the sphere of rights became wider. That is to say, what are being termed as 'fundamental rights' today were not there till yesterday, and if at all they were, they were no more than mere yearnings which had no sanction at their back. Every one of these rights became a right in the true sense of the word only when the law of the land and the constitution recognizing it conferred validity on it.

Now let us take stock of another aspect of the western concept of rights. So to say, the western people claim upholding of the fundamental rights for the whole mankind but their attitude is practically against this assertion. Their concept of rights is based on their theory of nationality and racial discrimination. The fundamental right which they want guaranteed for their own nation and the white race, they do not consider other nations and races deserving of those. When the French Charter of Human Rights was incorporated in the constitution of 1791, it was also clarified:

> "Although the colonies and the. French possessions in Asia, Africa and America form part of the French

Empire, the constitution, aforesaid still does not extend to them."

This makes it evident that the charter which has been termed "The Charter of Human Rights" is in reality the charter of the Rights of the French people. No other nation, rather, the non-French people living in the French possessions, had any right to make and demand for them. And we find the countrymen of Rousseau perpetrating such beastliness and barbarism in Algeria, Vietnam and other possessions, which constitute one of the blackest chapters of modern history.

The same holds good for Britain. The rights enjoyed by the British citizens in its unwritten constitution, were never allowed by the British masters to be incorporated in the laws framed by them in their colonies; their Magna Carta, their law of Habeas corpus and their Bill of Rights were all for them alone. So it would be a mistake and misleading to term them documents of Human Rights as the rights conferred by these documents were confined to the citizens of Britain alone. If any other nation demanded these rights for themselves from the British rulers, it was branded as an act of rebellion and treason and those making the demand were made the target of tyranny and barbarity. Even today the treatment meted out to the black natives in South Africa and to the subjugated white citizens in Northern Ireland is a proof of the British people's duplicity that speaks for itself.

On 30th November, 1972, when the General Assembly of the UNO passed a resolution to make racial discrimination a cognizable offence, among four dissenters, along with America, South Africa and Portugal, Britain was also one.

America is no different from Britain and France. The white colonizers of America effected the entire race of aborigines of that continent, the so-called Red-Indians. For the building up and development of their "New World" they caught African blacks like animals and enslaving them, transported regular shiploads of them to America. These slaves were regularly sold and purchased. The African coast from which they shipped the freshly caught slaves in Africa, came to be called the Slave coast.

The surviving race of descendants of these one-time slaves, has not so far succeeded in attaining equal rights with the white men of America. Whenever it referred to the American constitution and demanded for themselves enforcement of the "Human Rights" mentioned therein, their demand was ruthlessly crushed. Robert Dewey's biting sarcasm on this state of affairs is worthy of note:

> In a colony of 500,000 slaves and thousands of white indentured servants, Thomas Jefferson, a wealthy slave-owner, sat down and wrote the memorable words of the Declaration of Independence.

Apart from this racial discrimination internally, when we take stock of the American role in the world outside, the picture becomes all the more grim. Hiroshima, Nagasaki, Korea, Vietnam, Combodia and the Middle East, do tell the harrowing tales, of the fundamental Human Rights being trampled with impunity.

Now let us take the fourth upholder of Human Rights, communist Russia. This is the cradle of Socialism that had stood up with the banner of liberation of humanity from the American and British imperialism and from every sort of exploitation, and with the promise to bring to mankind happiness of peace, prosperity and true freedom. But when it, for the first time, had a chance to put up a show of its "Virtues" and "Blessings", its twilight gave way to the ruddy sun from behind a huge mound of seventeen million human corpses. And when its ways illumined the East and the West Hungary, Eastern Germany, Poland, Czechoslovakia, occupied Turkistan and all those other regions where communism had an opportunity to enter, were bathed in blood. The Russian expert of Social Sciences and philosopher. Professor Pitririm Sorokin, giving details of the loss of human lives during the Russian Revolution, says:

> The total number of direct victims of the Red Terror of the Communist Revolution in the year 1918-22, according to a conservative estimate is at least 6,00,000, more than 1,00,000 a year. And this excludes the victims of the civil war, including the White Terror, and all the direct victims of the revolution itself. In one way or another, fifteen to seventeen millions of human lives were thus sacrificed to the ideal of the revolution.

The New Encyclopaedia Britannica writes :

> A far greater number of persons, perhaps 2,000,000, mainly of the educated upper and middle classes, were lost to Russia by emigration to escape Communist rule.

These incidents amply reveal the fact that the concept of rights of the western countries is not that of the rights of the humanity as a whole, but is bedevilled by racial, territorial, national and ideological prejudices. The rights which they consider essential for themselves, they do not believe in granting the same to other nations. They nave with al their might and main tried to withhold the same from others and to keep those exclusively for themselves.

Socialist Concept : Along with the consideration of the western concept of rights, it will be in the fitness of things to just have a look at the Socialist concept of rights. According to Marx and Lenin, the real fountain-head of the fundamental rights is the dialectical process of history. These rights have not been conferred on man by nature but are the product of this process. Playing their role in the various stages of history they must finally come to an end in the communist classless society. To begin with, these rights helped the bourgeois class in overthrowing the feudal society and establishing the capitalistic society. Later on, the proletariats used them as a weapon in their class struggle against the capitalists. Now under the Socialist order these rights are protecting the interests of the toiling people, and finally for the sake of freedom and equality these will cancel themselves out under communism.

According to this philosophy these rights are neither natural nor the essential part of man's person, nor are they inalienable. They have no special significance or importance. They are a part of the general law of the land. Only the ruling party which is the caretaker of the interest of the working people, and the only means of the fulfilment of their aspirations has, the authority to determine the same. Enforcement of the basic rights can be allowed only to the extent to which it is in accord with the interest of the working people. Barring this fundamental principle, the demand for these rights in any other contract is altogether unlawful and unconstitutional. The social interests of the working people is the one principle of determining all the fundamental rights.

And this interest is determined by the communist party, since it is the only party comprising the progressive and responsible representatives of the workers and it alone can be expected to keep the interests of the workers in view, to make certain their social welfares, and to frame appropriate laws which include determination of the fundamental rights. Andrei Vishinsky elucidating the Russian philosophy of law, writes;

Soviet 'Socialist Republic is one of the most important branches of Soviet socialist law, which we have previously defined as the totality of the rules of conduct, established in the form of legislation by the authoritative power of the toilers and expressing their will-the application of said rules being guaranteed by the entire coercive force of the socialist state to the end (a) of defending, securing, and developing relationships and orders advantageous and agreeable to the toilers, and (b) of annihilating, completely and finally, capitalism and its survivals in the economy, manner of life, and consciousness of people, with the aim of building communist society.

The expounders of the Russian constitution, Grigorian and Dologoplov present the following definition of the fundamental rights:

> The basic right and duties of Soviet citizens are an expression of the socialist spirit of Soviet state.

It means the state has complete supremacy over the individual which has the authority to determine his rights which in turn are not above the sphere of common legislation.

This concept of rights is entirely different from the western concept of the fundamental rights rather diametrically opposite to it. In the western countries the real purpose of these rights is to offer protection to the individual against the state. So in the west these rights are given a higher position than the common laws framed by the state. By incorporating them in the constitution the legislative powers 'of the state are limited, and the Judiciary is entrusted with enforcement of the fundamental rights.

As against this, let us turn to C. D. Kering to see what the position of these rights is in Russia and other Socialist countries:

> The Eastern concept on the other hand derives fundamental rights from the objective law imposed and enforced by the State. Any justification on the grounds of natural law is firmly rejected. It is impossible to guarantee the citizen effective protection against the state in this way because the degree of projection is dependent on the normative will of the state.

"Barring Yugoslavia, in all communist countries, ordinary courts provide very limited legal protection. And there is no international institution for the protection of human rights. The protection of civic rights through the public prosecutor is a fraudulent, put up show, since these public prosecutions are not independent, but abjectly follow the directives of the government."

The fundamental rights mentioned in the Russian constitution are the following:

(1) The right to work.

(2) The right to rest.

(3) In old age, sickness or some other disability, the right to the supply of necessities of life.

(4) The right of education.

(5) The right of equality between man and woman.

(6) Apart from national and racial distinction, the right of equality among all the citizens of Russia.

(7) Freedom of conscience.

(8) The right of expression, through speech and written word, assembly, holding meetings, and the right of demonstration.

(9) The right to join organisations.

(10) The right of non-intervention in the affairs of individuals, families and correspondence and

(11) The right to seek asylum.

Alongwith these rights the Russian constitution also prescribes obligations which are as follows:

(1) Honouring the constitution, abiding by the laws, consideration for the organisation of labour, a reasonable attitude in relation to the social obligations and respect for the principles of the Socialist society.

(2) The protection of the Socialist properties and their consolidation,

(3) Compulsory military service and the defence of motherland.

The list of rights in the Russian constitution does not include the right of forming parties. Elucidating this point Andrie Vishinsky says:

> The Soviet State, in granting freedom to citizens, starts from the interests of the toilers and naturally does not include freedom of political parties in the enumeration of these freedoms granted in as much as this freedom, in the conditions prevailing in the USSR, where the toilers have complete faith in the Communist Party, is necessary only for agents of fascism and foreign reconnaissance, whose purpose is to take all freedoms away from the toilers of the USSR, and to put the yoke of capitalism upon them once more.

In Russia and other communist countries, the one party system, the control of the ruling party over all the institutions and over the entire resources of the state, the absence of any moral and metaphysical concept of the fundamental rights, the state having all the powers of determining the rights, and the absence of the powers of judiciary to secure these rights or to enforce them, have rendered even those nominal rights, which have been shown in their constitutions totally meaningless. In a communist country, no citizen deprived of the rights conferred on him by the constitutions, can go to a court of law against the State, since neither any courts exist for the redressal of such grievances nor can the state, being the fountainhead of all rights be made the defendant in a case. Whatever it deems right must be accepted as such. And that which it does not recognise as a right or after its recognition cancels, limits or suspends it, it is no more a right that the State may be charged with its denial to anybody. Here right is the other name of the will of the State. Outside the sphere of this will no right has any existence of its own.

This concept of rights, in fact, is based on the concept of man in the socialist philosophy. The concept of life among Socialist thinkers is purely materialistic. To them, like other material objects of this universe, roan is also a material entity and his value is determined by his productive capacity. Just as any part of a machine for the demonstration of its working and productive capacity needs electrical energy, water, lubricating oil and proper care etc; man, also for the development of his productive capacity and its practical demonstration needs support in the matter of food, clothing, education and care.

This support can be had only in a system in which all the individuals of the society may be performing their functions as the productive factors, and a central administration be looking after them and meeting their needs of board and lodge, clothing and other material necessities of life.

More than a productive factor, man has no value. Religion, morality, soul, belief, the life hereafter, are all terms coined by the capitalists and their agents for the exploitation of the people. Lenin says:

> "We refuse to have any thing to do with morals based on divine injunctions by the capitalists. We reject all such moral values whose basis is above human and class consideration. We say it is a fraud, and the peasants and workers are defrauded to serve the interests of the feudal lords and capitalists. We declare that our moral values follow the class strife of poor. The source of our moral values is the interest of the class strife of the poor. That is why we say that there are no moral values outside the human society."

According to the Socialist concept man is the sum total of a stomach and matter, and economic struggle is its only goal of life. When this position of man in society has been determined what other rights are there to be conferred on him save food and shelter, and clothing and treatment. The communist countries guarantee only these material rights and do not recognize any other right based on moral values, it is the logical outcome of their outlook on life. Unless and until they change their view-point in relation to man, they cannot be expected to extend and expand the sphere of fundamental rights.

The West And Islam : People in the West have the habit of attributing every beneficial development in the world to themselves. For example, it is vociferously claimed that the world first derived the concept of basic human rights from the Magna Carta of Britain which was drawn up six hundred years after the advent of Islam. But the truth is that until the seventeenth century no one dreamt of arguing that the Magna Carta contained the principles of feral by jury, Habeas Corpus and control by Parliament of the right of taxation. If the people who drafted the Magna Carta were living today they would be greatly surprised to be told that their document enshrined these ideals and principles.

To the best of our knowledge, the West had no concept of human and civic rights before the seventeenth century; and it was not until the end of the eighteenth century that the concept took on practical meaning in the constitutions of America and France.

After this, although there appeared references to basic human rights in the constitutions of many countries, more often than not these rights existed only on paper. In the middle of the present century, the United Nations, which may now be more aptly described as the Divided Nations, made a Declaration of Universal Human Rights, and passed a resolution condemning genocide: regulations were framed to prevent it. But there is not a single resolution or regulation of the United Nations which can be enforced if the country concerned wants to prevent it. They are just expressions of pious hopes. They have no sanctions behind them, no force, physical or moral, to enforce them. Despite all the high-sounding resolutions of the United Nations, human rights continue to be violated and trampled upon.

When we speak of human rights in Islam we mean those

rights granted by God. Rights granted by kings or legislative assemblies can be withdrawn as easily as they are conferred; but no individual and no institution has the authority to withdraw the rights conferred by God.

The charter and the proclamations and the resolutions of the United Nations cannot be compared with the rights sanctioned by God; the former are not obligatory on anybody, while the latter are an integral part of the Islamic faith. All Muslims and all administrators who claim to be Muslim have to accept, recognize and enforce them. If they fail to enforce them or violate them while paying lip-service to them, the verdict of the Holy Quran is unequivocal:

> "Those who do not judge by what God has sent down are the disbelievers Kafirun (5:44) The following verse also proclaims:
>
> "They are the wrong-doers zalimun." (5:45) A third verse in the same chapter says:
>
> "They are the perverse and law-breakers fasiqun." (5:47)

In other words, if temporal authorities regard their own words and decisions as right and those given by God as wrong, they are disbelievers. If, on the other hand, they regard God's commands as right but deliberately reject them in favour of their own decisions, then they are wrong-doers. Law-breakers are those who disregard the bond of allegiance.

Bibliography

Adams, C.C. : *Islam and Modernism in Egypt,* Oxford University Press, New York, 1953.

Ahmad, Bherhan : *The Mujaddid's Conception of Tauhid,* Feroz Pub., Lahore, 1940.

Ahmad, Imtiaz : *Divorce and Remarriage among Muslims in India,* Manohar Publishers, New Delhi, 2003.

Ahmad, K. N. : *Muslim Law of Divorce,* Kitab Bhavan, New Delhi, 1988.

Ahmad, Manzuruddin : *Islamic Political System,* Kitab Bhavan, New Delhi, 1991.

Ali, Chiragh : *The Proposed Political Legal and Social Reform under Muslim Rule,* Popular Prakashan, Bombay, 1883.

Badrul, S. : *Muslim Behaviour,* Kitab Bhavan, New Delhi, 1991.

Bahedur, Kalim : *The Jamaat-i-Islami of Pakistan,* Progressive Books, Lahore, 1978.

Baksh, S. K. : *Politics in Islam,* Kitab Bhavan, New Delhi, 2003.

Bawer, Raymond : *The New Man in Soviet Social Psychology,* Oxford, New York, 1990.

Berger, M. : *Islam in Egypt Today : Social and Political Aspects of Popular Religion,* MacMillan, London, 1970.

Bernier, Francois : *Travels in the Mogul Empire,* MacMillan, London, 1916.

Bukhsh, S. K. : *Contribution to the History of Islamic Civilization,* Kitab Bhavan, New Delhi, 2000.

Charles, Howard : *The Constitutionalism,* Great Seal Books, New York, 1947.

Chave, F. : *Islamic Histroriography,* Cambridge University press, New York, 1990.

Davids, Waines : *An Introduction to Islam,* Cambridge University Press, New Delhi, 1995.

Durrani, F.K.K. : *Muhammad (PBUH) the Prophet,* Oxford, New York, 2001.

Enayat, Hamid : *Islam in the Political Process,* Cambridge University Press, Cambridge, 1993.

Engineer, Asghar Ali : *A Rational Approach to Islam,* Gyan Books Pvt. Ltd., New Delhi, 2001.

———: *Islam : Challenge in Twenty-first Century,* Gyan Books Pvt. Ltd., New Delhi, 2004.

Guillaume, A. : *The Traditions of Islam,* Khayats, Beirut, 1966.

Hassan, Ali : *Observations on the Musulmauns of India,* Macmillan & Co., London, 1832.

Helmut, Reifeld : *Islam in South Asia : Adaptation, Accommodation and Conflict,* Social Science Press, New Delhi, 1999.

Houtsma, T. : *Encyclopaedia of Islam,* Macmillan, London, 1934.

Irfan, Habib : *The Agrarian System of Mughal India,* Popular Prakashan, Bombay, 1963.

Jafar, Sharif : *Islam in India,* Oxford, New Delhi, 1972.

James, Burges : *The Muhammadan Architecture of Ahmadabad,* Bernard Quaritch, London,1900.

Jha, V. : *Indian Society: Historical Probings,* Rawat Pub., Delhi, 1974.

Joseph, and Bosworth, C.E. : *The Legacy of Islam,* Oxford University Press, New York, 1979.

Karl, Jaspers : *Man in the Modern Age,* Routledge & Kegan Paul Ltd., London, 1997.

Katharine, Scarfe : *Perception of the Islamic Word,* Cambridge University Press, New Delhi, 1992.

Lewin, Roger : *In the Age of Mankind,* Simithsonian Books, Washington, D.C., 1956.

Lewis, Richards : *Universe,* Harmony Books, New York, 1973.

Martin, Lings : *A Sufi Saint of the Twentieth Century,* Century Pub., London, 1971.

Mirza, Waheed : *The Life and Works of Amir Khusrau,* Kaveri Pub., Calcutta, 1935.

Mortimer, Edward : *Faith and Power, the Politics of Islam,* Oxford, New York, 2002.

Muhammad, Iqbal : *Six Lectures on the Reconstruction of Religious Thought in Islam,* Royal Pub., Lahore, 1930.

Nabith, A. : *The Foundations of the Articles of Faith,* Feroz Pub., Lahore, 1963.

Nasr, Seyyed H. : *An Introduction to Islamic Cosmological Doctrines,* Cambridge, 1964.

Nicholson, R.A. : *Literary History of the Arabs,* Kitab Bhavan, New Delhi, 1994.

Nusservanji, D. : *Zoroastrian Civilization,* Oxford, New York, 1922.

Oage, Charles H. : *The Society,* Macmillan & Co., London, 1959.

Padwick, C.E. : *Muslim Devotions,* MacMillan & Co., London, 1960.

Phillips, O. Hood : *Reform of the Constitution,* MacMillan & Co., London, 1970.

Pierce, R.A.: *Russia in Central Asia, 1867-1917,* University of California, Berkeley, 1960.

Qadir, Abdul, : *Criminal Law of Islam,* Kitab Bhavan, New Delhi, 1999.

Qazi A. Qadir : *The Changing World of Islam,* Royal Pub., Lahore, 1992.

Rizvi, Hasan Askari : *Islami Reassertion : a Socio Political Study,* Progressive Publishers, Lahore, 1981.

Robert, D. : *Exploring our Living Planet,* National Geographic Society, Washington, 1989.

Saukat, S. : *Human Rights in Islam,* Kitab Bhavan, New Delhi, 2001.

Sharma, Arvind : *Women in World Religion,* New York Press, New York, 1990.

Syed, M. H. : *History of Muslims in India,* Anmol Publications, New Delhi, 2003.

——— : *Islamic Terrorism : Myth or Reality,* Gyan Books, New Delhi, 2002.

Tarn, W. W. : *The Greeks in Bactria and India,* Cambridge, London, 1938.

Thomas, Arnold : *The Legacy of Islam,* Oxford University Press, New York, 2000.

Thompson, H.R. : *Sculptures and Inscriptions of Darius the Great on the Rock of Behistan,* Oxford, London, 1907.

Tritton, A.S. : *The Caliphs and their Non-Muslim Subjects,* Oxford, New York, 1930.

Tutsch, Hans E. : *Facets of Arab Nationalism,* Wayne State University Press, Detroit, 1965.

Underhill, E. : *Mysticism : a Study in the Nature and Development of Man's Spiritual Consciousness,* Oxford, New York, 1956.

Usmani, J.M. : *The Authority of Sunnah,* Kitab Bhavan, New Delhi, 1998.

Von, Edmund : *Modern Islam,* University Press, Los Angeles, 1952.

Von, Grunebaum : *Unity and Variety in Muslim World,* Oxford, New York, 2003.

Waheed, Akhtar : *Sufi Approach to the Problem of Alienation,* Wilson & Co., New Delhi, 1975.

Weiner, Myron : *Sons of the Soil : Migration and Ethnic Conflict in India,* University Press, Prineton, 1978.

Williams, Michael : *Outlines of World Military History,* Oxford, New York, 1996.

Wilson, Lambron : *Traditional Modes of Contemplation and Action,* University Press, Tehran, 1977.

Wolfson, H.A. : *Glimpses of Medieval Indian Culture,* Popular Pub., Bombay, 1959.

Yahanan, Friedmann : *Tolerance and Coercion in Islam : Interfaith Relations in the Muslims Traditions,* Cambridge, New York, 1990.

Yazbeck, Haddad : *Islamic Values in the United States,* Oxford, New York, 1997.

Zaehner, R.C. : *Hindu and Muslim Mysticism,* Oxford, London, 1960.

Zahid, Malik : *Subjects of Quran,* Kitab Bhavan, New Delhi, 1998.

Zahurul, Hasan : *Tarikb-i-Sufiya-i-Gujarat,* Jamil Academy, Ahmadabad, 1981.

Zaki, Azam : *The Ideas of Arab Nationalism,* Cornell University Press, New York,1956.

Index

B

C

D

E

F

H

I

M

P

□□□